REPURPOSING ᴛʜᴇ PAST

How a Former Farm Boy and Marine
Helped Give Bucks County a 21st-Century Facelift

BOB WHITE

with ALLAN SLUTSKY

Repurposing the Past: How a Former Farm Boy
and Marine Helped Give Bucks County
a 21st-Century Facelift

Published by Bob White Books

repurposingthepast.com

Library of Congress Control Number: 2021903057

Paperback: 978-1-7366296-0-4

eISBN: 978-1-7366296-1-1

Cover and Interior Design: GKS Creative

Project Management: The Cadence Group

Copyediting and Proofreading: Kimberly A. Bookless

All photos courtesy of Bob White except for the two Penn Salt photos on page 245 (courtesy of Sally Sondesky of the Historical Society of Bensalem) and the "Trenton Makes The World Takes" bridge photo on page 246 (courtesy of Todd White from scenicbuckscounty.com).

Dedicated to the one I love:
my wife, Gladys Mendieta White

CONTENTS

Preface vii

Co-Author's Foreword xiii

PART ONE   **1**

Chapter 1. A Full House in Bucks County 3

Chapter 2. A Reluctant Yankee in Virginia 13

Chapter 3. Back on the Chain Gang 23

Chapter 4. Semper Fi 31

Chapter 5. Viva La Revolución 39

Chapter 6. 8th and I 43

Chapter 7. Four Days in November 47

Chapter 8. I Ain't Gonna Work on Grandad's Farm No More 51

PART TWO   **63**

Chapter 9. Welcome to the RDA 65

Chapter 10. My New Toolbox 77

Chapter 11. Learning the Ropes 93

PART THREE   **107**

The RDA Files: The Bob White Years 109

Morrisville Vulcanized Rubber Mill 111

A. B. Murray Inc. 119

Corell Steel 131

Levittown Shop-a-Rama 137

Stainless Steel Inc. 145

Howell Hardware 155

Longhorn Steakhouse 161

The A. E. Staley Site 167

Riverfront North 173

Bristol Steel 191

The U.S. Steel Fairless Works and the Port Of Bucks 197

Rohm & Haas / Maple Beach 213

The Grundy Powerhouse 225

The U.S. Magnet Factory 233

The Penn Salt Manufacturing Company 243

Action Manufacturing 251

Miller Trailer Park 257

All in a Day's Work 263

PART FOUR   **277**

Chapter 12. Finishing Touches 279

Appendix 289

Testimonials and Accolades 295

A Heartfelt Thank-You 303

About the Co-Author 307

PREFACE

Under the cover of a moonless, starless night, a barely visible 220-foot silhouette silently emerged from its sanctuary inside the massive concrete submarine pens at L'Orient, France. It belonged to U-202, a type VIIC German U-boat, the principal culprit associated with the Kreigsmarine wolfpacks that preyed on Allied shipping convoys in World War II. But on May 27, 1942, this 750 tons of malevolence and destruction headed out into the shadowy depths of the North Atlantic Ocean with a singularly different mission: to land four Nazi spies on the East Coast of the United States with the intention of using acts of sabotage and terror to diminish America's industrial capabilities.

Their intended targets included major hydroelectric plants, essential railroad tracks and bridges, Jewish-owned department stores, and in particular, an ominous-looking factory with a jagged, saw-toothed roof known as the Pennsylvania Salt Manufacturing Company. Its home base was located on the banks of the Delaware River, a stone's throw north of Philadelphia in a town called Bensalem.

In the years leading up to America's entry into World War II, a number of northern Philadelphia municipal and suburban neighborhoods became hotbeds of German American Bund activity, and this factory had been under their surveillance for some time. What had attracted their attention? Local Nazi sympathizers had observed that no insects, shrubs, or even a single blade of grass were to be found within several hundred yards of the building. What could possibly have been going on inside that was so utterly toxic?

George John Dasch, the 39-year-old American expatriate and leader of the submarine's quartet of saboteurs, knew the answer to that question. It was something that had far more dire circumstances for Germany than poison gas or some other variant of chemical warfare: The Penn Salt Company was the sole domestic manufacturer of a synthetic chemical called cryolite, an essential component in the production of the lightweight aluminum America used to build its military airplanes. German intelligence's high command quickly deduced the logical, inescapable conclusion: *no cryolite—no US Air Force.*

Standing in the darkness on the deck of U-202 smoking a last cigarette before the ship submerged, Dasch reviewed the details of his mission. In two weeks, he and his co-conspirators would land on America's East Coast. If the destruction of this factory cost them their lives, they were prepared to make the ultimate sacrifice for the Fatherland.

OK, by now, I'm sure you're wondering how the heck you wandered into the middle of a Tom Clancy spy novel. Indulge me for a few more paragraphs, and hopefully, you'll see where I'm going. In real life, every story doesn't always follow a lengthy script of heart-pounding, edge-of-your-seat action and intrigue. There is no heroic Jack Ryan figure in the tale of U-202. In fact, its ambitious, promising start quickly turned anticlimactic and then ended with a dull thud a few weeks later.

After crossing 3,000 miles of ocean, Operation Pastorius, as it was known, sprung into action shortly after midnight on June 13. With their sub sitting 100 yards offshore of the Long Island, New York town of Amagansett, Dasch and his co-conspirators paddled ashore in two inflatable rubber dinghies loaded with waterproof crates containing weapons, explosives, detonators, changes of clothes, and a large amount of cash for living expenses.

Within minutes, the operation was compromised. As the other three members of the landing party were burying the crates in the sand for later retrieval, George Dasch was spotted by a young Coast Guard sentry on a routine patrol. An attempt to pass himself off as a stranded fishermen went nowhere. The sentry's suspicions were immediately raised when he heard co-conspirator Ernest Burger call out to Dasch in German.

After shouting at Burger to shut up, Dasch considered killing the young sentry but instead opted to offer him a $260 bribe to keep silent about what he'd seen. Accepting the cash, the young man naturally went directly to his Coast Guard station and alerted everyone (including the FBI) about what had just transpired. The saboteurs had already scattered, boarding a Long Island commuter train to Manhattan.

Within 24 hours, George Dasch discovered that his dedication to the Fatherland wasn't as strong as he'd previously thought. Worried about the consequences he would face if caught, he contacted the FBI and offered to turn himself in and provide all the details about the mission. Ernest Burger similarly lost his nerve and followed the same path.

The FBI and the Coast Guard were already way ahead of the game. They'd unearthed the buried munitions, and J. Edgar Hoover had organized the largest manhunt in the history of the United States. Several days later, all four men were apprehended, tried, and convicted. Dasch and Burger were given 30 years at hard labor, and the other two saboteurs died in the electric chair of the Washington, DC district jail. Dasch and Burger never served out the full length of their sentences. Both were deported in 1948 and were looked upon as pariahs when they returned home to Germany. The Nazi high command was so rattled by the mission's failure that they never planned any similar course of sabotage on US soil for the remainder of the war.

Other than the stubborn persistence for a few years of local Bucks County grandfathers' tales and rumors of Nazi submarine sightings in the Delaware River and the nearby Neshaminy Creek, Operation

Pastorius had no legs. It was a dead story of no impact, other than providing a minor footnote in some history books.

So now you know what this book is *not* about. What it *is* about has to do with the fate of the Penn Salt Manufacturing Company. More than half a century after the end of World War II, that same building with the distinctive saw-toothed roof profile still remained on the banks of the Delaware River. It had deteriorated into an abandoned carcass from a bygone industrial age: a blighted eyesore riddled with a variety of environmental problems. But unlike Operation Pastorius, the Penn Salt building still had a story to tell.

That's where I came into the picture. In 1996, the job of cleaning up the site and transforming it into a beautiful thriving community for the 21st century and beyond was placed squarely on my shoulders.

So there you have it. At the age of 80, I decided to tell the story of how a farm boy, who did little else besides milk cows for the first 18 years of his life, came to be involved with the Cold War, the Cuban Missile Crisis, and President John F. Kennedy's funeral before finally becoming the executive director of the Redevelopment Authority of the County of Bucks, one of the most successful programs of its type in the entire United States.

If this were merely a vanity project, I never would have put pen to paper. But as someone who was raised to abhor waste, I had a hard time accepting that everything I've experienced and learned over the years would just vanish into the mists when I'm no longer here. There are over 1,000 redevelopment authorities (RDAs) across our country. The thought that my story and the material contained in this book's pages might possibly help other communities and inspire other RDA industry folks—or even people outside the field—gives me a great deal of satisfaction.

There's nothing ingenious about what I did throughout my RDA career in Bucks County. I like to think of it as utilizing good common horse sense, but I do profess to have had a few tricks up my sleeve that I developed over the years, so feel free to borrow at will. I also like to think that some of the case studies of projects I worked on are entertaining tales unto themselves: stories of small town politics, visionary developers, and ambitious, colorful personalities, with a fair share of heroes and villains thrown in. They may not be as riveting as the characters and plots Tom Clancy created in his best-selling submarine thrillers, but in the end, they just may give you a lot better mileage.

Bob White
BRISTOL, PENNSYLVANIA
OCTOBER 2020

CO-AUTHOR'S FOREWORD

To say I felt like a fish out of water was putting it lightly. My three previous books had been a biography about 1960s teen idol Bobby Rydell, a musical transcription book tracing the history of rhythm and blues icon James Brown's backup bands, and a biography of Motown Records' legendary '60s studio bassist James Jamerson. Come to think of it, *all* of my previous dozen books before these three were also about musical subjects. So how in the world did I get into a predicament where I might be writing about a public official who worked for the Bucks County Redevelopment Authority, an arm of the county's government that was responsible for cleaning up toxic, abandoned industrial sites and finding new uses for them?

It would be an easy out to blame things on a friend of mine named Jim Gorecki, who worked in the real estate field in and around Bucks County. A musical ally and a fan of my Bobby Rydell bio, Jim told me an acquaintance of his named Bob White was looking for someone to help him write a book about his career. Acknowledging that the subject wasn't my usual fare, he assured me that if I would just meet with Bob, I'd be instantly hooked.

Although I've principally been a working musician for over half a century, the writer side of me couldn't help but be intrigued by the meeting's setting. The sign outside the Bristol, Pennsylvania restaurant read: "The King George II Inn: Est. 1681." A quick google on my iPhone informed me that this was *the* oldest continually operating restaurant in the United States. If Jim's intention was to get me "hooked," this wasn't a bad place to start.

Like the King George II, I instantly perceived Bob White as very real and very impressive. After decades of backing up and working with celebrity actors, singers, dancers, comedians, and producers, I've come to recognize and accept that undefinable aura that surrounds the movers and shakers in this life. Unlike the celebrated Henry David Thoreau quote, "The mass of men lead lives of quiet desperation," these are people who, for want of a better description, just have "it." Despite taking their lumps like all of us do from time to time, the members of this select club are able to mold life to their needs and goals—or at least successfully navigate its rougher waters far better than the average person.

Appearing somewhat larger than his stated five-foot-eleven frame and dressed completely in black with a matching cowboy hat, my first impression of Bob was that he was the Johnny Cash of Bucks County. But, unlike a stereotypical 1980s hair band whose members sit in their dressing room in unremarkable jeans and T-shirts and then walk on stage costumed in skintight spandex with teased-out hair the size of a football helmet, Bob dresses the same way every day. It's just who he is.

Another detail I was quick to recognize came from our initial meeting and all the subsequent breakfast research sessions that took place at a variety of roadside diners in and around Bucks County: Bob always attracts a crowd. I wouldn't say it bears comparisons to the parade of people who sought an audience to ask favors from *The Godfather*'s Don Corleone, but I don't think a single one of our research sessions ever transpired without several people stopping by our table to say hi, pay their respects, or ask for advice. Aside from his approachability and affable nature, people just seemed to like and trust him. Most of all, they knew if they wanted to get something done in Bucks County, Bob was their go-to guy. Comfortable in his own skin, he always seemed to be as relaxed while joking with a waitress or busboy as he was talking business with a local contractor or politician.

For the first few months of this project, I found myself traveling through Bob's depiction of the winding back roads and endless rolling fields of rural 1940s and 1950s America. In spite of coming from a completely foreign world with a different set of values and belief systems, it was tough for me to ignore or disagree with the valuable, homegrown life lessons he absorbed from his formative years as a farm boy and later as a Marine. They weren't framed as pedantic, condescending lectures; in fact, they weren't framed in any specific way at all. It was just Bob graciously sharing a collection of entertaining stories, freely offered general knowledge, and common sense perspectives you couldn't help but accept and internalize while drinking coffee and buttering your toast.

Although it may appear so at times, making his tale come off as an idealized Norman Rockwell portrayal of a vanished American way of life was not my intent. The true worth of Bob's story lies in the way he so successfully fused and adapted the simple values of that life into the complex, professional world of his later years. So, in the same way he welcomed numerous early morning diners into our writing sessions, I hope readers of this book will reap some of the same benefits that 600,000 of his Bucks County neighbors got to experience and enjoy during Bob White's two and a half decades at the Redevelopment Authority.

Allan Slutsky
CHERRY HILL, NEW JERSEY
OCTOBER 2020

PART ONE

CHAPTER 1

A FULL HOUSE
IN BUCKS COUNTY

I was born to work. Now please don't interpret that as arrogance or conceit on my part. I'm not trying to paint myself as some mythical folk hero like John Henry, the "spike-drivin' man" who burst his heart attempting to beat the railroad's steam-powered rock drilling machine in a race. When I say, "I was born to work," I mean it literally. I was born October 21, 1940, and lived on my grandfather's 200-acre farm in Bucks County, Pennsylvania. America was just emerging out of the Great Depression and needed to get back to work to heal itself. Further complicating the USA's economic situation was the imposed rationing of food and fuel once we entered World War II. Like many small private businesses, family-owned farms desperately needed workers but often couldn't afford to pay them. The most cost-effective answer to their workforce problems was a common practice as old as the hills: have lots of children.

That's exactly what my parents did. Harry L. and Harriet White had six of us—five boys and one girl—with me being the fourth in line. Home was a large, four-bedroom farmhouse located at the junction of Newtown Township and both Upper and Lower Makefield Townships. The house was divided into two halves with two separate stairwells.

Grandad Bill and Grandma Mabel lived on the left side of the house, which consisted of two bedrooms and a bathroom on the second floor and a kitchen, dining room, and a window-lined sunroom on the first.

My mom and me in the winter of 1941.

The rest of us lived on the right side, with an upstairs bedroom for my parents and a very large second bedroom with six separate beds arranged in a row around two of the walls for my siblings and me. Downstairs was a kitchen and a living room.

The place I was born: Grandad's farmhouse (as it looked in 2020).

Notice something missing . . . like . . . a bathroom? Both sides of the house shared my grandparents' single bathroom. You can imagine the line down the hallway when 10 people got up in the morning. That's why there was also a four-seater outhouse out back, although I never recall seeing more than a maximum of two people being in there at the same time.

Grandad was a walking contradiction: a devout, prayers-at-every-meal, churchgoing Christian whose principal adjective was *goddamn*. I'm sure he used some other descriptive words from time to time, but that's the one I remember the most. Grandma always used to say to him, "Billy, why would you ask God to damn that wheel barrow"—or whatever else he was working on at the moment—"when you're trying to fix it?"

That was one of Grandma's roles: to correct her husband. When he would tell his oft-repeated story about how the snow from the blizzard of 1888 came up above his knees, she was always quick to point out, "Billy, you were only a four-year-old during that blizzard. No wonder it came up above your knees." Years later, a similar blizzard would still have covered most of his lower body. Grandad was barely five feet tall—a white-haired dynamo and part-time tyrant who always seemed to be in a hurry. In spite of Grandma being a one-woman correction bureau, she was very supportive of him and all he did. They were very close, although I can't ever recall seeing him hug or kiss her. It just wasn't their way. They kept their feelings for each other under wraps.

Grandma and Grandad dressed up in their Sunday best.

There's a reason why I mentioned Grandad before all the other members of my family: For better or worse, he had the most significant impact on me and was the family member I spent the most time with during the first two decades of my life. Grandad bought his farm in the early 1900s, a property he'd previously worked on as an employee. As a sign of how different and trusting those times were from the world in which we currently live, Ben Burris, the previous owner, allowed Grandad to buy it with no money down and let him make annual payments that came from the profits his crops generated. If somebody had given me a deal like that, I'd have been happy as all get-out, but not Grandad. Other than sporadic visits across the road to talk with the owners of the local country store, or watching *The $64,000 Question* on the 10-inch TV set he bought in the mid-1950s, there wasn't much room for anything in his life other than work.

Any rare moments of joy on his part were limited to the times he was driving his 1954 Farmall Super-C tractor in the fields. It was his pride and joy. If there were ever a true love affair between man and machine, this was it. An easy, natural flow always existed between the two of them. Grandad's man-to-family relationship? That was something he struggled with.

Now don't get me wrong; in no way was he an evil or mean-spirited guy. He could be very kind and downright charitable at times, as he was with poor neighbors in the area during the lean years of World War II. Grandad extended a great deal of credit to them for milk, produce, and other necessities that came from his farm—debts that often went uncollected. Outside of that, he was a sullen, serious man who had to have his way in all things and didn't see the need for (or was incapable of) showing his family any warmth or affection. It was all about the work, seven days a week, twenty-four hours a day.

More than any other family member, some of that work ethic was passed on to me. Since I couldn't be left alone in the house when my parents and older brothers were out working, Grandad started giving me chores to do just after I turned four years old. It was simple things at first, like shaking out straw for the cows' bedding or carrying lightweight things around the barn. But as I grew older, that workload gradually—no, *greatly*—increased.

7

I drove my first tractor when I was five years old. My feet couldn't even reach the clutch or brake, so I had to stand up in the seat to steer. My dad would put the tractor in first gear and then jump off. All I had to do was steer the tractor toward the field where they were cutting corn. When I reached the spot where they were working, Dad or one of the other farmhands would jump back on and stop the tractor, change wagons, and send me back to the barn with a fresh load. First gear was very slow, so even if I ran into something, the tractor would just stop. I started out on an International Farmall BN, a small tractor with a potent exhaust. One time, it caused me to fall asleep at the wheel and I hit a tree. No damage done. My three older brothers were also working the fields and one of them came running over, shut off the engine, woke me up, and sent me off with another load.

Not too many kids can lay claim to driving a tractor and starting elementary school in the same year, but I could. In 1945, I was enrolled at the Washington Crossing Elementary School, a two-room schoolhouse for first and second graders. On day one, Mrs. Rykosky, my teacher, quickly discovered I was having trouble seeing things on the blackboard and sent me home with a letter to my parents suggesting they take me to an eye doctor. Within a few days, I was wearing glasses as thick as coke bottles.

It may seem to be a mundane detail except for one thing: Back then, kids would pick on you and call you "four eyes." They didn't have stylish Gucci and Oakley frames like they do nowadays. Industrial-looking wire rims were the only available choice, and I bent up many a pair in the fights with classmates that followed. The situation didn't improve much when I moved on to the third and fourth grades, which were taught at the one-room Dolington School in nearby historic Dolington, Pennsylvania. That "four eyes" moniker continued to follow me.

Poor eyesight was not the only deficiency in my life. Overall, our family was a contented lot, but it would have been nice if there were a bit more cultural stimulation around the house. No one ever read books to us when we were kids. In fact, there was very little book reading in general other than the Bible. The same with music. Other than the songs we sang in church and the few recordings of the day we could pick up on our battery-powered radio, music didn't play much of a role in our lives. Most of the time, that radio was more likely to be tuned to popular shows like *Tom Mix, Roy Rogers, Gene Autry, The Shadow,* and *Johnny Dollar.* When the sun came up though, the daily grind of farm life engulfed our lives once again.

Grandad was apparently grooming me for something. He had plans for me. By six, I was already milking cows and taking on new duties with my brothers, both in the fields and in the barn. Our parents compensated for that in our limited down time by letting us be kids. There wasn't too much drama or upheaval in our early lives. The traditional "spare the rod, spoil the child" disciplinary approach of the day was never used on us. I don't ever remember any of my siblings getting hit or slapped. I'm not saying we were always angels or anything like that. It was just that, with everyone always being so busy working, there wasn't much time to get in trouble. Still, trouble found us on a few occasions.

Maybe the worst of them was when my younger brother Dick and I almost burnt down the barn playing with matches.

Grandad's barn as it appeared in 2020. As an adult, it still looks immense to me, so you can imagine what it looked like through the eyes of an eight-year-old boy.

Even though the pile of hay that caught fire was quickly brought under control, we knew we'd just bought ourselves a world of trouble. After hiding out for almost four hours, we finally turned ourselves in. I couldn't have been more than five years old and Dick was only four, but our tender ages brought us no mercy. Mom was furious. She tied both of us to a couple of trees a few yards apart and then burnt our fingers with the flame from one of those long wooden matchsticks (which were, coincidentally, referred to back in the day as "barn burners"). OK, calm down, calm down—it wasn't as drastic or sadistic as it sounds. There was no damage done and no marks left. She just wanted us to feel the heat of what a fire could do.

Several years later, she used a similar aversion therapy technique after catching some of my brothers smoking. I'd never smoked, but you know how guilt by association works; I had to pay the same price as everyone else. She sat us all down at the kitchen table and made us smoke Camel cigarettes until we got sick as dogs. By today's standards, those two disciplinary incidents would probably be labeled as child abuse. I have to admit though, her methods were effective. I never played with matches again, and it would be years before I'd even attempt to smoke a cigarette.

Overall, I was the easiest of my siblings to raise. I was toilet-trained by age two—one of my brothers took until eleven—and I rarely spoke back to anyone. My dad wasn't very involved in our early upbringing. He'd started a construction business in the early 1940s and was usually working—mostly off the farm, except for the times Grandad needed extra help. Dad would bring over some of his workers to help with baling hay, combining grain, or carrying out any of the farm's other daily operations that needed some extra hands. Those days were some of my favorite childhood memories because I got to spend some quality time with my dad. Other than that, I never saw him that much. When he wasn't working, most of his spare time was spent drinking and running around being a ladies' man.

I have no recollection of him ever sitting down at the dinner table with us for a meal, although simple logic would lead me to deduce that he must have eaten with us at some point. Perhaps in the back of my young mind, it was upsetting so I blocked it out over the years. On the surface though, it all seemed quite normal to me at the time. I loved both my parents dearly and had no clue that anything was amiss between the two of them. Then, one fateful day in 1945, Grandma asked me to try and talk my dad out of leaving my mom. "He loves you. You're his favorite," she told me. "He'll listen to you."

There was no chance of that happening. At five years old, I didn't have the backbone or elocutionary skills to talk to an adult about such a personal, far-reaching decision. And even if he considered me his favorite son, he wasn't going to listen to a little pipsqueak like me. So I did the only thing a young child could: I cried and remained sad off and on for the next three years.

Me at seven years old.

Dad's womanizing eventually narrowed down to one woman: the wife of one of his close friends. Looking toward the future, he bought a farm that bordered on Grandad's 200 acres and relocated us into his new farmhouse. The "us" no longer included Dad. He settled down with his new girl in a bungalow in nearby Newtown.

My younger brother Dick, Mom, my sister Mary Jane, and me after we moved into the farmhouse my dad bought following his split with Mom.

I couldn't really comprehend what my parent's split meant until reality set in three years later in 1948 when they finally divorced. Mom was heartbroken and desperately needed to get as far away from Bucks County as she could. When a friend told her about a 168-acre farm for sale near a town called Hillsville, Virginia, she plunked down $5,000 from her divorce settlement and moved down there with all six of us kids in the spring of 1949.

CHAPTER 2

A RELUCTANT YANKEE
IN VIRGINIA

Did I mention something a few paragraphs back about living through my childhood years with very little upheaval? I guess that would be true if your definition of upheaval does not extend to having your living conditions regress by a century. There was an unspoiled, rustic beauty to our new home in Virginia. I might have appreciated it more if I were a landscape painter or a wilderness photographer, but I was just a simple farm boy who actually had to live in this idyllic picture.

The modest, Cape Cod–style farmhouse we were living in had no electricity, no sink or plumbing, no refrigerator, and no interior water supply. Our only source of light after the sun went down was either candles or kerosene lamps, and the bathroom was an outhouse out back that we all used. My mother and my sister, Mary Jane, were the lone exceptions. They had a potty in their room that my brothers and I were responsible for emptying several times a day. Our water came from a springhouse, a small wooden structure built over a natural spring in the ground, situated about 50 feet away from our front door. We always kept a bucket full of water with a ladle just inside the house's entrance, which constantly had to be refilled.

The inconvenience of it all complicated even the simplest of acts. In my first year in Virginia, I had an upset stomach one rainy night and wanted to take some Alka-Seltzer. The water bucket was empty and I didn't feel like getting soaked running out to the springhouse to refill it, so I just downed the tablet by itself. As I gagged while it exploded in my mouth and throat, I learned a valuable life lesson: Alka-Seltzer doesn't work too well without water. The things we took for granted back up north.

The same thing applied to the act of bathing, which became an entirely new experience for all of us. Saturday night was bath night in our new home. We'd place a galvanized metal washtub in the middle of a room, and Mom would fill it up with water she'd heated on the kitchen stove. Even though a few fresh buckets were added every so often to warm up the tub's contents, we all basically used the same water. The ladies went first and then the rest of us boys took our turns. The last person to wash up did so using the seven previous family members' dirty water.

We may have been short on the amenities we enjoyed in Bucks County, but a *shortage* of water certainly wasn't one of them. Hillsville was at the end of the Blue Ridge Mountains near Route 100. Our house was situated in a valley referred to as "bottom land."

Our Virginia farmhouse. The house was built on stilts because of the recurrent threat of flooding from the surrounding hills.

It was a natural drainage basin for the mountains and cliffs that surrounded us. The locals named those highlands "Coon Ridge" because of all the hunting that went on there. Very often, we could hear the high-pitched yelps of the hunters' coon dogs when they were hot on the trail of a fox or some other small animal.

We were living on an "inside farm," meaning other farms surrounded us on all sides. The only way anyone could get to our property was to cut across someone else's land. Further isolating us from the rest of the world was a 30-foot-wide creek that ran past our house and continued on right through the middle of the mountains. To cross it, we had to walk over a long footlog with a guide wire attached at each side of the creek. It was the only way to get in and out of our farm. Several times a year after big rainstorms, that footlog would either wash away or be inaccessible, stranding our entire family until the waters subsided.

Our connection to the outside world: the footlog over the creek.

Under normal circumstances, the creek's water was so deep that only big trucks or horse-drawn wagons with high undercarriages could navigate the expanse, and even then, it was only at a shallow ford where stones had been placed to raise the level of the creek bed. A standard car would have been washed away. It didn't matter though, because cars never came by; the nearest blacktop road was two miles away.

One of the most enduring impressions from my Virginia experience was how cold we all felt from the late fall to early spring. That would seem to make no sense, since we were almost 500 miles *south* of Bucks County, but our house had no insulation, and the limited heat we did have came from a potbelly stove in the living room and a woodburning cooking stove in the kitchen. We always wore a lot of clothes in that house. The second-floor bedroom I slept in with my brother Cooper would have been uninhabitable for half the year if not for the chimney that came off the stove downstairs. We had to climb up a ladder to reach the room, and we'd sleep under a big quilt called a feather tick. It sounds impressive, but the tick's ability to keep us warm was diminished because the construction on the eaves of the roof had never been finished. Snow used to blow in when there was a blizzard outside, so the heat radiating off the chimney that ran through our room was a godsend.

I'd be remiss if I didn't mention the overwhelming friendliness of everyone in our little valley. A few people in the surrounding hills and the mile-long dirt road leading to the roadway were still Johnny Rebs fighting the Civil War and trying to figure out why their Confederate dollars were worthless. For the most part though, they were OK and didn't get on me too much about being a Yankee. Besides, within a short time after arriving, I'd picked up the distinctive twang of a Southern accent, which helped me fit in with the locals.

My brother Jerry didn't adjust as well. He was a disciplinary problem in Hillsville's school and kept getting kicked out. Mom always managed to talk his way back in, but she couldn't help with his academic standing. Jerry finally quit school in the eighth grade. He had flunked so many times, I actually caught up to him and was going to be in the same grade. No way was he gonna put up with that. Can you picture a 16-year-old like him squeezing into a desk made for much younger students while his 12-year-old little brother sat across the room in a desk with his feet barely reaching the floor? I can't blame him when I look back on it. I'd have been embarrassed too.

A 12-year-old Yankee in Johnny Reb land.

The rest of the family and our just-getting-by, day-to-day lifestyle blended right in with our new neighbors. A lot of people in the valley were struggling with the same economic challenges. Mom was doing the best she could to hold things together with the periodic child support payments Dad mailed us. She always tried to convince us that the Virginia move was the best thing in the world, and because our faith in her was so strong, we never questioned her.

At least there was one aspect of our Hillsville life that was not a step down: our food situation. Unless you're talking about agrarian lifestyles during the dustbowl, Depression era, there's usually plenty to eat on a reasonably functioning farm. Our Virginia operation was much smaller than Grandad's, but we had enough chickens, ducks, cows, and pigs in and around the barn to put meat and dairy products on our table. We also got fish from the creek, and a two-acre garden provided all the produce and vegetables we needed. We just had to work a lot harder than most folks to make it all happen.

Because we had no tractors or any other heavy machinery, we had to do everything the old-fashioned way. When we plowed our fields, it was with an old team of workhorses and a lot of backbreaking effort. No cultivator meant weeding and seeding was by hand, and the lack of a freezer necessitated curing and canning most of our food to preserve it. Breakfast was usually eggs, bacon, and homemade biscuits, with gravy that was made from fatback and milk, thickened with flour and seasoned with salt and pepper. On Sundays, Mom would also whip up a big batch of pancakes. All of our other meals were basic meat, potato, and one vegetable type affairs. You learned to eat what was available. There wasn't a lot of variety, and it certainly wasn't as fancy or haute cuisine as what you'd get at Maxim's in Paris, but by no means were any of us undernourished.

In fact, we were all remarkably healthy compared to people today, when everyone immediately runs to the doctor as soon as they get a common cold, the sniffles, or a cough that persists for more than a few days. We couldn't afford that, and we didn't have a lot to choose from when it came to readily available patent medicines. Other than some highly questionable "miracle" tonics, aspirin and Alka-Seltzer were the only things you saw on the shelves of the general stores. Home remedies ruled the day. Mom once gave me a spoonful of sugar with two drops of kerosene in it to help me get over some simple ailment. It was obviously a bogus cure. You can call it a placebo or mind over matter, but somehow, it worked. We're much cleaner and hygiene-sensitive today with all the hand sanitizers and what not, but back then, our houses were much more breathable, with air changing constantly through open windows. All today's high-tech insulation, air conditioning, filters, and storm windows do is keep playing around with the same trapped air. That's my theory anyway, for whatever it's worth.

We really didn't need much past Mom. She was a mother hen type of woman who always managed to see to all our needs, whether it was cooking around the clock or miraculously creating pants, shirts, and other garments out of the large cloth bags in which our animal feed was delivered. Even so, the child support payments only went so far. It really bothered her that she couldn't take care of us in the way she would have liked. When she turned to the farm to make up the financial deficit, we all did our part, selling eggs and buttermilk to our neighbors, picking wild blackberries to use as barter for goods we needed at the general store a few miles away, and raising and selling off some livestock. It helped, but money was still tight, so my brothers and I generated extra funds by plowing and harrowing other farmers' fields with our horses and mowing and stacking more hay than I'd like to remember—all this in addition to doing the same things for our own farm.

Don't let the smile on my face fool you. Stacking hay gets old really fast.

One of my money-raising specialties was taking a horse into the woods to drag logs to the local sawmill. Even though I gave most of the money to Mom, I was able to save enough over time to buy a portable typewriter for the princely sum of seventy-nine dollars. I was only 11 years old, but I taught myself how to type. I was already a go-getter with a developing fascination for numbers and clerical pursuits. That doesn't necessarily mean I was a good student. With all my chores on the farm and the nightly difficulty of reading by a flickering kerosene lamp, I rarely did any homework. I guess I just wasn't cut from the same read-by-candlelight mold as Abraham Lincoln. In spite of that deficiency and my habit of rarely doing homework, I still excelled at mathematics. As for why I wanted a typewriter, I have to look forward in time rather than backward to comment on that. To this day I have an insatiable appetite for gadgets and other technologically advanced toys, although I have no idea where that hunger came from.

Eventually, our family's situation improved substantially with the addition of electricity during our last three years in Virginia. Its effect was dramatic, immediate, and wide-ranging. We finally had a freezer and refrigerator to keep our food fresh, and a new electric stove replaced the old woodburning one we had. That put an end to our kitchen turning into a sauna whenever Mom cooked during the summertime. We no longer had to churn butter by hand, and receptacles throughout the house brought electric clothes irons and plug-in radios into our lives. I even lost my excuse for being a lousy student with the addition of electric lamps at night, and we could now work in the barn after sunset. Before then, we were never allowed anywhere near the barn with a kerosene lamp unless there was a nighttime emergency with the livestock.

Overall though, we still couldn't maintain the pace necessary to pay all the monthly bills. Mom was wearing down, and some of my brothers were beginning to develop different ideas about what they wanted to do with their lives. I'm sure one of the principal culprits for our growing dissatisfaction was our geographical location. Any supplies that came out of our farm had to cross the creek and then be carried—whether by hand or horse and wagon—up a steep, half-mile-long hill just to get to a dirt road. That was only half of the story. We also had to do the same thing in reverse when supplies were brought in. Getting to our all-12-grades-in-one-building schoolhouse in Carroll County followed the same course, with an additional, often muddy mile-and-a-half walk tacked on just to get to the school bus. It all became such a grind.

Still, not everything was bad about my Virginia farm years. I'd been given four ducks to raise that hatched out dozens of offspring. Since no one in our family liked to eat duck, their population swelled more than tenfold. Their only natural predators were the foxes, possums, skunks, and hawks, which they were exposed to when they hung around and swam in the creek. I really loved raising those ducks, and I also got a lot of enjoyment out of learning to work with our horses. With all the opportunities for seclusion offered by our natural surroundings, my brothers and I had some epic games of hide-and-seek—even though they teased me to no end. One time, when he was on my case, I broke my brother Bill's arm when I hit him with a tree limb.

But outside of our immediate family, our social life was nil. We worked way too much to develop any close friendships, and the long distance from our past life in Pennsylvania drastically limited visits from family members up there. I only saw my dad once a year for the entire five years I spent in Hillsville. It was no surprise that—after five years of southern life—we were all overjoyed and relieved when Mom told us we were moving back to Bucks County.

CHAPTER 3

BACK ON THE CHAIN GANG

I was the odd man out, or I guess I should say the odd *child* out. It was a complicated situation. My older brothers Cooper, Jerry, and Bill had moved back to Bucks County ahead of Mom and the rest of us to start their new lives. I couldn't move into the newly purchased farmhouse we lived in just before we migrated down to Virginia because my dad had moved in there with his new wife and her two kids. That would have been really awkward. My mom had taken Dick and Mary Jane and moved into the home of her Aunt Nell in Brownsburg, Pennsylvania. Nell was a retired missionary who had spent 30 years in India. A true believer, she contributed so heavily to Billy Graham's crusades throughout her life that the reverend actually came and visited her once. It would have been better for me if she had allocated a few of those bucks to build an extra room onto her house, but that never happened. Consequently, there was not enough room in Nell's house for me to move there either.

The only vacant room for me was in the empty farmhouse in Hillsville, Virginia. As self-sufficient as I'd become from all the farmwork skills I'd developed since the age of five, it was a real stretch to even think my parents would allow a 14-year-old kid to stay there by himself. My parents eventually made the housing decision for me: I had a choice between sleeping in a cornfield or returning to Grandad's and joining my brothers Jerry and Cooper, who were already living there and working on the farm. The Hillsville property would sit dormant for quite a few years until my brother Jerry bought it off of Mom for $5,000, paid as a combination of cash and a used 1961 Ford Fairlane.

Mom began her new life back in Pennsylvania as a practical nurse at the Bucks County Home for the Poor. She had the perfect skill set: a combination of having a natural feel for healing along with a strong empathy for people's suffering. I had firsthand experience with her medical talents back in Virginia when I seriously cut my foot on some broken glass. Mom saw I was rapidly losing blood, so she cleaned the wound as best as she could, wrapped my foot in two towels, and kept the pressure on until she got me to the local doctor. If not for her expert ministrations, I might not have made it. Mom was no less attentive to the complete strangers she had as patients in the home for the poor. It wasn't uncommon for her to scold their relatives for not visiting enough, and when they passed away due to illness or old age, Mom took it personally and cried as if she'd just lost a member of her immediate family.

She was doing important work that greatly benefited the lives of impoverished and elderly residents of our community. My life back in Bucks County wasn't quite as rewarding—at least, it seemed that way at the time. The value and long-term implications of what I would experience during my teenage years at Grandad's would not reveal themselves to me until I was considerably older.

When I enrolled in the tenth grade at Council Rock High School, I felt like a man without a country. Down in Hillsville, the kids called me a Yankee. Now, because of the southern accent I'd picked up while living down there, my Council Rock classmates called me a rebel. It was all harmless fun and I made some good friends, although I wouldn't see them too often. Most of the social, academic, cultural, and athletic pursuits high school kids regularly participate in would be unavailable to me. Living on Grandad's farm saw to that. This time around, I wasn't a cute, innocent little kid playing with farm equipment around the barn like I was before going down to Virginia. Living in Grandad's house was no free ride anymore. I was there to work, seven days a week, from before sunrise to after sunset. I understood and accepted my new lot in life: If I didn't work, I wouldn't have a place to stay.

During my five-year absence, Grandad's operation hadn't changed that much except for him replacing his beloved Farmall C tractor with a brand new Oliver Super 88. It was the emperor's new throne. No chance I, or anyone else, was going to ever get our hands on that baby. The old Farmall C and a new but slightly less powerful Oliver 77 were my weapons of choice as I took on a slew of daily, weekly, monthly, and seasonal tasks around the farm. Mowing and cutting back the brush and weeds from road banks, baling hay, fixing fences, cultivating and weeding the cornfields, bagging grain on the combine, and harvesting all the different crops would seem to be an overwhelming number of tasks, but by the terms of the ball and chain pact I'd made with the devil, these were just the appetizers.

The main event was the livestock. Grandad had 17 dairy cows that had to be cared for and milked twice a day, and he also had 30 steers. The steers were easy. You just fed them and let them graze all day until they reached a thousand pounds and were sold off to local slaughterhouses. The dairy cows, on the other hand, were extremely high maintenance. It was a 365-day-a-year job. They had to be milked and have their udders washed at 4:45 a.m., and then the same process was repeated 12 hours later. They also had to be fed, their stalls needed to be cleaned out and bedded down with fresh straw, the milking equipment and pails had to be cleaned, and then the milk had to be delivered to Torbet's Dairy in Newtown for processing. Despite being too young to have a driver's license my first two years back in Bucks County, most mornings I was the delivery boy, driving three miles on the back roads to Newtown in a 1946 Chrysler sedan with the back seat removed to accommodate all the milk cans. The roads were usually deserted that early, and the local police and everyone else knew us so they looked the other way.

All of the work was hard, but hard work never fazed me. Work that traumatizes you for life is another story entirely. As you can imagine, a large number of edible crops in one place would attract a variety of insects and animals. One of my frequent chores was shoveling corn out of the corncrib. On one occasion, when I'd shoveled to the point where there were only a few bushels left at the bottom of the crib, the corn suddenly started to move and out scampered a dozen rats of all sizes. Shaken to my core, I scrambled up to the top of the crib until they ran off. That wasn't the end of my critter problems; it was just round one of an ongoing battle.

A much worse experience awaited me on a frightful day some months later. I was grinding feed for our cattle in the upper part of the barn, which was situated under a hayloft. It was a bitterly cold day, so I was wearing several layers of clothing to stay warm. Walking from the barn back to the house after finishing the job, I felt something crawling on my back. Reaching back, I grabbed it, pulled my coat and all my clothes off over my head, and began jumping on the pile to kill whatever was inside. Thinking I was crazy to be undressing in subfreezing weather, my grandfather came running over to see what was wrong. I shook out the clothes, and a huge dead rat fell to the ground. From that day on, I tied my pants legs at the bottom and wore tight clothes around my chest and neck so nothing could go up or down my body. To this day, the image of that dead rat is something I've never been able to completely drive out of my head.

In a strange sort of way, my battles with these critters was a welcome diversion from the repetitive tasks and the sameness of every day. Getting up each morning before the sun broke the horizon and going to school smelling of manure started to get to me. So did Grandad's general demeanor. He was not a particularly nice man to work for, criticizing my every effort. No matter how I raked hay, milked cows, or plowed a field, it was no good. The concepts of encouragement and compliments were as foreign to him as Zen Buddhism and astrophysics.

School and any outside life I may have had was just an inconvenience to Grandad. To maximize my available work time, he worked out an arrangement with the school bus driver that I was to be the last student picked up on his route in the morning and the first one dropped off after school. The extra time didn't matter; the road in front of me was an endless conveyor belt of tasks. No matter how hard and long I worked, I was never done. *Never done* is a tough place for a teenager to be.

I rarely complained, although Grandad was smart enough to eventually sense my unhappiness. When I reached 16, he made a few compromises and threw in some minor consolation prizes to keep me from quitting. I was allowed to hang out and go to movies and parties with my friends on Saturday nights, and Grandad gave me a weekly allowance of 10 bucks, which he later increased by another 5 dollars. When I finally got my driver's license, I bought my first car, an old Nash with a stick shift, overdrive, a convertible roof that slid off the car, and a radio that didn't work half the time. Not a great choice. I traded it in for a '52 Buick—a big piece of iron, but it got me around. At least I didn't have to walk three miles into town anymore just to meet up with my friends. Hoping to keep me home as much as possible and distract me from thinking too much about missing almost my entire teenage experience, Grandad bought a new TV for the house. His strategy worked to a point, but that didn't mean I wasn't mapping out my future in my few moments of free time—a future that definitely wouldn't include farmwork.

I had no set idea what I wanted to do as a career, but I had a feeling that typing and bookkeeping courses would come in handy at some point. I did well in those classes, although my grades in my other academic courses suffered as a result of my heavy work schedule. I eventually flunked a grade, which enabled my younger brother Dick to catch up to me. Unlike Jerry, who got angry and dropped out of school after the same thing happened to him in Hillsville, I just told everybody Dick was really smart and had skipped a grade.

I was going nowhere for the moment, but I had an unshakeable belief that great opportunities awaited me if only I was sharp and decisive enough to recognize them and seize the moment.

ROBERT O. WHITE
Bob   Newtown
Dancing Club 10, 11; In-
tramurals 10, 11.
   Bob's favorite hobbies
are going on hunting and
fishing trips and working
with cars. At present he
is working on a dairy farm
but in the future would
like to be an accountant.

*Left: Typing class at Council Rock High School. I wasn't a great student, but my fingers could really fly on a typewriter keyboard. **Right:** My senior picture and bio in Council Rock High School's yearbook. Dancing Club?*

Many young people today would view the portrayal of my childhood and formative teenage years as a representation of a prehistoric era. It's easy to understand why. Coming of age in the 1940s and '50s, most of the living conditions I experienced (except for the heavy machinery) were not that dissimilar from those that could have occurred in a similar coming-of-age story from the 1800s or even earlier times. And you know what? I wouldn't have had it any other way. I consider myself very fortunate to have grown up when I did, even though talking about it risks venturing into run-of-the-mill cliché territory about the nobility of hard work and the dedication I picked up along the way. At the very least, my connection to those simpler times—even though it may have taken me years to realize it—has kept me grounded throughout my life. Reducing life's equation down to just working the land with your own hands from dawn till dusk can do that to you.

But it's often the less expansive, smaller-scale experiences that deliver some of our most valuable lessons. When I was a ten-year-old fourth-grader in Virginia, I was minding my own business at a recess one day when I was suddenly dragged into my classroom by the school principal, bent over a desk, and given five hard, humiliating whacks on my butt in front of all my classmates. The weapon of choice was a wooden paddle with holes in it, designed to cut down on air resistance and deliver as painful a blow as physically possible. Then I had to make an equally embarrassing apology to the teacher in front of everyone.

What in the world had I done to deserve a punishment as severe as this? My teacher had asked one of the other boys in my class to go outside and ask me to come into the school so she could talk to me about something. To this day I have no idea why, but he told her, "Bob said you should go fuck yourself." I never said anything of the kind. I didn't even think it, but the damage was done. I was a kid from a broken family, a Yankee no less, in rebel land, and my older brother Jerry had been thrown out of the same school when he was in eighth grade. They figured I was trouble. The response was swift and traumatic. I still shudder when I think about the unfairness of it all. The long-term lesson that resulted took a while to sink in but was no less valuable. I learned not to take anything for granted. If you want life to be fair, you better grab the bull by the horns and have some say in its outcome.

CHAPTER 4

SEMPER FI

I didn't protest or fight for my rights after my public spanking, and I took the same passive stance all the years Grandad bullied me and took away my youth. I was on the outside looking in, just a powerless bystander watching my life go by. But I was also an 18-year-old farm boy desperate to get the hell away from milking cows and smelling like manure. It was time to man up. When a marine recruiter showed up at Council Rock High School in February of my senior year, I saw my path to freedom. His sales pitch was short, direct, and persuasive:

> *I'm from the US Marine Corps. We build men. If you want*
> *to be a man, come see me in the back of the auditorium.*

The low wages offered by the Marines didn't faze me. The possibility of getting paid *at all* would be a big change for me. And being paid while being built into a man? That was a lure I couldn't resist. Three months later, on May 5, 1959, I joined the reserves and entered active duty on June 15, just five days after graduating from high school. And you can bet your bottom dollar I milked cows every one of those last five days. There was no celebratory going-away party or anything like that. Instead, there was a lot of anger and guilt being thrown my way. I waited until the last few days before my departure to tell my grandparents. They were understandably shocked but were also—unfairly, in my opinion—very pissed off. I knew they'd feel that way, so I postponed the issue until it was unavoidable. I had no stomach for dealing with their resentment and hostility three meals a day for several months leading up to my departure for basic training.

"What are we gonna do with all these cows? You know your grand-mother and I can't do all the work," Grandad repeatedly complained after being informed of my imminent departure. Knowing all they cared about was getting the farm's work done helped me cope with their insinuation that I was being ungrateful. Yeah, they fed me and gave me a place to live, but for the amount of work I'd contributed to their farm, the conditions under which I had to live, and, most of all, the sacrifice of *all* my teenage years, a deaf, dumb, and blind man could see they'd gotten the better part of the deal by a country mile.

If there was any gratitude that needed to be shown, it was me toward my father, who rescued me by stepping in and promising Grandad my chores would be handled by some of the workers from his construction company. That really meant a lot to me and made me feel much closer to him. During the five years I was down in Virginia, our relationship was almost nonexistent, but it had warmed up significantly since I'd moved back to Bucks County. His bailing me out of this uncomfortable situation was the icing on the cake. It was the best going-away present I could have had.

There was, however, one other going-away present I should mention. The Marine representatives who recruited me and some other local guys took us out to eat at Philadelphia's famous Bookbinder's Seafood Restaurant, courtesy of Uncle Sam. It seemed liked a condemned man's last meal before meeting the hangman. The last sweet sensation of our desserts hadn't even faded from everyone's taste buds when the recruiters drove our group to 30th Street Station and put us on a train headed for Parris Island, South Carolina.

I was actually looking forward to getting screamed at and ordered around for 16 weeks. You know about the dread many Marine recruits feel in the pit of their stomachs when they first see the crimson and yellow entrance sign to Parris Island? That fear didn't apply to me. After Grandad's around-the-clock bitching, my feelings weren't going to get hurt by a drill sergeant screaming in my face. I was as strong as an ox from years of farm work, and as for spending a few months getting up before dawn to march five miles, I'd damn sure rather do that than spend the rest of my life milking a dozen cows at 4:45 a.m.

I kinda got a kick out of some of the stereotypical aspects of Marine recruit life. Like when I knocked on the drill sergeant's closed door to ask him a question and he bellowed, "I CAN'T HEAR YOU!!!" I couldn't help but think, *How in the world would he know someone was knocking if he didn't hear me?* That's the logic of life on Parris Island. It's better not to think too much and just do as you're told, especially when it comes to the DIs (drill instructors). Back then, they were allowed to hit you if you got them pissed off. I saw one DI make a recruit eat a letter from his girlfriend as punishment for some minor infraction. One time I got an earful from a DI for saying "thank you" to him. "Do I look like a female sheep to you?" he barked at me. It would *not* have been a good idea to try and explain that I meant Y-O-U, not E-W-E. You just had to shut up, take it, and remember to never say "you" again.

The one fear all of us recruits had was being "set back." If you broke a serious rule or underperformed, they'd transfer you to another company and make you start boot camp all over again. It didn't matter whether or not you had already completed one week of training or fifteen. It was back to the beginning if you screwed up. I had no intention of being sent back to week one, so I embraced my Parris Island experience, particularly their efforts to instill each recruit with a sense of pride in themselves, their company, and the long tradition of the Marines. Eighty young, roly-poly high school boys got thrown together in a company and emerged as a disciplined, hardened team of men with a firm knowledge and respect for the Corps' history and traditions. A move that started out for me as a simple escape from my grandad and his farm became a life-changing experience.

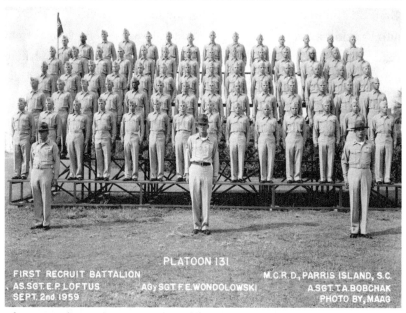

PLATOON 131

FIRST RECRUIT BATTALION   M.C.R.D., PARRIS ISLAND, S.C.
AS.SGT. E.P. LOFTUS   AGy SGT. F.E. WONDOLOWSKI   A.SGT. T.A. BOBCHAK
SEPT. 2nd 1959   PHOTO BY, MAAG

If you're wondering where I am in the middle of the wall of khaki in this photo, I'm standing in the next to the last row on the far right. Of the three drill instructors standing in front of our platoon, Sgt. Loftus (on the far left) was, by far, the most ornery. Any Marine recruit who got on his bad side was in deep trouble.

The Corps had no time for my overblown, dramatic assessment of the 16 weeks I'd just completed. To them, I was just another jarhead going through the developmental process of becoming a valuable asset to the Marines. Before I had a chance to catch my breath, I was shipped off to Camp Lejeune in North Carolina in September 1959 to complete four weeks of infantry training regiment (ITR) training. I felt like a big tycoon. The seventy-eight dollars a month Uncle Sam was paying me was better than the allowance I was getting at Grandad's, the work was easier, and I was still getting all my food, lodging, and clothing for free. The only thing missing was a good set of wheels to get me around. When the Marines gave me a 30-day leave after completing ITR training, I traveled back home to work for my dad's construction company and earned enough money to buy a used 1955 Plymouth Belvedere. I also came back to add to my experience in operating heavy construction machinery. I thought it might come in handy with the military.

You'd have to search far and wide to find a Marine who wouldn't admit to being filled with pride every time they put on their dress blues.

As I drove back to the base, I wasn't sure where I'd be assigned, although I hoped I could land my butt on top of some massive military excavators, dozers, and backhoes. At the very least, I figured I'd get motor pool duty, driving armored transports and reconnaissance vehicles.

Sixty days of mess duty washing dishes on the graveyard shift (2:00 a.m. to 11:00 a.m.) for C Company, First Battalion, Eighth Marines wasn't what I had in mind. I was placed there because of a predictable military snafu. The tests I took when I first joined the Marines indicated I could type 60 words a minute. That was the kiss of death for my heavy machinery dreams. Anyone who can type that fast in the military is undoubtedly going to be given a 0141 military occupational specialty (MOS) designation for clerical work. Once the company commander finally found out where the office clerk he'd requisitioned had been misassigned, I was quickly transferred to the company office.

It was a blessing in disguise. Because of my daily proximity to the company commanders, executive officers, warrant officers, and ranking enlisted personnel, I got to know many of them quite well. The officers were treated like gods in the Marines. They were usually highly educated college grads who were commissioned, and their general behavior separated them from the lower-ranked enlisted Marines. A sergeant might snarl something like, "Move that goddamn table!" when he was talking to a lower rank, while an officer would calmly say, "I'd like that table moved." They were always respectful and were expected to be officers and gentlemen.

For an ambitious kid like myself, the company office was the place I needed to be. I did everything I could to make the most of the opportunity, including reading all the Marine manuals cover to cover. I also was meritoriously promoted from lance corporal to corporal E4 after taking a Marine Corps test and scoring 99 out of 100. The result of all this was my startling discovery that, in the real world outside of Grandad's farm, people actually give out compliments when you work really hard and get results! I certainly appreciated them, but the "attaboys" I received in the Marine Corps didn't mean as much to me as you might think. I was always thinking ahead to the next task or project that waited for me around the corner.

I didn't have to wait for too long. In May 1960, Company C shipped out for the first of two tours of duty in the Mediterranean Sea with the Seventh Fleet. WOW! Spain, Italy, Sicily, France, Turkey, Greece—it was all very exciting for a kid whose lifelong travelog couldn't list much past the Carolinas and some farmland in Pennsylvania and Virginia. We shipped out on LST 1178, a landing vessel designed for dropping off troops and amphibious vehicles in shallow water and on beachheads. We were lodged six bunks high in cramped, dimly lit sleeping quarters, but it didn't matter; nothing could dampen our enjoyment of being on a ship at sea in such exotic settings. Youthful innocence, however, blinded us to the strategic gravity of our deployment. With the Cold War in full bloom, the US felt it was of the utmost importance to maintain a strong presence in the Mediterranean.

If I'm making it sound like we were just a bunch of teenage kids on a vacation, that wasn't really the case. Any deficiency we may have had in understanding and appreciating the United States' long term global policy was offset by some measured doses of reality. If being caught in a hurricane four days out into the Atlantic Ocean on our way to the Mediterranean didn't put the fear of god into us, then we had a second chance when a fire broke out on board that threatened to set off the ship's ammunition magazines. Moving all our company's gear and records from one side of the ship to the other while being pounded by a hurricane was no picnic. Thankfully, we ended our tour without sinking or being blown up.

Once we were back in Camp Lejeune, the last remaining visions of white sand beaches, sun-drenched cliffside dwellings, and beautiful European women faded into the monotonous olive drab and brown of Marine Corps life. I worked every weekday at the company office until it closed at 4:00 p.m. Afterward, there was little to do other than lift weights, play cards, or shoot pool. Saturdays and Sundays provided a break from it all, and with gas costing less than twenty cents a gallon, I could afford to drive back home when I didn't have weekend guard duty. Then Monday mornings arrived and the cycle started all over again. Military life can be incredibly boring and predictable in between assignments—until something unpredictable happens.

Loading up the trunk of my 1955 Plymouth Belvedere for a trip back home.
I'd been given a weekend leave from Camp Lejeune.

CHAPTER 5

VIVA LA REVOLUCIÓN

I entered military service during the peacetime conditions that existed between the Korean and Vietnam Wars. I wasn't expecting to be involved in any monumental events with worldwide implications, but history has a way of finding you whether you expect it or not. The entire western hemisphere had been on edge since January 1959 when Fidel Castro's guerrilla forces overthrew Cuba's US-supported Batista government. The tension ratcheted up for the next two years and reached a new peak when the CIA, fearing an encroaching communist threat, tried to remove Castro from power in the ill-fated April 1961 Bay of Pigs invasion. In less than 24 hours, 1,400 US-trained Cuban exiles were killed or captured by the new Cuban dictator's far-superior army.

That military success did little to calm Castro's growing fear of another US invasion. In a secret agreement reached in July 1962, he was able to coax an already angry Russian Premier Nikita Khrushchev into placing ballistic missiles on the island of Cuba. He didn't need much convincing; Russia was already viewing a recent deployment of American ballistic missile sites in Turkey and Italy as an existential threat and sought to level the playing field. After an American U-2 spy plane established the existence of the Cuban missile sites, the US initiated a naval blockade of the island on October 22 with the intent of discouraging any further Russian missile deliveries to Castro.

While the outside world wrung its hands in anguish over the increasing possibility of a nuclear confrontation, Camp Lejeune just continued going through its usual paces. Soldiers marched, file clerks typed, and daily drills progressed. A company reinforced by a weapons platoon was routinely on standby every week, as were the military exercises and mock amphibious landings at nearby Onslow Beach. In October 1962, one of the company drills was significantly different.

My company happened to be the one chosen for standby duty. We all fell out as usual, thinking we were embarking on another drill to test our battle readiness. They'd usually load us onto a Sixby two-and-a-half-ton transport vehicle and drive us around the block before returning to base. This time though, they kept on driving until we reached the coast. We were loaded onto LPH-4, a Marine Corps helicopter ship, and transported to the US naval base at Guantanamo Bay, Cuba. Our marching orders happened to coincide with the day a US Navy vessel fired a warning shot over the bow of a Soviet freighter trying to run the blockade with a new shipment of missiles.

This was no drill! It was quite a shock to many of my comrades who felt we weren't properly prepared for an excursion like this. Welcome to the armed services, boys! That's the way it always begins. All the marching and battle simulations in the world can't get you ready for the real thing. We had conscientious objectors in our ranks, as well as gung-ho yahoos who just wanted to shoot guns and get into a fight. In the end, the discipline that was drilled into us from our first day at Parris Island prevailed. So did our confidence in the experienced commanding officers in our midst. We believed in them.

Our mission was to assist in the security of the naval base, so we were posted on the opposite side of the bay from the US naval facility in an area that bordered Cuba. Castro's forces had already cleared out all the shrubbery on their side of the six-foot chain-link perimeter fence so they could spy on what we were doing. I found it odd that the Cuban field commanders didn't realize that by clearing away all the shrubbery, it also allowed us to spy on them, particularly all the comings and goings of ships in the Cuban port just behind Guantanamo.

Either way, it was a standoff. Cuban soldiers stood no more than 300 feet away from us. Our guard stations faced their guard stations. But we had massive bunkers protecting us and they didn't. No one was going to push us off the island. The early doubts and jitters the company experienced when we first landed in Guantanamo quickly faded. In their place was a growing, unmistakable feeling of patriotism that ran through our entire company. We were there to protect the people and the interests of the United States of America.

Thirteen days of fear and tension gripped Washington, DC and the rest of the world as negotiations between the two superpowers plodded on. We all had a sense of how serious the situation was, but predictably, the Marines stoically treated our security mission as they did any other day. *Maybe* we exhaled a little bit when President Kennedy and Khrushchev finally reached a deal on October 28.

The Cuban Missile Crisis standoff officially ended on November 21 when Russia dismantled their offensive weapons in Cuba and the US did the same in Turkey and Italy. Even though the immediate threat was over, our company remained in Cuba for another five months. I spent most of the time working in the company office, so I didn't pull too much guard duty. In our downtime, we were able to travel by boat to take advantage of the facilities at the naval base across the bay. My company's seven-month deployment in Cuba proved to be a great experience, although once things calmed down, life wasn't much different than on any other military base.

I knew I'd need a change of scenery when I returned to Camp Lejeune and, by happenstance, the Marines were good enough to read my mind and provide it for me. I found out I'd been transferred to the Sixth Marines and would be working at Regimental Headquarters S3. Though it may sound like a lot of military jargon and numerical gibberish, I couldn't have planned it any better. I was the unit diary and orders clerk, recording all the daily events, typing out orders for transfers, and preparing court martial papers and any of the other needs of the legal staff, but working at S3 also enabled me to view all the MOS requisitions that came through the headquarters' office. One of them was for an 0141 clerical position at the Marine barracks at 8th and I Street in Washington, DC. I jumped at it. Thankfully, I was selected, but it entailed extending my enlistment to qualify for the transfer.

There was a reason behind my desire to be transferred to Regiment S3: I'd met a girl named Patricia Kennedy at a church social in 1957. We dated for a few years until she wrote me a "Dear John" letter while I was in Parris Island. I'd like to think it was the unforgettable, dashing image of me in my military uniform, but for whatever reason, we reconnected in the summer of 1961 and made love for the first time on Christmas Eve of the same year. As luck would have it, our romance was cut short a few days later when I was shipped out to Vieques, Puerto Rico, for maneuvers and a two-month tour. While I was away, Pat discovered she'd become pregnant, so we got married when I returned and she moved down to Camp Lejeune to be with me.

Our first home was a one-bedroom trailer in the base's crowded trailer camp. These cookie-cutter residences were separated by only 10 feet of open space on each side and were staggered on angles so you and your immediate neighbors wouldn't be staring into each other's windows. The two of us put up with the claustrophobic surroundings for a while until Pat decided she wanted to be closer to her family back home. By early 1962, Washington, DC started to look like a good fit.

CHAPTER 6

8TH AND I

The 8th and I Barracks took up an entire city block and housed 800 Marines, the Marine Corps band, and the Marine Corps Institute. This new assignment was a significant upgrade for Pat and me. Instead of shoe-horning ourselves into that Camp Lejeune trailer, our new residence was a three-bedroom house on Alabama Avenue SE. We sure needed it since, in short order, there were three of us. Pat and I were married in March 1962, and our son Randy was born shortly thereafter on September 23.

I felt like I was a wealthy Greek shipping tycoon when my pay grade increased to $225 a month after receiving a promotion to corporal E4. Being married and living off base also qualified me for a basic allowance for quarters (BAQ) that gave me an additional monthly stipend of ninety dollars. I was moving up in the car department too, after purchasing an almost-new 1961 Plymouth with a slant six motor, a working radio, wind-up-and-down windows, and of course, power steering by Armstrong (slang of the day meaning *no* power steering). Hell, I was living the life of Riley, as they used to say.

The sleepy DC neighborhood I returned to every night was in stark contrast to the hustle and bustle of the Marine barracks where I worked during the day. The barracks was a hotbed of activity, and it was my job to document all of it in the unit diary. My Camp Lejeune habit of reading every Marine manual I could get my hands on continued at my new location. I read and mastered the intricate processes and requirements for reporting daily movements in the company and learned as much as possible about the Uniform Code of Military Justice. Many of the same clerical duties assigned to me at Camp Lejeune continued at 8th and I but on a much higher level. It was necessary to become proficient in all phases of the documentation of Marine personnel records. Perfection was required on every document to ensure any and all Marine personnel involved in a deployment would receive the proper benefits as they moved through the Corps.

To the layman, I'm sure all this sounds like boring, mundane work, but I had a passion for it, with an encyclopedic memory and a gift for organization. My typing skills had evolved into an art form by this point—a heckuva good thing, considering the daunting typing requirements. In the pre-computer age, making corrections was not easy. Finally getting a shot at working with electric typewriters made things easier but only so much. We weren't permitted to use the recently invented whiteout / liquid paper concoctions, and everything I typed was a sextuplet situation facilitated by six pages of carbon paper. You really had to hit those keys with some power to get through to the last copy of each page. And any time you made a mistake, you had to correct all six versions of the same page by hand with an eraser. On top of that, only three mistakes were permitted per document. Once you exceeded that amount, the entire document had to be retyped.

The long-term implications of all these highly developed skills were easy to overlook because I was doing double duty. I still had to take part in all the same drills and annual conditioning training as the rest of the guys in my company. Every year I was on active duty, I spent enough time on the firing range to qualify as a rifle marksman and a sharpshooter with the .45-caliber pistol, and I had to participate in all the long marches with a full pack and rifle. The only difference was once we were done, the other guys in the company could rest up; I had to record all these maneuvers in the Marine Services Record Book. Everything started to blur together, but in the midst of all the clerical work and the military drills that occupied my daily life in Washington, DC, history was once again about to interrupt the daily flow of events and take center stage.

CHAPTER 7

FOUR DAYS
IN NOVEMBER

The 1961 Cuban Missile Crisis was not the first time President Kennedy came into my consciousness. I was only 20 when he was elected, so I couldn't vote for him—a fact I've always considered to be nonsensical, since I was deemed old enough to be in the Marines and possibly die for my country but was deemed too young to be allowed to vote for our commander in chief. Senator Kennedy had to fight through a similar age discrimination issue coming from journalists and assorted political analysts who felt he was too young at 43 years to sit behind the Resolute desk in the Oval Office. Equally questionable was the commonly held opinion that a Catholic could never be elected president of the United States. JFK proved them all wrong on both counts.

Within a few months of his first year of service, it was impossible for me not to be impressed by his honesty, his overall demeanor, and the dignity that he brought to the office. Everyone—Republican or Democrat—was in love with his wife, Jackie. What a First Lady she was! Years later, it's common knowledge that President Kennedy had numerous affairs with other women, but during his all-too-brief presidency, JFK, Jackie, and their two children appeared to be the perfect American family. I greatly admired that, while also being a bit envious. You'd have to use the word "family" very loosely when referring to the haphazard atmosphere and conditions in which I was raised.

I wasn't fortunate enough to have ever met him face to face, but I did get to see him quite a few times when he showed up at the 8th and I Marine base to view the summer parades or when his weekend visits to the presidential retreat in Camp David coincided with the times in 1962 and 1963 when I was assigned to security duty there. He always had a good word for the guys in the guard shack at the retreat's entrance. I used to do a fairly respectable JFK imitation, but I never got the chance to lay it on him. I doubt the Secret Service would have been too fond of that.

On that fateful day on November 22, 1963, I was on a 96-hour pass driving home to Bucks County to visit my family. My car radio was not working (some things never change), so I was completely cut off from the events of the day. When I pulled off the road to get some gas, the station attendant informed me that President Kennedy had been assassinated. I called my mom on a pay phone, and she told me the base had called with orders for me to immediately return to the barracks. Overwhelming feelings of sorrow and despair accompanied me on the ride back. I just kept thinking, *This can't be true.* When I returned to base, the same solemn atmosphere permeated everyone and everything. Lee Harvey Oswald was already in custody, but no one knew for sure who was behind the plot. The Russians? Castro? The Mob? Not knowing who was responsible and what could be coming next had everyone on high alert.

Once Lyndon Johnson assumed the presidency, stability was restored and I was given a new task. I was assigned to assist the Marine Corps officer in charge of the funeral procession. We were responsible for scheduling and properly locating the military cordon and the various military bands that would be playing along the procession's route from St. Matthew's Cathedral to Arlington National Cemetery. For four straight days leading up to the burial, the work was nonstop, but I looked upon it as a great honor. I'll never forget viewing the president's casket in the Capitol rotunda and praying for him and his family. Even more haunting for me was the image of the eternal flame being lit at his graveside. I'm aware of the effect it had on the millions of Americans who watched in anguish as the black-and-white, two-dimensional image of our shared national agony appeared on their television sets. Imagine what I felt on November 25, seeing firsthand the full-color, three-dimensional version of the same image punctuated with the scent of the newly lit flame as it filtered through the chilly fall air.

President Johnson sent letters of commendation to me and the other members of our team for the work we'd done and then proceeded to get on with the business of running the country. That's what is so great about America—the rock-solid strength and integrity of our institutions. A foe may attempt to defeat us by killing our commander in chief, but someone will always step in, fill the position, and make sure our country's life goes on without interruption.

History and I parted ways during my last two years of service at 8th and I. Predictably, the drills, clerical work, and assorted assignments continued with their customary precision, although there were some minor deviations. One change was a matter of casting. On the weeks when I was on security detail at Camp David, I was now, regrettably, guarding President Lyndon Johnson instead of JFK. Now, don't get me wrong; I had nothing against President Johnson. It was just that the gaping wound that came in the wake of the Kennedy assassination had not come close to healing.

If I wanted some drama, it was there for the taking in my personal life. Pat's family never approved of me and didn't even show up at our wedding. Still, she had a right to want to be near them. She'd been working as an executive secretary for the government while we were living in Washington, but I could tell she'd grown weary of being a Marine wife. I loved being in the military and probably would have made it my life's career, but I had a family to think about and my wife had dreams and

49

desires of her own. I resigned from the Marines and moved Pat and my son back to Pennsylvania into the house of an aunt who had recently died. I still had five months of service to go, so I only saw them on weekends—and even then, only on the ones when I wasn't on security detail at Camp David. It was a difficult time for us.

On March 8, 1965, 3,500 Marines came ashore at Da Nang, South Vietnam, to augment the 25,000 US military advisors already stationed there. It was the first wave of actual US combat troops to arrive in that fractured country. Although undeclared by the US Congress, everyone knew we were at war once again; they just hadn't yet recognized the extent of the nightmare to come. But this new fight would fall on the shoulders of other young men. I was released from active duty on June 12, 1964 and was placed in the inactive reserves for a year until my honorary discharge from the Marines came on May 9, 1965.

I was a civilian in Bucks County once again. Grandad was suffering from cancer and had a colostomy, which necessitated selling off all his cherished cows except for one that was Grandma's favorite. I rarely visited him after I returned from military service, and on the occasions I did, he still didn't have a good word for me. I think he was still bitter about my leaving the farm for military service. Grandma, who lived to be 98, never tired of telling family members that the Marines had ruined me. If finally having a mind of my own and refusing to submissively work until I dropped dead was her idea of me being ruined, then there's not much I could do about that.

Worrying about things that were out of my control was no longer on my menu. I had more pressing matters to deal with. Two doors from my past had just closed. The question that loomed in the air awaiting an answer was: *What was I going to do with the rest of my life?*

CHAPTER 8

I AIN'T GONNA WORK ON GRANDAD'S FARM NO MORE

It wasn't as epic a decision as I seem to be implying. A return to serfdom at Grandad's was out of the question, so I thought about being a cop for a moment. That was a field that a lot of ex-servicemen pursued, but I really wanted to go into the construction business. The perfect fit was staring me right in the face: the Harry L. White Construction Co. My dad's business would give me the opportunity that had evaded me in the Marines.

I started out as a basic laborer and truck driver, hauling stone and blacktop in a six-wheeler capable of hauling ten tons at a time. I got a reprieve from that duty one day when Dad asked me to assist someone who would be operating the backhoe to dig a hole for an on-site septic tank. The guy was late, so I just hopped on the backhoe, played around with it for a while to get the hang of it, and then dug the hole myself. My dad showed up at ten o'clock and was so impressed he made me the backhoe operator for the next few years.

The next big challenge he placed in my path was learning to operate a D6 bulldozer on a highline electrical installation, for which it was necessary to prepare paths for concrete trucks to come in and out of a very muddy construction site. Dad gave me a 30-minute tutorial and then basically threw me in the water and said, "Now swim." It was all on me for the next six months to carve out temporary roadways and build stone-based fords in the small creeks around the site to allow all the construction vehicles to come in and out.

I had a distinct advantage over most beginners in the construction business because my father owned the equipment. I don't think I would have had the guts or arrogance to just jump on someone else's expensive backhoes, loaders, cherry pickers, graders, and rollers and risk damaging them while teaching myself how they worked. Yet, that's exactly what I did with Dad's gear. The school of hard knocks proved to be extremely beneficial to me, and so was the expertise and generosity of the other on-site workers, project managers, and superintendents I befriended. I'd show up an hour before I needed to, just so I could pick everyone's brains about reading blueprints, using transits to set stakes for vertical steel structures, how to bid jobs, and any other construction-based knowledge I could absorb. Dad was thrilled to see me learn the business and encouraged it all.

My dad was the owner and boss of his construction company, but that didn't stop him from shoveling asphalt with the rest of his workers. He was always a hands-on type of guy. That's him on the lower left.

My career was in full bloom. I couldn't have been happier with how things were progressing. Regrettably, the same thing couldn't be said for my personal and family life. I'd entered the Marines with a lot of good habits and left with some bad ones. Except for the avoidance therapy incident when Mom force-fed Camels to all five of us White boys, I'd never been a smoker. The Marines didn't care about my smoking history; in fact, they were complicit to some extent in getting me started. It's hard to believe by today's standards, but in the late '50s, a carton of cigarettes was standard issue along with your uniform when you entered the service. Still, I resisted. Then I noticed that the drill instructors gave smokers periodic breaks from marching that the nonsmokers didn't get. In the blink of an eye, I was the Marlboro Man.

Five or six years after I returned home to Bucks County, I started noticing that my fingers had become discolored by an ugly yellow stain, so I quit cold turkey. I was doing great for a while until I picked it up again. While playing in a softball game, a hot-looking girl I'd wanted to meet offered me a Tareyton cigarette. Accepting it from her was one of the dumbest things I've ever done. The girl became a distant memory in no time; I became a three-to-four-pack-a-day smoker until 1979. I finally said, "Enough of this," and gave up smoking for good that same year after a significant increase in the cost of a carton of cigarettes. I figured I could do a lot better things with $7.50 than pollute my lungs.

My wife Pat bore the brunt of dealing with that and the other bad habits in my arsenal. You'd think I would have developed some common sense after years of watching the way my Grandad ragged on my father about drinking and smoking. That didn't happen. Drinking and I partnered up when I was in the Marines—nothing big mind you, just a few Rolling Rock beers here and there. By the mid-1960s though, I was buying a dozen cases of beer every other Saturday and loading up the cooler in the back of my pickup truck so I'd have a seamless, uninterrupted supply. The image of an out-of-control, falling-down drunk did not apply to me. I was more of a sociable, life-of-the-party type guy, talking my head off to people at the bars until two thirty in the morning.

Back then, people often drank on the job at construction sites—not just the hired workers, but *me* too. With all the background checks and liability issues of today, that would never be allowed. Luckily, since there were far fewer cars on the road in the 1960s, we all got home safely, even when impaired. One time during that era after a hard day of working and drinking, I was driving home when I stopped at a traffic signal in a nearby town. I thought I'd been sitting there a normal amount of time when suddenly, I heard a knock on my window. I rolled down the window and lo and behold, it was the chief of police, who I knew quite well. "What's up, Chief?" I asked him.

He bristled. "What the hell are you doing?"

I told him I was waiting for the light to turn green.

"How green do you want it to get?" he snarled. "It's turned green seven times. Now go home!"

And of course, I did just that.

In spite of my daily workaholic schedule, somehow I always found time for nocturnal drinking and carousing. And as diligent as I was on the job, I was equally negligent about taking care of my "home work." After putting up with my antics for longer than I deserved, Pat threw in the towel and left, taking Randy and our second child, Kimberly. They moved to Florida first before eventually resettling in Norwalk, Connecticut.

For two years, I had no idea where my kids were. I was devastated when I found out where she was, got drunk, and started driving north on I-95 toward Connecticut with bad intentions on my mind. By the time I got to the George Washington Bridge, I'd sobered up enough to realize I couldn't drink anymore, turned around, and went home. I went on the wagon in my midthirties, too late to save my marriage. Pat and I finally filed for divorced in 1968 and made it official in 1972—my fault, not hers.

Along with any remorse I may have had about not being a better husband and father, I had two other major regrets. When we were still together, Pat and I moved into a house in Wrightstown, Pennsylvania that I was able to purchase for only $12,900. It had septic problems, which was the reason behind the property's ridiculous, below-market asking price. A problem like that would typically scare off most people, but I wasn't most people. With my construction skills, I had the problem solved and corrected in no time.

A local bar owner who had always admired that house tried to talk me into trading it for a building she owned that had living quarters on the second floor and a bar called the Chain Bridge Tavern on the ground level. Not wanting to live above a bar, Pat talked me out of it. Some years later, the property sold for well over $1,000,000. Missing out on a seven-figure profit was tough to stomach, but I probably would have just been a drunk bar owner. I needed to leave that world, and besides, I had decades and numerous opportunities ahead of me to make money.

More disappointing to me was the finality of my resignation from the Marines. If I'd known Pat and I weren't going to make it, I'd have stayed in military service for the rest of my career. They were five of the best years of my life.

There has always been a simple antidote to any turmoil and personal struggles I've had throughout my life. Work has always been my solace and source of comfort; it's the foundation I can always return to when things start going bad. In the second half of the 1960s, that foundation was rock solid.

Almost everything about working for the Harry L. White Construction Co. was a plus, including the deepening relationship I had with my dad after being apart from him for so many years. However, there was one big negative that eventually proved to be insurmountable: My brother Jerry became my immediate boss. I knew that situation was doomed from the start. Jerry was the only one of my brothers I had a hard time with. We were OK with each other when I was really young, and then it all changed once we moved to Virginia. He was the kind of guy who would ask to borrow a pair of dress shoes and then return them six weeks later, torn up and covered in mud, with nary an apology to be found.

When I moved back into Grandad's after Virginia, Jerry was still living there. Unlike my seven-days-a-week work schedule on the farm, he didn't have the same "If I don't work, I won't have a place to stay" mentality that I did. Most of the time, he just lived there, worked when he felt like it, and occasionally disappeared for months at a time, driving semi-trucks back and forth across the country. The anger issues he had and his hard drinking and partying were getting him into trouble more and more. He finally hit rock bottom one day when he got arrested and sent to jail for six months after getting into a knife fight with another motorist in the Lincoln Tunnel going into New York City. Dad recognized Jerry was headed for a bad outcome, so he saved him from himself by making him the head of his construction company.

Jerry was a tough man to work for. Nobody ever did anything right in his eyes. I'm sure he picked up that characteristic from being around Grandad, but Grandad was critical in a matter-of-fact kind of way. Jerry, on the other hand, would play the blame game, say mean-spirited things, and put you down. Like, if I was behind the wheel of his rickety truck and it broke down, he'd typically say, "Asshole! What the hell were you doing driving on this road anyway? Besides, you know you're supposed to pull on the choke when the damn engine starts to stall out." Then when we'd get the engine to turn over, he'd add, "Now you think you can keep this truck on the road for the rest of the day without screwin' things up all over again?"

I tolerated that kinda crap for around four years until I'd finally had enough. By that time, all of my other brothers were also in my dad's employ. There were just too many bosses and not enough workers for my liking. One day in 1969, I walked off the job. My brother followed me down the street screaming, "Where you goin'? Where you goin'?" He knew, because I just kept walking and never came back.

I've never been unemployed and never received workers' comp—a streak kept alive by some fortunate circumstances and a lifelong inclination toward having multiple jobs and projects going on simultaneously. I had a restless soul, but I wasn't stupid. I always made sure I had a secure job waiting for me before I left the previous one. Toward the end of my tenure at my dad's company, I was living in Doylestown. An insurance salesman came to my house, and I liked his sales pitch so I purchased a policy. It seemed like a solid, challenging field of work, and since I'd been looking to make a career change, I asked him to introduce me to his manager. In January 1970, after going through their training course and getting my license, I started selling insurance for the Independent Order of Foresters. Sounds like the name of a cult don't it? But the company was a respected fraternal benefit organization that had been around since 1874.

In an effort to avail myself of every possible tool that could help me succeed, I started taking Dale Carnegie salesmanship and self-improvement courses. I even carried around three-by-five cards in my pocket with inspirational sayings like "Whatever the human mind can conceive, it can achieve," and "You can't win the past, but you can win today." They may sound trite and corny, but they helped me. So did my unorthodox approach to sales. I didn't use the prepared lines and pitches I was fed during the insurance company's training course. I talked to people as if I were the local farmer that I'd been through so much of my life.

You had to be a caring people person to connect with them, although you also had to be a bit of a scammer. I was a committed devotee of W. C. Fields's "Dazzle them with brilliance or baffle them with bullshit" line. Sales techniques aside, the product I was selling was a good one, and I never forced a policy on anyone who didn't need it. The combination worked for me. I got more appointments and sold more insurance than anyone else in the district.

Six months after I began, they offered me the position of district manager. My new office oversaw five counties and was soon grossing over $1,000,000 a month in sales. Along with the successes came a nasty case of burnout. I continued in health and life insurance sales for almost 10 years, but I knew I'd have to make a move at some point.

In preparation for my eventual exit, I started adding a dizzying array of overlapping part-time and full-time skills and occupations to my resume. In the process, I became the heavyweight champion of functioning on only three to four hours of sleep. I bartended, plowed snow for the state department of transportation, prepared people's income tax returns, and drove tractor trailers for UPS.

My insurance salesman look. I maintained my Marine crew cut until I reached my early thirties, when I finally let my hair grow out. It was a better look for my Independent Order of Foresters' career and for my pickup bartending gigs.

Still a farmer at heart with a need to plant and see things grow, I took some of the money I made in insurance and bought a flower shop in nearby Morrisville. From 1978 until 1985, I grew geraniums and mums in its quarter-acre, glass hothouse until "restless soul syndrome" struck again. The flower shop evolved into a landscaping business in 1982 that eventually expanded into land development, paving, and a construction business called Dunrite Construction.

I was following in my father's footsteps as the owner of an impressive lineup of trucks, loaders, backhoes, excavators, and pavers, with over a dozen people working for me. Sadly though, Dad's footsteps ended in 1988. He was suffering from leukemia and had driven himself to the hospital for a transfusion on the day he died. A few days before he passed—and 43 years after Grandma had asked me to talk my dad out of leaving my mom—I was called on once again to try and talk some sense into him.

He had always been a heavy drinker and smoker. It wasn't uncommon for him to drink several boilermakers and light up half a dozen cigars in a single day. My stepmom Betty knew his bad habits would be the death of him. As in our previous encounter four decades before, there was nothing I could say that would make him change his ways. Besides, his smoking and drinking were mere drops in the bucket. His leukemia situation didn't need any outside help to do its job. He was 79 when he passed. I put together a three-foot-by-four-foot bulldozer made out of yellow mums for his funeral.

Sixty percent of Dad's company went to Jerry, and the rest was divided up between my other brothers, my sister, and me. Once again, Jerry, the problem child of the family, hit the lottery. The first time happened in the late 1970s when he was able to buy Grandad's farm for a mere $200,000. The yearly taxes on the farm had actually exceeded the amount Grandad originally paid for the place in the early 1900s, so he unloaded it. These are just facts. I have no bitterness or envy toward my brother Jerry. If I'd have stayed with Grandad from high school throughout my adult years, that farm probably would have been mine. But why in the world would I want to inherit something that brought me nothing but misery?

I was proud and happy with the path I'd chosen and believed in the reasons behind the continuing string of successes I'd been compiling. The core values behind every move I made were simple: When working for others, treat everyone else's business as if it's your own; in your own business undertakings, treat your clients the way you would want to be treated; and, above all, get along with everybody, even if you have a disagreement.

Dunrite was an important stepping-stone and turning point in my career, although for a while, it appeared to be my undoing. My hands-on participation as a member of the company's workforce brought about its demise. I hurt my back working on a site and needed major surgery. I couldn't work at all. It was a bleak period. I had married for a second time in 1979, and my wife Trudy was 18 years younger than I was. How was I going to keep up with her and also support the two of us?

I sold off everything to keep my head above water until I healed up and then started a new company in 1990 called "Bob White Construction Management Consulting." Instead of muscling heavy machinery and tearing up my body carrying lumber and bulky bags of concrete, I was lifting pencils and using my brain. My new company was built around using my years of acquired knowledge of the local building codes and the construction and financial communities to provide consulting services for developers, contractors, and private individuals who owned land and wanted to build a custom-made house.

At the time, the standard move for folks like that was to go directly to a builder they'd seen in an advertisement somewhere, but they would never get a locked-in price that way. All my business came from word of mouth. I'd connect the client with an architect, take care of acquiring all the necessary permits and licenses, help them get a mortgage if necessary, hire a contractor, and research and find the best prices on all the raw building materials. (After one bad experience, I always had the owner pay those costs directly to the supplier.) Then I'd act as the foreman to oversee the proper sequencing of plumbers, electricians, tin knockers, and other skill positions. For all that, I'd get a set fee agreed upon in advance, and within three to four months, the client had a beautiful new home at an unbeatable price.

My new company also offered consulting services for small stores, businesses, and strip malls to redesign, modernize, and reconfigure existing spaces that had become outdated—a service I referred to as "Adaptive Re-use Consulting." I had actually started taking on those types of projects in the mid-1980s and worked with numerous developers and builders, including a Bucks County businessman named Pat Deon Sr. and his father Pasquale. They both became good friends of mine and Pat Sr., in particular, was an important mentor for me.

I first worked for them in 1985 when they were building a strip mall called Deon Square. They hired me to assist in the land development by grading the stone, preparing all the curbs, sidewalks, and grassy areas, and then paving the parking lot. We hit it off right away, and consequently, I worked with the Deons on numerous other projects over the next eight years. On one of them, Pat Sr. introduced me to an upper-level Bucks County politician and afterward told me about a job that had opened up in the county's redevelopment authority. Unable to picture myself in the role of a political appointee, I didn't take the offer seriously until Pat pulled me aside some months later and said, "Aren't you tired of paying for your own insurance?"

PART TWO

CHAPTER 9

WELCOME TO THE RDA

Pat Deon's friendship and concern for my well-being was much appreciated. The $10,000 benefits package he mentioned that came with the redevelopment authority (RDA) job would certainly come in handy. In hindsight though, job benefits were way down at the bottom of my list of deciding factors when I finally walked into the RDA's office and filled out an application for the position. I'd come to realize that an endless stream of one-off home building and reconstruction projects could only take me so far. I wanted to improve and change the lives of more than one person at a time. To do that, I needed a much larger stage—a more expansive canvas on which to paint, so to speak.

Pablo Picasso's greatest works and Spain were inseparable; for Frederick Remington's artistic vision to come to life, he needed the old American West; and Vincent Van Gogh found his most famous subjects in the South of France. My calling was a bit more humble and closer to home; in fact, it *was* home. And while not quite as exotic as those far off places I just mentioned, it was just as essential to any success I might have at the RDA.

There are over 3,000 counties in the United States. So what's so special about Bucks County? When you think about it, how much mention do you hear about any counties outside of the one in which you may currently live? I think you'd agree that very few come to mind. Orange County, California is certainly one of the select few because of the density of its population and its renown reputation as a long-standing bastion of conservative Republican politics. (Disneyland and scenic seaside resorts like Laguna Beach and Huntington Beach ain't too shabby either.) Illinois' Cook County has a population larger than 28 individual states in the continental US, and everybody knows about Cook County Jail, one of the largest prison facilities in the country. Miami-Dade has the Everglades, almost 700 miles of pristine beaches, and a very large, influential Latino population. And then there's Bucks County, Pennsylvania.

Every election season, Bucks County seizes the national spotlight as one of the most important voting barometers in America. Traditionally, political pollsters and pundits have relied on its population as an important indicator of how voters are leaning during campaign season. The county's rustic natural beauty and quaint antique villages annually draw hundreds of thousands of tourists. For more than 100 years beginning in the early 1830s, it was an essential transportation and shipping hub for the northeast section of the US because of the Delaware Canal that ran from Bristol to Easton, Pennsylvania. And . . . oh yeah . . . can't leave out that George Washington crossing the Delaware River business. Not too many counties anywhere in the country can lay claim to that level of historic pedigree.

Yet, while all those characteristics were factually significant and impressive, none of them specifically spelled out *O-P-P-O-R-T-U-N-I-T-Y* to me—at least, not until I focused in on the lower third of Bucks County around boroughs like Morrisville, Tullytown, and Bristol, and also the townships of Bensalem, Bristol, and Falls. The county had 54 different municipalities (23 boroughs and 31 townships) that were in the RDA's jurisdiction. The upper two-thirds of its territory was made up of relatively affluent residential areas with a lot of wide-open spaces. They didn't need much help, but that lower third did. During the early part of the twentieth century up until its decline in the 1960s and '70s, Lower Bucks was an economic powerhouse and manufacturing center. The aftermath of that decline left numerous underused, and sometimes abandoned, blighted hulks of once-thriving factories that formerly employed thousands of Bucks County residents and contributed to the prosperity of the towns in which they were located. *This* was my calling—this was my canvas.

Unfortunately, the Bucks County Redevelopment Authority (BCRDA) had no such lofty vision or goals of working on large-scale projects as the 1990s approached. It was primarily involved with rehabilitating individual, run-down houses. The 1945 Pennsylvania Act 385 (the Urban Redevelopment Law) gave Pennsylvania municipalities the authorization to set up RDAs to assist businesses, developers, and homeowners in rehabilitating blighted and deteriorated properties and finding new uses for abandoned or underutilized industrial, commercial, and residential sites. Bucks County was late in entering the game.

When the Bucks County RDA was finally established by the county commissioners in 1962, it was initially set up to deal with a dilapidated low-income housing project of 1,500 units in Warminster named Lacey Park. The development was built in 1943 by the US government to house workers at the nearby Johnsville Naval Air Development Center. Rents were as low as thirty-five dollars a month.

Two decades later, it was no longer in the hands of the feds. A slum-lord had purchased it and, as a result, most of the units were in a sorry state. Broken windows and walls were common, and some of the units actually had dirt floors. Crime was rampant and house fires were frequent. There were over 10,000 separate health and safety violations. When the state department of environmental resources (DER) finally raised hell in 1975, the Bucks County RDA became involved. In 1986, ownership of the property was taken over by a housing cooperative known as the Warminster Heights Home Owners Association (WHHOA), who worked with the county and the RDA to renovate some units, but eventually 750 of the units had to be torn down.

In 1993, when I first walked through the doors of the RDA's office in Yardley, it was still entrenched in that same rehabbing mode of operation. A five-person, all-volunteer board of directors met once a month and supervised all their activities. They interviewed me on several different occasions during the summer, and, although they were a bit leery of my coming in with only Pat Deon Sr.'s reference, they finally offered me the job of running their Owner-Occupied Housing Rehabilitation Program in August 1993. You could say I was underqualified for the job degree-wise, but I was overqualified ability-wise.

What they wanted me to do was not that much different from what I'd been doing. My new duties included inspecting the houses of low and moderate income homeowners, making sure they qualified for the programs we offered, and preparing write-ups for the needed repairs and items to bring the homes up to code. The term "black ice" had come into usage during this period because an unusual amount of freezing rain had descended on Bucks County that winter. It made for a lot of leaky roofs, but many of the jobs we did also required everything from the installation of new heaters, to plumbing, electrical, and drywall repairs.

We needed to advertise what we were doing, so I'd put signs on the houses we were rehabbing that said, "This project supported by the Department of Housing and Urban Development (HUD) and the Bucks

County Redevelopment Authority." Some of the homeowners didn't want the signs, so I'd joke with them and say, "You want your neighbors to think you robbed a bank or inherited a big wad of money?" That usually made them think twice before taking them down.

Miraculously, thanks in part to HUD's zero-interest homeowner loans, we completed 43 of these projects in my first year. I say "miraculously" because there wasn't much help coming from the two-person RDA office staff. A used-car salesman, who was about to retire after 18 years on the job, was running the housing rehab program. The other full-time employee was an office manager who did little other than typing up any contracts or write-ups—but *only* if I wrote them out in longhand first. There were also a few political appointees who theoretically worked part-time, although they rarely showed up. To this day, their qualifications and job descriptions remain unknown to me.

One of the 43 completed projects from the RDA's early Owner-Occupied Housing Rehabilitation Program.

I was a virgin to this political appointee concept, but I quickly surmised that political appointments and qualifications for the job don't necessarily have to coincide. On one of the first interviews I conducted at the RDA, I spoke with a woman who came highly recommended by a prominent Bucks County political figure. I needed an administrative assistant, and she seemed to fit the bill. She'd made a very strong impression on me during her interview, and I wanted to close the deal. As a last step, I told her I needed to administer a typing test so I could get an idea of her speed. She floored me when she revealed she didn't know how to type at all.

It would be disingenuous to portray the dismal state of affairs in the office any other way, but in fairness, there were also a few shining stars affiliated with the RDA who had a profound influence on me. Pat Bachtle was the board's vice chairwoman when I first arrived at the RDA until she eventually rose to the top spot on the board. She was (and still is) a sharp, soft-spoken lady who listens, thinks things through, and knows how to execute. You set her on a rabbit, and that rabbit is as good as caught. Throughout my RDA career, I knew I could rely on her knowledge and rock-solid judgment.

The same could be said for Rich Snyder, our solicitor, who taught me the intricacies of the RDA law and how the authority operated on a day-to-day basis. Rich was appointed to the acting executive director post in 1992 when his predecessor abruptly resigned. It was a temporary position until they found a permanent replacement. I didn't include him in my description of the office staff because he was hardly ever around, and when he was, he'd become unavailable by noontime. Let's just say he liked the ponies and leave it at that. Nevertheless, we became good friends and I'm indebted to him for his coolheaded demeanor and the valuable info he gave me during my early years at the RDA.

There was one area in which Rich had no expertise though. The state of technology in the RDA's office was so behind the times that we might as well have been conducting our business out of a cave. Since Rich never even owned a cell phone, he was the last person I could turn to for help. Our office manager was still using a typewriter. The RDA had yet to purchase a computer or word processor for her, and it wouldn't have mattered if they did. When I discussed purchasing one, she refused to even *learn* how to operate it. "I'm too old to start learning newfangled stuff like that," she told me. Hell, even a onetime farm boy like me had already been a computer owner for eight years. I was hooked from the moment I bought a Tandy 4000 from a RadioShack back in 1986.

Further complicating matters were the office forms she was using. They'd been photocopied so many times they were barely legible. I'm talking like . . . 25th generation! No one had ever thought about keeping a clean, virgin master form to copy from. The homeowners and senior citizens we were dealing with had great difficulty in reading them and often just signed out of frustration without really knowing what was involved.

As someone who always took pride in the quality of my work, I was stunned when I inspected some of the shoddy workmanship of the building contractors the RDA had been using. On one of the jobs, a contractor had done all the interior work first and then fixed the roof afterward. Not too smart a move, considering it rained before the roof was completed and the already-finished living room ceiling was damaged by the water. His workers tried to cover up the problem with gobs of spackle, but it looked like crap.

I refused to pay the contractor until he made things right. He was haranguing the homeowner for the money and she was begging me to pay him to get him off her back. I told her I wasn't going to pay for shoddy workmanship and she shouldn't accept such a poorly executed job. Then I notified the contractor he had 10 days to fix the ceiling or I'd get someone else to do the work and I'd pay the new guy by deducting the funds that were due to him. That's the way it played out. The original contractor's response was to tell me he'd never work for the RDA again; mine was to tell him he'd never have another chance to bid on an RDA project.

Job after job, I was finding similar quality control problems: greasy fingerprints on unfinished kitchen cabinets that would never wash off, corners that were not perfect 45-degree angles, poor paint jobs and drywall finishes, and amateurish installations of replacement windows. Contractors would also try to sneak in some "extras" after the fact. I had never allowed them to stick me with add-ons that weren't in their original spec sheets and job quotes when I had my own construction company, so I certainly wasn't going to tolerate that practice on RDA projects.

Job after job, contractors offended by my refusals to accept their work and their questionable business practices told me they'd never work for the RDA as long as I was in charge. If this kept up, I was going to have to widen my search outside of Bucks County to find people willing to work with me. I stopped banging my head against a cinder block wall the day I came to the realization that it wasn't all their fault. They had no idea what was expected of them because they'd never been provided with a specifications book that explained how and to what level of quality the work was to be completed.

Illegible work orders, no computers or printers, and no contractor's spec book? This was no way to run an RDA. I went to the county's community development department and asked them for one of their old computers and a dot matrix printer. They made me jump through the usual bureaucratic hoops, but they agreed to loan them to us as long as the RDA's board of directors signed off on it. Hallelujah! We'd finally exited the Stone Age. Within a few weeks, I'd rewritten all the work forms, stored them on the computer, and printed them out for immediate use. Then I set out to write, print, and distribute the official *Bucks County RDA's Contractor's Specification Book* to all the local contractors we used. The dot matrix printer fonts didn't make the document look like a work of art, but it was good enough to do the job.

Things didn't go well at first. There were hard feelings. Many of the contractors felt they were experts in the field and told me I should not expect the same quality they delivered in upscale neighborhoods when they were working on low-income housing. I stood my ground and told them that if they wanted to work on RDA projects, the level of their workmanship would have to be consistently of the same high quality *regardless* of the neighborhood. Knowing there would be a good deal of work coming up, they backed off but tried to save face by saying, "I don't need the book. I know what to do."

It was time for me to stop being such a hardhead. I met them halfway, replying, "I wouldn't be hiring you if I thought you didn't know what to do. I just want you to know that I'll be inspecting all work and want you to have the book as a reference so you'd know what I expect." That seemed to work. They accepted the books and signed off on them.

I'd won my first few battles, and even though I was working *for* the RDA, I came out of it as my own boss. Of the 43 completed housing projects during my first year, most of them came in at an average cost below $8,800, with the funding coming from the county's community and business development department. In the end, we went from having a waiting list of several dozen people who needed our rehab services to a waiting list of *zero*. In its place were 43 happy homeowners. We also gutted and rebuilt 15 housing units for the Warminster Housing Authority. What I'd accomplished must have impressed somebody upstairs in the Bucks County hierarchy: On August 9, 1994, the RDA's board of directors appointed me as the authority's permanent executive director after a unanimous vote.

The upward trajectory of my RDA career was not as smooth as I just made it sound. There was talk around the office during my first year that if the fortunes of the authority didn't improve, it was going to be reduced to an "as needed" agency that would go into operation only when (and if) a job presented itself. A consultant had been hired to drum up business because no one in the office was going out into the county to search for properties that needed to be redeveloped. So what kind of an idiot would want to stay in a job whose future looked as bleak as that? The kind of idiot who's talking to you right now.

Hell, I wasn't scared of the RDA being downsized. Even before I was offered the executive director position, I knew I could turn things around. What did scare me though, was the $32,500 salary I'd been making. I couldn't survive on that. I was moonlighting all through my first year, consulting on the building of two new homes—one in Buckingham, Pennsylvania and the other in Princeton, New Jersey. I'd be on the building sites by 6:00 a.m. and would work at the RDA from 8:30 a.m. to 4:30 p.m. Then I'd go back to the building sites to see how things were going. My evenings at home concluded with prepping for the next day. It was going to be tough to keep up with a schedule like that for any length of time.

I think the RDA's board of directors sensed my displeasure and also realized the quality and quantity of work I was giving them was way above my pay grade. After six months on the job, they gave me a $5,000 raise, but my eyes were still wandering. That abruptly ended when I was told the executive director's position came with a $50,000 annual salary. I decided to drop anchor and stay for a while; it was time to roll up my sleeves.

I'm doing myself a bit of a disservice with the last few paragraphs. After beginning this chapter with some lofty rhetoric about taking the RDA job so I could improve and change the lives of people in Bucks County, I'm starting to sound like a real mercenary. So my desire to help people bears repeating.

Still not buying it, huh? Can't say I blame you. We live in cynical times where our politicians will say anything to get elected, endless TV and internet ads promise miracle cures they can't deliver, and scam artists rule the day. So let me just throw a simple truth out on the table: *I was raised that way.*

Think about it: Mom's work at the Bucks County Home for the Poor, Aunt Nell's missionary work and charitable contributions, the sense of fairness my dad brought to the table in dealings with his employees, the way poor local farmers helped each other during my time in Virginia, and Grandad's generosity toward hungry neighbors during the tough times of World War II—these are all things I witnessed and took for granted as I was growing up. I thought everybody behaved that way. So why should I have changed the way I've always lived my life just because I got a promotion at work?

Speaking of Grandad, I think it's time to tie up some loose ends on that matter. When my story parted ways with him a while back, his health was deteriorating and he still held a grudge over my leaving the farm for the Marines. The numerous gripes I've voiced about him were more than justified, but the years have given me a deeper appreciation for the man and the gifts he left me.

There's no doubt he was cold, selfish, and self-centered, yet—unintended though they may possibly have been—those gifts have proven their worth time and time again throughout my life. I'm not talking about the obvious ones like work ethic, sense of responsibility, and determination. Regardless of them being by-products of going through the Grandad experience, I would have picked them up anyway. The Marines tattoo those same qualities on your soul with the endless drills and in-your-face lectures delivered by the Parris Island DIs.

Grandad's delivery was far more subtle and nuanced than the Marine drill instructors, yet its impact for me was more profound and long-lasting. You could say allowing a five-year-old child to drive a tractor is reckless and dangerous, but placing that amount of responsibility on my shoulders at such a young age gave me a sense of self-worth and confidence that few children ever achieve. And as annoying as his ceaseless criticisms were, they taught me to always try to do a job the right way, *without* the expectation of compliments or recognition. That, in itself, is a very liberating concept that helped shape my career, both as an employee and an employer.

Personal shortcomings notwithstanding, Grandad was a very success-ful and respected man. There was a basic reason for that, which he put into words during the last years of his life. He'd been fighting cancer for a long time and was eventually placed in a nursing facility. No one expected him to make it, and yet that tough old bird proved everybody wrong by having a miraculous turnaround that enabled him to return home and live for almost two more years. The last thing in the world the doctors wanted him to do was work, so of course, he climbed back on his tractor and went out into the fields. In response to Grandma's frequent protests, he said, "If I'm gonna die, it's gonna happen when I'm doing something I love." He finally passed away at the age of 87 in 1979 when he was no longer capable of carrying on with that love affair.

I didn't come from an affluent, moneyed background, so I've never understood that world. If getting rich is your only goal, working for a municipal redevelopment authority is unquestionably the wrong place for you to be. More importantly, if you don't love what you do and your goals don't match up with what a job has to offer, you're not going to be successful. Grandad recognized that fact early on and put it into practice throughout his life—right up until the very end.

CHAPTER 10

MY NEW TOOLBOX

I'm sure you've noticed by now that I'm fond of dropping a folksy adage or two when the mood strikes me. *Be careful what you wish for—you just might get it,* might be the appropriate thing to say at this point. When I owned my own construction company, I was hiring and interacting with construction people who had a work ethic and a way of thinking that was familiar to me. They could be crass and unrefined at times, but I knew how to navigate those waters. Working in an office atmosphere with people who were far more polite and sensitive took some adjusting on my part, but I've always taken pride in my ability to get along with everybody. Within a few weeks, I was comfortable. Coming to grips with the steep learning curve my new executive director position required was another matter entirely; that transformation would not happen as quickly.

By comparison, the work requirements I had to contend with at Dunrite Construction and Bob White Construction Management Consulting were one-dimensional. We rarely (if ever) had on-site environmental problems, and there were no dealings at all with the US Environmental Protection Agency (EPA) or the Pennsylvania Department of Environmental Protection (PADEP). No grants or government programs were applicable for the projects I was doing; the only municipal and governmental demands on me were obtaining building permits and adhering to the local building codes; political involvement was nonexistent, and the paperwork for each job was minimal. As for the financial situation, it was as simple as could be: My clients paid for the building supplies directly to the suppliers and then paid me by check or cash for my services, and out of that, I paid my workers. End of story. Now flip all that around 180 degrees and you get a picture of the new world I was facing when I assumed the leadership of the RDA.

Pennsylvania was part of the Rust Belt, a region in the upper half of the US extending from central New York, through the Great Lakes states, and running as far west as the eastern border of Iowa. These states formed the backbone of American industrial might and power for almost a century, but by the beginning of the 1980s, the advent of automation and the shift toward a service and high-tech economy brought about deindustrialization, urban decay, and in some cases, population loss. Bucks County suffered the same fate.

When our industries and manufacturers went out of business, it wasn't a clean break, like when a homeowner decides to sell their house and move to a different neighborhood. These defunct industries and manufacturers usually left behind abandoned, run-down buildings with a wide assortment of environmental toxins that threatened animal and human life in the municipalities in which they were found. The jobs and taxes they once generated for their host community were now things of the past, and nobody wanted to buy these properties because of the liability and legal issues that stemmed from their environmental problems and the hazardous conditions of the buildings and their surrounding grounds. *Welcome to your new life, Bob White. Now go find a way to make a decrepit property that's worth less than zero into a beautiful new office complex or residential community worth millions.*

Work ethic, determination, and a deep résumé that included extensive knowledge of operating heavy machinery wasn't going to be enough; understanding building codes and knowing how to read blueprints wouldn't get me there either; nor would my communication and managerial skills or my deep-rooted knowledge of Bucks County and its people. What I really needed was a new vocabulary and a whole new set of tools.

I hope you'll indulge me for a little while as I interrupt the storyline with a "show and tell" of my new toolbox. Even if you just skim the material, that follows, it'll help you to understand and appreciate the narrative that's coming up.

Terminology

BLIGHT—a blighted property is a deteriorated, vacant, underutilized, or completely abandoned building, although it could also be a plot of land in the middle of a neighborhood. Often these buildings are boarded up, have broken windows or caved-in roofs, and generally present a variety of perceived or actual hazards to the local community that bring down the property values of the surrounding real estate.

A building must meet one or more of the eleven categories used to establish blighted properties under the guidelines of the Pennsylvania Urban Redevelopment Law of 1945 (PA ACT 385). These include properties that are:

- fire hazards
- unfit for human habitation
- public nuisances (particularly dangerous "attractive nuances" to children and teenagers)
- tax delinquent and vacant for more than two years
- strewn with trash and debris that attract rodents and vermin
- lacking water, gas, and other utilities
- environmentally contaminated and hazardous
- not compliant with local building codes
- burdened with municipal liens exceeding 150% of their appraised value.

BROWNFIELDS—abandoned or underused commercial and industrial properties that often contain a variety of contaminants in their soil, in groundwater, and in the buildings themselves. While posing serious risks to the environment, wildlife, and humans (along with substantial legal and financial burdens to the surrounding community), these sites also offer significant opportunities for improvement and reuse.

The brownfield designation can apply to major factories like steel mills, refineries, landfills, and chemical plants, as well as smaller, neighborhood operations like dry cleaners or gas stations, which tend to produce high levels of subsurface contaminants. It is a legal classification that places conditions, restrictions, and incentives on the redevelopment of these types of sites. The term "brownfields" came into being in the early 1990s but didn't become an official act until 2002 when George W. Bush signed the Small Business Liability Relief and Brownfields Revitalization Act (the "Brownfields Law").

GREENFIELDS—undeveloped, unfenced, open fields in a city or rural area that have been left to evolve naturally. They contain no industrial or other man-made contaminants and are generally kept off limits to the general public by private entities or governmental agencies. Pastures, apple orchards, and natural wooded areas would fall into this category. Private developers can try to purchase or develop these areas, but redevelopment authorities can work only on blighted or brownfield properties.

Environmental Contaminants

It was common practice in the 1930s and '40s to dump or bury waste materials, chemicals, and scrap metals on the grounds around industrial sites. There was no malice in it; they just didn't have any awareness back then that the earth's capability to absorb contamination is not unlimited. Just like the prevalence of cigarette smoking through much of the first seven decades of the twentieth century, no one had any idea of the consequences and carcinogenic effects of what they were doing. When I was a kid, people used to dump used motor oil on driveways and highways to keep the dust down. Since some of these were unpaved, it seemed logical at the time, but now we know better.

It wasn't until the late 1960s that the federal government finally began to wake up to the toxicity presented by these contaminants. Federal and state agencies like the EPA (founded in 1970) and the PADEP (founded in 1995) were established to regulate and, if necessary, enforce the proper remediation and disposal of toxins that threatened the environment and human health.

The following is a list of substances the RDA typically finds when we work on redeveloping the buildings and grounds of Bucks County's brownfield sites:

VOLATILE ORGANIC COMPOUNDS (VOC)—most solvents fall into this category. Common examples are benzene, ethylene glycol, formaldehyde, methylene chloride, tetrachloroethylene, toluene, xylene, and butadiene. They usually have a noticeable aroma when released into the air.

PERCHLOROETHYLENE (PCE)—a VOC used as a solvent in a wide range of industrial and commercial applications. The most common is dry cleaning chemicals for clothes. Although production of this chemical is decreasing, its persistence in the environment makes it a significant groundwater and air pollutant that poses a serious threat to humans. Efforts are underway to reduce the use of PCE in the dry cleaning industry by the development of green technologies.

TRICHLOROETHYLENE (TCE)—a VOC that is a clear, colorless liquid. It has a sweet odor and evaporates quickly. TCE is an extremely toxic chemical that is used primarily to clean steel but is also used in refrigerants and automotive engine and transmission repairs. It usually finds its way into the first aquifer (underground layers of water-bearing rock) and contaminates it. It then can continue down to lower levels through fractured rock.

SEMI-VOLATILE ORGANIC COMPOUNDS (SVOC)—a subgroup of VOCs that are of concern because of their abundance in indoor environments and their potential for negative health effects on humans. SVOCs have a higher boiling point than VOCs, so they don't evaporate into the air as easily. They often sit on top of dust piling up over time after being released into the air from dry cleaning and paints.

POLYCHLORINATED BIPHENYLS (PCBS)—man-made chemicals that are generally oily liquids or solids with no smell or taste. They are very stable and resistant to extreme temperature and pressure. PCBs were used widely in electrical equipment like capacitors and transformers, voltage regulators, and fluorescent lights ballasts. Their use was banned in the US in 1979 due to the unintended impact these chemicals could have on human and environmental health.

POLYCYCLIC AROMATIC HYDROCARBONS (PAHS)—organic compounds containing only hydrogen and carbon that tend to stay in the environment for long periods of time. They occur naturally in coal, crude oil, and gasoline and are also produced when tobacco, garbage, wood, oil, and coal are burned. PAHs are also used in the manufacturing of tar, dyes, plastics, pesticides, and naphthalene, which is used to make mothballs. Many PAHs have carcinogenic properties.

HEAVY METALS—lead, iron, mercury, arsenic, copper, chromium, and cadmium.

ADDITIONAL CONTAMINANTS—asbestos, pesticides, lead-based and anti-fouling paints, and hydrocarbon spillage (the basic components of petroleum products).

ACT 2 (Pennsylvania's Land Recycling Program)

Before 1995, Pennsylvania had a glut of abandoned former industrial and commercial properties that *no one* wanted to touch with a 10-foot pole. Why? Well . . . put yourself in the shoes of a potential developer:

You have a concept in mind for a beautiful multiuse office complex in a certain municipality. There's plenty of greenfield, open space land in the area, but building there would be expensive because there's no water, electric, or sewer service nearby and also no roadway infrastructure. All of that would have to be developed, along with constructing the necessary buildings from the ground up. So you decide to go in a different direction and look for an abandoned former industrial or commercial site that might suit your needs.

The pluses are obvious. All the necessary surrounding infrastructure that the greenfield sites lacked are already in place, so you're left with the option of either rehabbing the existing building or demolishing it and building a new one from scratch—whichever one is more cost effective and better suits your needs. You've found a site that looks perfect so you decide to take things to the next level by contacting the local municipality and sending out specialists to assess the property and its grounds.

In short order, you realize you've opened up a Pandora's box of problems. The building is structurally sound, but the property is loaded with pollutants and toxins for which you'd be legally responsible. The EPA requires a 100% remediation of the problem, which could cost millions of dollars and potentially take an unlimited amount of time to complete, and—not wanting to be in the chain of ownership and liability—banks are refusing to give you a loan. Under the circumstances, there is no way to turn a profit on the project, so the developer's choices for a path forward are clear: either build on a greenfield site or find a different location in a state with less restrictive environmental laws and regulations.

Hundreds of scenarios like this one were costing Pennsylvania millions of dollars in tax revenues and job losses, and nothing at all was being done to address the environmental risks that still remained on all the state's "mothballed" blighted properties. Developers were taking their business elsewhere; something needed to be done.

Enter one M. Joel Bolstein, attorney at law, to the rescue. Joel was the deputy secretary for special projects at the PADEP in the mid-1990s when Tom Ridge was the state's governor. During that time, he was front and center in the writing and implementation of the state's groundbreaking ACT 2 legislation (and its associated ACTS 3 and 4), the programs that freed developers, investors, and banks from the crippling environmental regulations and legal liability issues that had scared them off for years. It achieved this by providing predictable, key elements that helped remove the risky "unknowns" from the redevelopment process:

SETTING STANDARDS AND TIMELINES. In 1980, the Comprehensive Environmental Response, Compensation and Liability Act (commonly known as "the Superfund" or CERCLA) was established to deal with cleaning up large-scale hazardous waste sites. It was an all-or-nothing type of situation; every last molecule of the offending contaminants and toxins had to be removed. That took unlimited amounts of time and money which, as previously mentioned, chased away any potential developers and investors.

ACT 2 set standards on exactly how clean a property needed to be in order to guarantee the safety of all human and animal life in the local environment. For example, setting an allowable toxin level of 1 in 10,000 parts might be considered too risky. On the other hand, a level of 1 in 1,000,000 parts would be overkill, because that's 10 times more than the cancer risk of just being alive. So ACT 2 took the middle ground and settled for 1 in 100,000. This allowed developers to know what they were getting into, how long the cleanup process would take, and how much it would cost.

PROVIDING RELIEF FROM LIABILITY AND FINANCIAL ASSISTANCE. ACT 2 was a voluntary program. It wasn't a mandated law that was imposed on everyone. If you were interested in developing a property, you had the option of signing up for the program to take advantage of its developer-friendly assistance features. The property owners who originally polluted a site were not eligible for ACT 2 benefits. Their only options were to either sink a lot of money into cleaning up the site or sell it. But who would want to buy into a property that would make them inherit the same problems that made the previous owner want to unload the property?

The same reasoning applied to mortgage companies who had always been reticent to foreclose on deadbeat owners because they didn't want to take on the liability issues. ACT 3 broke through that logjam by limiting the legal exposure of new owners from being held liable for any environmental problems and contaminants left on the grounds by the original owner.

ESTABLISHING REMEDIATION PROCEDURES. ACT 4 provided grants for up to $1,000,000 through the Department of Community and Economic Development (DCED) to help pay for the assessment and cleanup of a property's environmental problems. An additional 25% of the amount of the grant (called matching fees) was to be contributed by the developer. The assessment course of action was broken down into two stages:

PHASE ONE included a walk-through, visual inspection of the site and research into its past uses, including examining any existing aerial pictures of the property from different time periods. If a building was constructed before the 1950s and had never been renovated, there was a good chance of existing asbestos and lead paint problems; a large black spot on the grounds or a patch of land where nothing grows was often a giveaway sign of some type of underground contamination; deep stains on wood floors or discolored concrete also needed to be investigated; and if a site was previously a dry cleaning operation, the presence of PCE was a common occurrence.

PHASE TWO was a more active procedure that included digging numerous test pits (both shallow and deep wells) on the grounds of a site and sending out soil and water samples to laboratories for analysis. The lab tests are often quite expensive. Once the results come in, a remediation plan and timeline needed to be filed with the PADEP. Developers found additional help when ACT 2's writers included the proposed reuse of the property in determining how extensive the cleanup procedure had to be. For example, the standards for commercial and industrial usage of a property were less stringent—and consequently less expensive and time consuming—than those used for residential usage.

ACT 2 also allowed for a money and time-saving remediation procedure. The pathway for a source of contamination in the ground may be blocked from reaching and affecting the public and the surrounding environment by placing a fabric shield over the site and then capping it with either blacktop, concrete, or two feet of clean fill (gravel, sand, topsoil, crushed brick or concrete, or a mixture of any of these same materials). On moderate to lightly contaminated properties that are intended for nonresidential use, this is a PADEP-approved alternative to the 100% removal of all pollutants.

LOSS LEADER. What Joel Bolstein accomplished in ACT 2 was not that much different than an established marketing strategy known as "loss leader." You know how department stores sometimes put specific goods on sale at drastically reduced prices that makes you scratch your head and say, "How in the world can they be making any money on this?" The stores are deliberately selling these products at a loss so they can draw people into the store who might also buy more profitable items while they are on the premises. It's the old "Gotta give up something to get something" concept. If the problems of abandoned industrial sites, lost taxes and jobs, and lack of municipalities' economic growth were to be solved, the state needed to give developers some good reasons to keep them from taking their businesses elsewhere.

Hardcore environmentalists weren't thrilled with what Joel Bolstein and the rest of the architects of ACT 2 had done. They liked Superfund types of legislation that insisted on 100% removal of all contaminants. But Joel *was* an environmentalist. The difference was he was looking down the road at the bigger picture. If developers started building in greenfield land, open spaces and natural areas would diminish while the original problem of abandoned, contaminated industrial sites would still remain.

To sell that concept, Joel went barnstorming all over the state to convince municipalities, banks, developers, and RDAs that ACT 2 was enacted to help all of them. That's when I met him for the first time. We've been good friends ever since, and I even hired him as the Bucks County RDA's special environmental solicitor a few years later. Without hesitation, I believe I couldn't have accomplished half of what I did in my career at the RDA without Joel Bolstein's help and expertise.

Grants

DEPARTMENT OF COMMUNITY AND ECONOMIC DEVELOPMENT (DCED).

The DCED offers a wide range of state grants (from small to large amounts) intended primarily to aid developers, investors, and business owners who are engaged in projects that will stimulate economic growth and job creation in the retail, commercial, and industrial sectors.

Typical of some of the DCED's smaller community grant programs is a category sometimes referred to as a "facade grant." In order to get property owners in business and shopping districts to improve the appearance of their storefronts, the state will provide up to $5,000 as a 50% matching fee to what the owners spend out of their own pockets on the improvement. The process enables people to fix up their building for 50% of the actual cost; a $5,000 upgrade becomes a $10,000 upgrade. The intent is to bring in more customers and raise the property values of the surrounding buildings by improving the appearance of a business's facade.

INDUSTRIAL SITES REUSE PROGRAM (ISRP). This program provides grants and loans for environmental assessments (up to $200,000) and remediation (up to $1,000,000) to applicants who didn't create or contribute to an industrial site's environmental problems. The money comes from the PADEP. These grants require the property owner or developer to provide a 25% match of the total of all environmental remediation grants on the project. When the costs exceed the combined total of the grants and the 25% match, the balance of any funding required to clean up the property is paid by the developer or owner.

REDEVELOPMENT ASSISTANCE CAPITAL PROGRAM (RACP). These are grants targeted for construction and acquisition on projects that help encourage economic development and maintain or increase employment levels and tax revenues. They're also available to projects that have historic, civic, recreational, or cultural significance.

US ECONOMIC DEVELOPMENT ASSISTANCE (EDA). The recipients of these grants are typically private investors and developers whose projects bring about higher-skilled, living-wage jobs and advance entrepreneurship and regional competitiveness.

ENVIRONMENTAL PROTECTION AGENCY (EPA) AND THE PENNSYLVANIA DEPART OF ENVIRONMENTAL PROTECTION (PADEP). Numerous grants are available from both the EPA and the PADEP to fund the assessment and cleanup of contaminated commercial and industrial sites.

EPA BROWNFIELD PILOT GRANTS. These are available to communities for the initiation of their own environment-friendly startup programs.

COMMUNITY DEVELOPMENT BLOCK GRANTS (CDBG). A program administered by the Department of Housing and Urban Development (HUD) that provides grants to communities involved in redeveloping abandoned and underutilized industrial and commercial sites that are tied in to anti-poverty programs and affordable, low-income housing projects.

THE KEYSTONE FUND. Provides funding for projects that involve the restoration of historic buildings or properties that help preserve Pennsylvania's heritage.

PENNSYLVANIA DEPARTMENT OF TRANSPORTATION (PENNDOT). Provides grants for building railroad sidings and repairing railroad lines that help reduce truck traffic in residential neighborhoods.

Loans

PENNSYLVANIA INFRASTRUCTURE INVESTMENT AUTHORITY (PENNVEST). This low-interest loan program funds improvements and new construction of both public and privately owned drinking water, storm water, and sewage treatment facilities.

RDA REVOLVING LOAN FUND. The state of Pennsylvania offers grants to RDAs for the purpose of making loans of up to $75,000 to help small business. To qualify, a business has to create three new jobs, two of which are to be filled by low to moderate-income employees. These loans are somewhat risky because they often go to businesses that could not obtain grants or loans from other sources. The fund operates with an annual balance of $700,000, most of which is typically out on loan.

SECTION 108 LOANS. This feature of the CDBG program provides low-interest loans with flexible repayment terms for small businesses in underserved regions of the country. These grants help stimulate economic activity in these neglected communities while providing funds for housing rehabilitation and public facilities.

Incentive Packages

LOCAL ECONOMIC REVITALIZATION TAX ASSISTANCE (LERTA). This tax abatement program was created in 1977 to encourage outside investment and redevelopment in undesirable brownfield-type properties. The maximum allowable amount is a 50% reduction in real estate taxes over a period of up to 10 years, and it is allowed only on the improvements made to the property.

JOB CREATION TAX CREDIT PROGRAM. The Commonwealth of Pennsylvania will give employers anywhere from $1,000 to $3,000 per new employee hired by a business moving into or remaining at a specific site.

KEYSTONE OPPORTUNITY ZONES (KOZ), KEYSTONE OPPORTUNITY IMPROVEMENT ZONES (KOIZ), AND ENTERPRISE ZONES. These three fancy-named designations all attempt to do basically the same thing: grease the wheels for investment and development to flow into a designated geographic area (often old industrial parks and preexisting airports) by offering federal and state-sponsored tax breaks, grants, and low-interest loans. These incentives can take the form of tax exemptions, corporate income tax credits, and property tax abatements, and the loans can be as low as 2%.

There are more than 300 opportunity zones throughout Pennsylvania. Bucks County's enterprise zone lasted from 1996 through 2006 and covered the townships of Falls, Penndel, and Bristol and the boroughs of Tullytown, Morrisville, and Bristol. When its term ran out, it was extended for another 10 years, during which Penndel Borough was added to the zone. As of 2020, there is no enterprise zone currently in existence in Bucks County.

Eminent Domain

This is one of an RDA's most powerful but also most controversial tools. From time to time, I've jokingly referred to the process as "The

Hammer," but believe me, it's not something I take lightly. Reduced to its most basic meaning, eminent domain is the legal process by which an RDA or other governmental agency seizes or takes private property for the greater good of the public and then pays financial compensation (known as "just compensation") to the previous owner for his loss.

That "greater good" terms needs some explaining. One aspect of the greater good is the simple pursuit of progress. When a town hall meeting is convened to discuss traffic congestion and the solution arrived at is the widening of a road, there's a good chance someone other than the local municipality owns the property that's necessary for that purpose. The owner may not wish to sell but is legally forced to part with his property and is then compensated for it.

Protection of the public and stimulating economic growth and job creation also fall into the "for the greater good" category. A toxic, abandoned industrial site that threatens the health of nearby residents and also generates no taxes or jobs for the community is a typical candidate for the use of the eminent domain process.

Once a property is declared blighted by a municipality, the owner is notified. If the property owner does not provide a plan to cure the blight, apply for permits to make repairs within 30 days, and complete the plan in accordance with an acceptable construction schedule, a redevelopment authority can seize the property after it has been designated as a certified blighted area. The owner can contest the seizure in the courts and can also challenge the amount of financial compensation being offered. His rights are also protected by wall-to-wall regulations and restrictions that govern the process.

Not every eminent domain is a long, drawn-out, acrimonious process. If the owner is more than happy to part with his property, the process is termed "amicable eminent domain." The RDA often uses this practice to aid developers by temporarily assuming ownership of a property. That enables us to take it off the tax rolls while construction is proceeding, which saves the developer a lot of money. It also opens up the proposed reuse project to all the grants, loans, and incentives that only an RDA has the unique ability to acquire.

Got all that? Great! Now, back to my story . . .

CHAPTER 11

LEARNING THE ROPES

Once a Marine, always a Marine. I hit the ground running on my first day as the RDA's new executive director and immediately started reconnoitering the landscape. What I found out was sobering. There was only $32,000 in our coffers, with no public or governmental funds coming our way to pay for our operating expenses. The consultant who'd been hired to bring in business was generating next to nothing, and if I passively waited for the townships and boroughs to bring us projects, I'd be playing a losing hand. I had to make something happen—and fast.

Rich Snyder had helped me a great deal during my first year, but if I were to have any chance of turning things around as the new executive director, I needed to expand my knowledge of exactly what an RDA was. Just like I used to study all the Marine manuals at Parris Island and Camp Lejeune, I began devouring Pennsylvania Act 385 (the Urban Redevelopment Law), reading it over and over until I understood every facet of how an RDA operates.

We were a nonprofit organization that wasn't a line item on the state or any municipality's budget, and because we were a municipal organization, we didn't have to pay taxes. That being said, we ran the RDA like a small *for-profit* business. The responsibility for paying our employees and our office's mortgage and utility bills rested solely on whatever income its executive director could generate through innovation. Having lived under similar "If you don't work, you don't eat" conditions on the farm, I was very experienced and comfortable with that setup.

Most of our money came from invoicing the municipalities and developers for the administrative services we performed for them. Those included everything from consulting, interfacing with the DEP and the EPA, overseeing environmental assessments and remediations, putting together creative financing packages of grants, loans, and tax incentives for developers (the loss leader concept), and conveying information to the public in the municipalities in which the projects took place. Sometimes, there was also leftover grant money if a project came in under budget. If the state allowed it, we'd put it in our revolving loan fund or use it to redevelop and remediate other properties in our pipeline.

By themselves, the executive director's title and the power that came with it were of little value to me, but the opportunity they gave me to help improve the quality of life in Bucks County meant everything. John Boehner once remarked, "You've got to learn to use your power and lead. If you lead and no one's following you, you're just a guy out for a walk." I'd like to say his thoughts on the wise and efficient use of power had an effect on me in the mid-1990s, except he said it sometime during his 2011–2015 tenure in Washington, DC as Speaker of the House. Regardless of whether you're a Democrat or Republican, it's hard to argue with the truth of that statement. If I was going to lead the RDA, I needed to do a lot more than just understand things; I needed to begin assembling a network of people and procedures.

Good fortune smiled on me early on when I made two critical hires. Heather St. Germain became the RDA's new administrative assistant and office manager, and in expectation of a lot more business coming our way, I gave a guy named Joe D'Adamo the job of bookkeeping. I was a tough but very fair boss. When I hired someone, I adopted them. I put them in a comfort zone where they wouldn't have to worry about whether or not they'd be able to afford their mortgages, their kids' schooling costs, car payments, and clothes and food bills. In exchange, I expected consistent, first-class work. Heather and Joe never disappointed me. The new stability they brought to our office situation allowed me to turn my attention to other needs.

Building personal relationships and creating a "brand" both for the RDA and me were two of the most pressing items on my to-do list. Success wasn't going to come by sitting all day in front of a computer screen and calling the shots from the safe confines of an isolated office. I needed to get out among folks and talk to them to find out their needs and what they were thinking. I started driving around the county looking for run-down business and industrial sites that could be upgraded; I attended Bucks County board meetings and joined the Bristol Rotary Club; and I made a habit of looking for potential leads in the *Bucks County Courier Times*, the *Morrisville Times*, the *Newtown Gazette*, the *Yardley Voice*, the *Bristol Pilot*, and all the other local municipal newspapers.

Down the road a bit as the RDA starting getting busy, I expanded my reliance on these publications by making sure we got press coverage on every one of our projects. It wasn't the pursuit of publicity for publicity's sake. I viewed every successful RDA job as a stepping-stone to get other projects and opportunities. It was also our job to keep everyone informed, particularly because we were the coordinators for the public's wishes and concerns. I didn't want anyone to be blindsided. Everyone affected by any actions we took needed to be informed.

As I started to become more familiar with the ins and outs of the redevelopment authority process, I began attending industry conferences and conventions that were held in-state in places like Pittsburgh, Hershey, and the Poconos. I've never had a problem with stealing a good idea if it could help me achieve a valuable end, so I figured those conventions would be good places to pick up some tips and forge some relationships with influential figures in the industry. The Pittsburgh convention was one of my favorites because I learned a lot about how different Pennsylvania RDAs handled lead paint and asbestos problems, their strategies for attracting developers, and how the Pittsburgh RDA tore down their steel mills and the financing methods they used to make that colossal undertaking possible.

Sometimes, I traveled a little further out. On a five-day redevelopment authority convention in Chicago, I picked up something that seemed trivial on the surface but over time proved to have lasting value. The event was a very congenial, chummy affair. Business cards were flying, ongoing projects were presented, environmental remediation strategies were discussed and debated, and yet, when I got back to my hotel room, I realized *I couldn't remember anyone*—except for one guy.

Like everyone else, I overpacked. I'd crammed my suitcase with an assortment of different-colored suits, shirts, and ties like I was going to a fashion show. Then all of us RDA-type guys made our appearances on the convention floor as an eminently forgettable blur of blue, gray, tan, brown, and black. How can you stand out in the middle of a mishmash like that? But this one guy sure as hell did.

On day one, and every single day after, he entered the room dressed head to toe in plain old brown. Did he come to Chicago with just the clothes on his back? Maybe he could only afford one suit; maybe that was a uniform his RDA made all its employees wear; maybe he was having the same clothes laundered every day at the hotel; maybe this, maybe that. And then I realized: *This guy was a genius.* Out of the hundreds of convention attendees, he was the only person in that faceless crowd who drew my attention. I struck up a conversation with him about it one afternoon, during which he let me know his choice of haberdashery was by design. "Bob, black or brown, but never both."

From that day on, my color of choice was black, with a few personalized touches thrown in. I'd always liked wearing cowboy hats on construction sites to keep the sun off my face, and I had an affinity for cowboy boots. That was the new me. I'd let other people worry about whether I could afford only one set of clothes or if I was just buying my black shirts, slacks, jackets, and boots by the dozens. As long as I was leaving an impression and making them think about me, I figured I was on the right track.

I knew my game plan was working one day when an article in the *Bucks County Courier Times* referred to me as "a beefy, fast-talking construction expert dressed in all black with a cowboy hat." The board of directors didn't like that description, but I sure as hell did. And even if I didn't, the last thing I wanted to do was get into a public spat with the press. That's always a losing battle. I had an ink pen; they have a barrel of ink. Besides, I had a lot of respect for what they do, and I think they grew to respect me too.

No doubt, all these networking efforts were valuable pieces in the mix, but realistically speaking, they were just supporting actors. I needed to find the catalyst that would set off the chain reaction I was looking to build. That meant finding "the Joe." In military circles, that means finding the person who has enough clout and prestige to cut through the layers of B.S. and make things happen. I was lucky enough to find two "Joes": Harry Fawkes and Mike Fitzpatrick. Harry was the county's Republican Party executive director. He also happened to be the anonymous Bucks County politician Pat Deon Sr. spoke to about bringing me into the RDA.

I first met Mike at an Irish festival when he was just a 31-year-old lawyer. By the time I was offered the RDA's executive director position, he'd become the county commission chairman. Our relationship became a solid bond when he happened to drive by a construction site on a Saturday and saw me digging a ditch with the rest of the work crew—more on that later. The point is, I now felt I could go into battle with some backup support.

A lot of time and thought was spent on getting all my ducks in a row and establishing my authority, but what about the actual redeveloping? As formidable an uphill battle as I faced early on, I did have some material to work with. We had never stopped helping Bucks County residents get government programs and rehab their blighted homes, and the RDA actually did have two substantial projects that had been on its slate for a while. Both were moving at a snail's pace. Something needed to be done with a three-acre site that once housed a portion of the Morrisville Rubber Plant down at the intersection of Bridge Street and Pennsylvania Avenue, and the Riverfront North site in Bristol Borough was a massive, long-term situation that also needed to get going.

These were the type of projects that could turn around the fortunes of both the county and the RDA. Rehabbing individual houses was just putting a band-aid on a much larger problem. The reason low-income residents weren't able to take care of their houses in the first place was because there weren't enough decent-paying jobs available in the county. Cleaning up and repurposing large, abandoned warehouses and factory sites offered the perfect solution. A lot of new, high-wage jobs are created on both the front and back ends when you transform 250,000 square feet of contaminated uselessness into an office complex, a shopping center, a hotel, or even a new residential community.

The details and stories behind many of the RDA's most memorable projects during my tenure will unfold in the next chapter, but suffice it to say for the moment that the Morrisville Rubber Plant was a relatively painless, quick fix that began in 1994 and was completed by 1996. I can't say it's typical of all of our ventures. Some sites can be remediated and repurposed within a year or two, while others, like Riverside North, the US Magnet site, and the Grundy Powerhouse, can take a decade or more.

Once we got busy, the only constant in our office was lots of overlapping projects. No matter how efficient and organized you are, it's a stop-and-start business. You'll always be waiting for something, whether it be funding, grant approval, political and municipal bureaucracy, environmental test results, or a multitude of other things. If you're the type of person who likes to completely finish one project before moving on to the next one, you ain't goin' nowhere in the RDA business.

In my office at the Redevelopment Authority, juggling half a dozen simultaneous projects with the phone glued to my ear.

But I did get to complete one early on, and it gave me a chance to prove my mettle to an as of yet unconvinced RDA board of directors and office staff. I said a while back that I couldn't afford to sit back on my heels and wait for projects to come our way, but I didn't say I wouldn't take one if it did. In 1995, State Senator Tommy Tomlinson and State Representative Tom Corrigan approached me with a proposal for a much-needed roadway through some of the industrial campuses in Bristol Township, specifically a manufacturing site that used to belong to the A. B. Murray Co.

Neither the board of directors nor our office staff were familiar with my extensive background in roadwork. Not being content to just do a good job on what Tomlinson and Corrigan had asked of me, I upped the ante and told the board I also wanted to develop a run-down office building on the site and use it for the RDA's new headquarters. For an organization usually content to leave well enough alone, moving our location was akin to heresy. At the time, our offices were based at Floral Vale in Yardley. That never made sense to me because Yardley was in Lower Makefield, a relatively affluent area that didn't need much of the RDA's expertise. We needed to be near the lower part of Bucks County where the majority of the blighted and underused industrial sites were located—places like Bristol, Falls, and Bensalem townships and the boroughs of Morrisville, Tullytown, and Bristol.

Everyone connected with the RDA expected me to fall flat on my face, and when I made a boast to the board of directors that this building would be the site of our next meeting, they told me I was out of my mind. The meeting was only six weeks away. To everyone's surprise (except mine), the meeting happened in the office building—as advertised. We got it rehabbed and turned around in record time. The roadway took a bit longer, but it was equally successful.

If there were any doubters left in the room, they were keeping it to themselves. I couldn't do anything during my first year at the RDA without going to the board for their approval. Always having to run back to ask Mommy had been hampering me greatly every time I had to conduct negotiations. Now I had some autonomy. I felt like I'd finally earned everyone's trust and support, and just in time.

When Pennsylvania's ACT 2 legislation was passed in 1995, the world changed for every redevelopment authority in the state. It was if someone removed the parental controls from our computers. With the stroke of governor Tom Ridge's pen, all the suffocating federal EPA regulations and antiquated practices that had scared off investment and limited our ability to deal with blighted, contaminated properties were removed. Over the next few years, offers began pouring in from developers all over the state. Thanks to a $200,000 EPA Brownfields Assessment Pilot Program grant, I had something to show them.

We'd already begun surveying the county for prospective brownfield sites. Joel Bolstein, the environmental attorney who had played such a dominant role in writing and implementing ACT 2, helped us devise a zero-to-three rating system in eight different categories—things like environmental problems, water and sewer service availability, proximity to highways, and structural condition of the buildings. The intent was to highlight the properties that had the best shot at getting redeveloped. We started out with a list of 20 different sites and then hired Langan Engineering to help us trim the list down to just eight: Riverfront North, the US Steel Fairless Plant, the US Magnet site, the Grundy Powerhouse, the Stainless Steel Inc. factory in Perkasie, the A. B. Murray warehouse, Corell Steel, the Levittown Shop-A-Rama, and the Penn Salt Manufacturing site.

Chalk it up to naiveté on my part, but I never realized how large a role politics would play in getting all those large-scale projects to the starting gate. I was a quick learner though. The most common political arguments usually centered on the issue of whether a project's redevelopment should be undertaken by a private business or by the municipal governments. Politicians usually don't want to spend money unless they have to, and the developers and investors won't want to get involved with a property if there is no profit margin. Outside of the issue of the grants and incentives that can be procured to make a project profitable, only governments can do something for the greater good of the public while operating at a loss. *That* is a very precarious decision for a politician to make.

During my first year as executive director, a friend of mine said, "Bob, there's an election coming up, and, when the Dems come back in, you're going to be out of a job." I didn't take it too seriously because I could get along with anyone, whether they were Democrats or Republicans. Besides, I had no political aspirations so I didn't pose a threat to either side. His warning did open my eyes though. If I wanted to avoid any political pitfalls in my new position at the RDA, I was going to have to acquire a deeper understanding of the nature and mindset of the political beast. Within a year or two, I'd developed my rules of engagement.

Rule #1: Forget about putting a politician in a risky position when there's an election coming up anytime soon. In general, politicians are scared of anything that is an unknown. However, the good ones will stick their necks out from time to time—especially after they've been reelected.

Rule #2: Everyone on the RDA's board of directors was a political appointee (mostly Republicans). After the first year or two, I got to a point where I knew what they would approve and what they wouldn't, so I avoided bringing them projects that had little or no chance of passing. Nothing ever moved forward during my tenure with less than a unanimous vote. You might call that a phony, prearranged record of success, but it was more a matter of simple logic: Why dig my heels in and go to battle on remediating and developing a property that had multiple environmental and political challenges when there were two dozen other less-problematic sites on the RDA's conveyor belt that equally needed our attention?

Rule #3: Always give the politicians credit on every project, even if their participation was minimal. They need those public acknowledgements to get reelected, and they'll remember you the next time a different project comes around for which you might need their support. Besides, the important people in the county who matter will know who really did the work anyway. I always used to say, "You take the credit. Just give me the funding."

Rule #4: It's not a bad idea to make politicians think a project you're trying to push through was their idea in the first place. Sometimes I'd meet with a councilman or councilwoman on a pressing matter, and at some point during the conversation,

I'd drop a vague reference to a different property or project—just to gauge their reaction. If I picked up any negativity, I'd return to the original matter at hand. Even if they showed some interest, I still wouldn't pursue the issue any further. I'd let some time pass and approach them at a later date and say something like, "You know, Jim, that idea you had to widen that road through the center of town is a great idea. How do you think we could make that work?" Even if they knew it was not their idea, I never had a single politician say it wasn't, and no one ever accused me of playing them.

There was no grand design behind all my random efforts to learn the particulars of the redevelopment authority business. I can't say I'd recommend my trial and error approach to everyone, but somehow, it worked for me. I got my first wide-angle view of what I'd accomplished 15 years down the road when my Deputy Director Jeff Darwak and I had to put together a report for the county commissioners. They wanted us to account for what the RDA had accomplished during the previous decade when Bucks County had an Enterprise Zone. Seven of the eight major sites identified on the brownfields list were well underway and—working with the county's Economic Development Corporation and the Industrial Development Authority—we'd created or saved over 16,000 jobs in total from all the different projects we'd been working on. The RDA's peak years came between 1999 and 2005, with 15 large-scale projects in progress and dozens more queued up in line waiting to get going. The overlap from all the simultaneous activity allowed us to amortize a lot of our costs and make beneficial deals with contractors by guaranteeing them years of employment.

During the stretch of time from my inaugural year in 1993 to when we wrote the commissioners' report, our yearly operating budget increased from $120,000 to $700,000 and our office staff grew from two to ten employees. Two members of our staff did nothing but handle the low-income home rehabilitation program, which freed up the rest of us to throw all our efforts into tackling the larger industrial, commercial, and residential sites.

Due to all our achievements and successes, the footprint and status of the Bucks County RDA grew within the industry, and so did mine. Offers began coming in for me to speak at conventions and other related events. I put together numerous presentations, during which I spoke to groups as small as 10 people all the way up to larger audiences of 300 folks. (I always liked when Joel Bolstein accompanied me because walking in with one of the country's top environmental lawyers always made me look good.)

Many of my more memorable speaking engagements took place during my first decade at the RDA's helm. At Joel's request, I traveled to Harrisburg on one occasion to address a senate committee from the state legislature about the success of the brownfields program. That was a big one for me, although several presentations I did for the EPA and the PADEP proved to be equally valuable.

One of my presentations to the PADEP in the early 2000s.

Not every property we worked on came with environmental problems, but the older and larger ones usually did. That meant EPA or PADEP involvement—and sometimes both. The presentations I gave to those two organizations afforded me the opportunity to build some important relationships with them, and also with the United States Army Corps of Engineers (USACE). The timing couldn't have been better because it was during the first decade of my career at the RDA that work began on some of the largest, most complex, and most contaminated sites in our four-decade history.

Riverfront North's 52 acres on the Bristol waterfront was the recipient of the unwanted byproducts of eight decades of heavy industrial usage; the transformation of US Steel's Fairless Works in Falls Township into a deepwater port necessitated numerous dredgings of the Delaware River and the tearing down of millions of square feet of contaminated buildings on almost 2,000 acres of land; and getting work crews to enter and clean up the toxic grounds of the Penn Salt Manufacturing Company in Bensalem was like asking the Marines to charge up Mt. Suribachi in the Battle of Iwo Jima. We needed all the help we could get, and the friends I made at the EPA, the PADEP, and the USACE were worth their weight in gold.

These were the good years. My annual salary had increased commensurate with the RDA's outstanding record of achievement, and my level of autonomy grew. There were three county commissioners—always in a two-plus-one arrangement with the "one" coming from the minority party. You could really get bogged down sometimes if they got involved, but I rarely had to deal with them unless we needed county money. The once-a-month board of directors meetings we had in my early years had the board members calling all the shots. But because of the confidence they had in me, I was now running the agendas, although the board still had to give the final approvals. It made a lot of sense; I was there every day while they were there only once a month. When you have trusting, honest relationships and a judicious flow of power back and forth, you can get a heckuva lot of things done in a short amount of time.

I was in a good place. Even so, nothing is ever perfect. I still had my shortcomings and my share of defeats. I struggled with personnel management sometimes, often as a result of trying to overpay or use promotions to get better job performances out of our staff. Begrudgingly, I had to accept that, now and then, you can promote a person to incompetence. Some people are just not capable of taking on more responsibility or raising their level of effort. I also had a hard time firing people, so I'd usually try and find them a new job elsewhere before I cut ties.

My biggest setbacks—the ones I took the hardest—came from overreaching. I've always believed I can pull off anything I set my mind to, so I have to step outside of myself to admit to that. There were a few projects, like the A. E. Staley property and Rohm & Haas's Maple Beach site, where I was asking for more than some businesses and people were willing or able to give. When you dream big, sometimes you fall big. Nevertheless, I wouldn't have done anything different.

PART THREE

THE RDA FILES:
THE BOB WHITE YEARS

The heart and soul of the RDA's story are the actual redevelopment projects we worked on over the years. I may have been the executive director who guided the ship on many of these, but none of them would have arrived at their eventual destinations without the help of my staff and the support, hard work, and input of all the developers, contractors, and numerous Bucks County politicians, councils, committees, and board members I've had the honor to work with.

Seventeen of our signature projects are contained in the following pages, followed by another 35 other exploits of various shapes and sizes. As a convenience, a list of the acronyms used in this section is provided below.

Government Agencies

DCED – Pennsylvania Department of Community and Economic Development

HUD – US Department of Housing and Urban Development

EPA – US Environmental Protection Agency

DEP (sometimes referred to as **PADEP**) – Pennsylvania Department of Environmental Protection

USACE – US Army Corps of Engineers

PENNDOT – Pennsylvania Department of Transportation

PENNVEST – Pennsylvania Infrastructure Investment Authority

Grant and Tax Incentive Programs

CDBG – Community Development Block Grants

ISRP – Industrial Sites Reuse Program

RACP – Redevelopment Assistance Capital Program

EDA – US Economic Development Assistance Grants

LERTA – Local Economic Revitalization Tax Assistance

KOZ – Keystone Opportunity Zone

Toxins

VOC – Volatile Organic Compounds

SVOC – Semi-Volatile Organic Compounds

PCE – Perchloroethylene

TCE – Trichloroethylene

PCBs – Polychlorinated Biphenyls

PAHs – Polycyclic Aromatic Hydrocarbons

MORRISVILLE VULCANIZED RUBBER MILL

START AND COMPLETION DATES: EARLY TO MID-1970S AND THEN 1994 TO 1996

LOCATION: The corner of Bridge Street and Pennsylvania Avenue in Morrisville.

HISTORY OF THE SITE: The Morrisville Vulcanized Rubber Mill was in business from the early 1900s through the early '60s, when it closed down. It stood vacant for more than a decade and posed a significant hazard to the community because kids playing with matches set it on fire several times. The site was put up for sale because of delinquent real estate taxes, but no buyers stepped forward. Consequently, it fell into the ownership of Bucks County, who gave it to the RDA. They demolished the building sometime in the early '70s.

Studies were enacted to explore the feasibility of building an attractive shopping center on the site, but expediency ruled the day. When a strip mall developer with a much less ambitious plan offered to purchase a portion of the property, the RDA took the only deal on the table and sold him the land. In the blink of an eye, a Pizza Hut and a 7-Eleven occupied the location where the Morrisville Rubber Mill once stood.

After the partial sale of the rubber mill site to the strip mall developer, three acres of unused, open land remained. It had been on the

RDA's slate of projects to be dealt with for more than a decade, but nothing was happening.

Then in 1994, my first full year as the RDA's executive director, the old Morrisville Rubber Mill site became active once again. The strip mall's owner contacted me and explained that he wanted to refinance the property and needed a completion certificate from the RDA before the bank would approve the deal. The completion certificate would confirm the developer had satisfied all the requirements of the redevelopment contract between him and the RDA that were stipulated at the sale of the property.

Morrisville, Pa., Vulcanized Rubber Mill.

The Morrisville Vulcanized Rubber Mill as it looked before World War I. The pond still exists in 2020, but half of it is overgrown with vegetation.

Being new on the job, I wasn't sure how to handle the situation, so I told him I'd look into it and get back to him. What started out as a simple bureaucratic matter became the first challenge to my authority as the RDA's executive director. My research found that the original settlement required the property's owner to build a park on a small, unused parcel of land on the strip mall's plot. He just ignored that contractual obligation over the years and then came to me figuring the RDA probably had forgotten all about it. It may seem like a petty, minor detail, but I wasn't going to start off my tenure by letting someone ignore their contractual obligations with the county and Morrisville Borough.

Once I informed the owner that we couldn't issue the completion certificate until he fulfilled his overdue contractual obligation, he offered no resistance and built the park shortly thereafter. It all worked out: He got his certificate, the bank refinanced his property, and the RDA was a step nearer to closing the book on the old rubber mill property. All that remained was finding someone to take the site's remaining three acres off our hands.

We didn't have to wait too long. Late in 1994 or early 1995, Rich Snyder, the RDA's solicitor, introduced me to a new developer who had been eyeing those three acres as a potential site for a Holiday Inn Express he planned to build. We sold him the property for $60,000 and then he promptly built his hotel; however, it's never quite that simple.

ENVIRONMENTAL AND/OR BLIGHT ISSUES: A seven to eight-foot-deep pit had been dug in the ground and was filled with old tires and waste rubber. There was also a small amount of petroleum in the groundwater. Compared to some other environmental problems I would encounter in the coming years, these were on the lightweight side, but as I was a rookie executive director, they provided me with a good opportunity to wade in and get my feet wet in a situation that wouldn't overwhelm me.

COURSE OF ACTION FOR THE CLEANUP: The hotel developer decided to perform his own Phase 1 and Phase 2 inspection before finalizing the purchase. He found what he thought was an abundance of petroleum in the ground and wanted a reduction in the property's sale price because he would have to pay out of pocket to remediate the problem.

Being new on the job, I still didn't look at myself as an "executive" working in the safe confines of an office. I was the same get-your-hands-dirty, do-it-yourself guy who ran his own small construction company a few years earlier. And so, I did my own Phase 2 inspection. I rented a backhoe for $350 a day, operated it myself, and dug my own test pits. I also hired a geologist named Harry Alsentzer to get some expert advice. He took a dozen water samples from the grounds and sent them out for testing. They all came back "non-detect," which basically cleared the petroleum condition but still left the buried rubber products to be dealt with.

Harry gave me my first environmental lesson during our inspection. I watched as he took a single drop of oil and dropped it into a puddle. The oil immediately spread out on the surface of the water. "Oil and water don't mix," he said. "The oil just lays on the top and looks much more polluted than it actually is." Between the non-detect tests and what Harry showed me, the RDA declined the developer's request for a price reduction.

In truth, $60,000 was an inexpensive, under-market price for the property, but we offered it at that price because we factored in the costs he'd have to pay to clean up all the site's problems. The developer didn't put up much of an argument, paid our asking price, and, after a short remediation period, Morrisville had a new Holiday Inn Express in its midst.

COURSE OF ACTION FOR THE REUSE: Unlike many other projects in which the RDA was involved from the start of the environmental assessment phase through the remediation and reuse stages, we were out of the picture once we sold the three acres to the hotel developer. From that point on, all aspects of remediation, planning, and development were his sole responsibility.

COSTS AND GRANTS:
- $0.00 for the transfer of ownership of the property from Bucks County to the RDA.
- An unspecified amount paid to Bucks County in the 1980s for a majority portion of the Morrisville Rubber Mill site by the developer of the Pizza Hut/7-Eleven strip mall.
- An unspecified amount paid by Bucks County for the demolition of the Morrisville Rubber Mill buildings in the early '70s.

- $350 paid by the RDA for the backhoe plus the geologist's fee. All other cleanup and reuse expenses were paid by the developers of the strip mall and the hotel.

- $60,000 paid for the site's remaining three-acre parcel by the developer who built the Holiday Inn.

- No grants, government programs, or tax incentives were secured for this project.

POLITICAL ISSUES: None.

STATUS OF THE SITE TODAY: Just as the Morrisville Vulcanized Rubber Mill is now just a footnote in Morrisville's long history, so is the Holiday Inn Express. It's changed hands several times and is now a Quality Inn. Change is part of a community's natural evolution, and the RDA plays a role in facilitating that change. But not every project we do results in a picture-perfect outcome. I certainly would have liked to see something more pleasing to the eye at the intersection of Bridge Street and Pennsylvania Avenue than a chain hotel and a Pizza Hut/7-Eleven strip mall.

An aerial shot of what the rubber mill's grounds look like today. The 7-Eleven strip mall is directly above the pond at the exact middle of the far-left border of the photo. The long diagonal roof of the hotel is in the lower half of the right side, surrounded by parking lots.

But consider the alternative. An abandoned fire hazard of a building with tires and rubber waste piled up on its grounds was contributing absolutely nothing to the community. The businesses that replaced it are all now on Morrisville's tax rolls. Travelers have a clean, modern hotel to spend the night. And let's face it: At 11:00 p.m., when you need a roll of toilet paper, a cup of coffee, or a quick slice of pizza, you don't want to drive several miles to an upscale shopping district or mall that would probably be closed at that hour anyway. You want a store that's right around the corner like a 7-Eleven or a Pizza Hut.

Best of all, the Morrisville Vulcanized Rubber Mill site was no longer the responsibility of the RDA, we now had $60,000 in our bank account for use on other county projects, and the everyday, mundane needs of a community are currently being delivered from a plot of land that delivered nothing for decades. I'd call that a successful project.

Upper photo: Mill Pond Center, the name given to the 7-Eleven strip mall, is a nod to the old rubber mill that once occupied the same location. Lower photo: The renamed Holiday Inn is now a Quality Inn. You can get a sense of the proximity of the two buildings from the elevated Quality Inn sign to the left of the 7-Eleven.

A. B. MURRAY INC.

START AND COMPLETION DATES:
1995 TO 1998.

LOCATION: Off of Green Lane in Bristol Township. The site was sandwiched between north and southbound railroad tracks and a residential area on the east side.

HISTORY OF THE SITE: Going back as far as the 1930s, A. B. Murray Inc. was in the business of manufacturing large and small heating boilers for both residential and industrial use. This required immense amounts of steel that was shipped into its factory via railcars on train tracks that ran right into the building. After operating out of Bucks County for more than four decades, the company sold its property to the Earle M. Jorgensen Company, a British warehousing operation for steel building products. Sometime in the late 1980s or early '90s, it withdrew from the warehouse business and became a landlord, leasing the property to other similar businesses, most prominently the Hartwell Warehouse Inc. organization. Hartwell had a contract with U.S. Steel's Fairless Works and was storing thousands of tons of rolled steel on the premises.

Much of the front of the 16-acre property was blacktopped to provide parking for the 40 to 50 trucks that brought goods in and out of the facility each day. The existing structures consisted of a 164,000-square-foot steel warehouse made up of three interconnected buildings and a 9,000-square-foot, single-story office building that sat about 30 feet away. The office building had been built decades earlier and was originally a 500-square-foot scale house that was used to weigh trucks as they entered and exited the A. B. Murray campus. The difference between the two weights was the method A. B. Murray used to keep track of how much steel was involved in every shipment.

Beginning in the 1980s, several additions were built onto the scale house as the Jorgensen Company's needs for office space increased. A final 5,000-square-foot addition was added to house a call center in the building. By the 1990s, the building had ceased to be a scale house for some time. Hartwell was using a small portion of it for office space while the rest remained idle with little or no maintenance.

HOW THE RDA GOT INVOLVED: Bristol Township had a serious traffic problem. An unbroken line of industrial manufacturers and warehouses covering 85 acres stretched across its northern landscape, beginning with the A. B. Murray site and continuing through the campuses of Robern Cabinet Company, Crownwood Industrial Estates, and Corell Steel. The lifeline that kept all of these businesses humming was a daily parade of 40-foot tractor trailers bringing steel goods in and out. In order for them to reach the properties behind A. B. Murray's warehouse, it was necessary for them to come up Radcliffe Street, turn up one of the smaller side streets, and then travel through several blocks of residential neighborhoods that were not built to handle industrial traffic.

It wasn't a good situation, particularly in the morning when kids were walking to school or waiting to be picked up by their school buses. The locals also didn't appreciate waking up to the loud engine noise of Peterbilt and Mack truck semis or the smell of burning diesel fuel mixing with their morning coffee. The township's officials wanted to have an internal roadway built that would connect all the aforementioned industrial sites, keep the trucks out of the nearby residential neighborhoods, and provide a more direct access to the Pennsylvania Turnpike entrance half a mile away. In 1995, they contacted the RDA in hopes we could help make that happen.

ENVIRONMENTAL AND/OR BLIGHT ISSUES: The grounds of the former A. B. Murray Company had become 16 acres of blight. The exact composition and remediation of any toxins or contaminants found there were unknown to us because they were discovered and dealt with before the RDA became involved in the project. When we first entered the site in 1995, the warehouse was active and in use, although its outer walls were discolored and rusted and there were some abandoned vehicles and tires strewn about the grounds.

The 9,000-square-foot office building adjacent to the warehouse had more substantial problems. It had a leaky roof, and because of that, all the interior ceilings, drywall, and carpets were deteriorated and ruined. An engineer had condemned the building, and it was scheduled to be torn down because it was in the path of the planned roadway.

COURSE OF ACTION FOR THE CLEANUP: The EPA forced the Jorgensen Company to clean up the site. They hadn't caused the contamination, but they inherited the responsibility for it when they bought the property from A. B. Murray. (This was what companies had to go through before ACT 2.) Once again, since Jorgensen's remediation was done prior to the RDA's involvement, we had no idea exactly what was done, although we were told it cost almost $1,500,000.

Perhaps the seven-figure loss they'd incurred from the cleanup was the reason they decided to finally part ways with the property. Then again, perhaps not, but in 1996, when the RDA offered $1,450,000 for the 16-acre A. B. Murray campus, Jorgensen agreed to sell. (The Hartwell organization agreed to purchase the warehouse from the RDA once all of our redevelopment efforts on the site were completed.) Our first move with this new acquisition was to come up with a land development plan that added a new industrial roadway from Green Lane to the rear industrial acreage of Robern Cabinets and Crownwood Estates. That would satisfy the needs of Bristol Township—which, after all, was the principal reason we got involved with the site to begin with.

While this process was ongoing, the RDA was negotiating to save the condemned office building. Everyone who saw it viewed it as the equivalent of a dead man walking. They saw a mildewed, water-damaged dump that was scheduled to be demolished within a few weeks. But that's not what I saw; I saw the future office of the RDA.

It was a well-built, all-masonry structure with metal bar joists. Once we got the approval from the powers that be to save the office building, we put on a new roof and power washed the outside of the building. Then a demolition company cleared out the inside and aired everything out. The building began to come back to life. It may have looked bad when the RDA first came on the site, but I knew all it really needed was a little bit of love and a makeover.

The former scale house that eventually became the RDA's headquarters.

COURSE OF ACTION FOR THE REUSE: The process of building the roadway was thrown a major curveball when it was decided the office building would be saved. The reason was immediately apparent: The proposed roadway's path was supposed to go directly through the 1.3 acres on which the office building was constructed. But now that it wasn't going to be demolished, the path of the roadway had to be moved. The new path required shaving 6,000 square feet off the end of the A. B. Murray warehouse, getting the approval of the township, and most of all, getting Hartwell to go along with the new plan.

Grading and leveling the proposed roadway with a bulldozer.

The roadway's construction was much easier than the back and forth negotiations that preceded it. Once all the necessary land development approvals came in, it was built in just three to four months between 1997 and 1998. Hartwell couldn't have been more cooperative. The road started at Green Lane and ended 1,500 feet away in a cul-de-sac underneath the Pennsylvania Turnpike bridge, with an entranceway for both Corell Steel and Crownwood Estates.

The only things that remained to do to the warehouse were walling off the gaping hole where the 6,000-square-foot section was cut away and adding of a new coat of blue paint. We also ripped up the blacktopped area in front of the building where all the incoming trucks used to park. It was rendered obsolete by the roadway. And as a final touch, we built new railroad siding that entered the back of the building, because the old siding wouldn't accommodate modern train cars. The roadway now subdivided the site: The warehouse took up 14 acres, the office building occupied its 1.3 acres, and the remaining portion of the site's 16 acres was taken up by the road itself. It was deeded to the township and named North Wilson Avenue, starting with the office building, which was given the honor of having the inaugural address number "1."

The new railroad siding we built that ran directly into the back of Hartwell's warehouse.

In 1996, we fixed up 1,500 square feet of the office building for the RDA's use and eventually expanded it to almost 9,000 square feet when we created an incubator office space for startup businesses. That rehab work was performed over time as we got tenants. We just gave them four walls and let them do whatever they wanted. In time, the building housed six suites including ours. One of the new tenants turned out to be an unexpected find for us. Transportation Management Associates (TMA) was a federal program that dealt with national transportation projects. They did a traffic study of the surrounding area and helped us figure out the best way to further reduce truck traffic.

The rehabilitation and reuse of the office building brought about some unintended good fortune for me. I had to bid out the installation of the water, gas, telephone, and electrical services and get them installed before we could move in. The quote came in way too high at $20,000, so I called a plumber I knew from my past life in home rehabbing. He brought in some extra labor to handle the non-plumbing-related tasks, and we did everything ourselves in just one day for a shade under $10,000. By 3:30 p.m., the backhoe operator was filling in the trenches, and by 5:00, we were out of there. But not before County Commissioner Mike Fitzpatrick happened to drive by and see me knee-deep in the dirt digging with a shovel—on a Saturday, no less. That hands-on moment earned me untold amounts of good will and political backing in the coming years.

THE DEVELOPER: The roadway was built by a construction company that is no longer in business. The RDA was the developer on this project.

COSTS AND GRANTS:
- $1,450,000 paid by the RDA to the Earle Jorgensen Company in 1995 to purchase the property.
- $1,450,000 paid in 1998 by Hartwell Warehouse Inc. to purchase the property from the RDA.
- $1,500,000 paid by the Jorgensen Company, who were forced by the EPA to clean up the site.
- $250,000 PennDOT grant used to fund the added railroad sidings for the warehouse.
- $850,000 of DCED money went to pay for the cost of land development for the roadway, removing the blacktopped area from the

front of the warehouse, constructing the storm sewers to catch and dispose of water, and the actual cost of building the roadway.

- Funds for cleaning and rehabbing the office building came from the sale of the RDA's old office building in Yardley and from a small mortgage we were able to secure on the building.

POLITICAL ISSUES: Many people in the community felt the $850,000 Pennsylvania DCED grant should have been awarded directly to Bristol Township instead of going through the RDA, but I was lucky that the A. B. Murray project came at a time of strong leadership in the county. State Senator Tommy Tomlinson, State Rep. Tom Corrigan, Bucks County Republican Party Executive Director Harry Fawkes, and County Commission Chairman Michael Fitzpatrick put their faith in me and decided if a project this complex was ever going to get completed, the RDA's new executive director was the man for the job. More than any one individual, I owed Harry for this one. I may have been paving the roadway, but he was the guy who got the office building off the chopping block, which paved the way for our new headquarters.

CHALLENGES AND/OR SETBACKS: I really lucked into the A. B. Murray project. It was a textbook case of right place, right time that fell into my lap because the politicians were familiar with my earlier experiences in road building. Even so—as described in the previous section—many folks thought I'd never succeed. Instead, I got it done in record time with complete support from the Jorgensen Company, Hartwell, and the township. You know what it means when everything goes that smoothly? LOOK OUT!

Landreth Manor was a residential neighborhood situated just east of the RDA's new office building. Separating us was a 50-foot-wide buffer zone of unlandscaped trees and natural vegetation that belonged to the township. Some of the homeowners on the border decided to cut down the trees on their side of the zone. Then they extended their lawns into the newly cleared land, and some actually erected garden sheds there, even though they were on public property. They liked the A. B. Murray property the way it was—abandoned junk vehicles and tires, blighted office building, and all.

All of that was between them and the township though. My mind had already moved on to the next project—or so I thought. Over Memorial Day weekend, the trees on our side of the zone were cut down by one of our crews. The intent was to provide room for a small parking lot for the rehabbed office building and for the excavation of a water detention basin that protected the area against flooding. That left a direct sightline from the residents' yards to the back of our facility. They could see and hear all the trucks idling with their lights on in front of the A. B. Murray warehouse.

The neighborhood exploded, accusing the RDA of using the holiday to camouflage what we were doing. The local press got involved, neighborhood realtors spread misinformation, and in nothing flat, everything got blown way out of proportion. Somehow—in the eyes of some Landreth Manor residents—a haphazard clump of rotted, gnarly old trees that no one had ever cared about before was transformed into a beloved, idyllic forest that the *villainous RDA* had callously cut down.

We had many meetings with the residents in an attempt to calm things down. Most of the locals were fine with what we'd done, but a small contingent wasn't giving in. In their defense, I could understand their complaint about the truck noise and lights, *but who the hell asked them to cut down the trees on their side of the buffer zone in the first place?* Only time would resolve the dispute. After a few weeks, the local papers moved on to other stories, and the controversy petered out.

Later on that same year (1999), the RDA won an award from the Bucks County Chamber of Commerce for being the region's best economic development agency. I wasn't looking for revenge or a stick-it-in-your-face exoneration, but I have to admit, it was comforting. I don't like debating and arguing with people. I'm not good at it, and it just takes up too much damn time and effort.

STATUS OF THE SITE TODAY: The Hartwell Company still owns and operates the old A. B. Murray steel warehouse, but the RDA is no longer located in the office building across the roadway. The former scale house continues to be office space and is currently run and maintained by the tenants, who formed an ownership LLC and bought it from us six years before we moved out to a new location in 2016. We certainly got our money's worth out of our stay there. For 20 years, all our bills were taken care of, courtesy of the $60,000 in rental fees paid by the tenants in the five suites we leased.

As for North Wilson Avenue and the new roadway we built—it's functioning as planned, isolating the local neighborhoods from the comings and goings of the trucks entering and exiting the 85 acres of nearby industrial sites.

The finished roadway runs in between the scale house and the large warehouse on the left. The 6,000 square feet that was shaved off of that building originally extended to approximately the midpoint of where the roadway currently stands.

The roadway was the type of project that isn't a reuse that turns into a moneymaker for someone or contributes to the municipal tax coffers, but its ultimate outcome helped a lot of people in the surrounding neighborhoods. Nevertheless, not everyone was happy about it. I imagine a few Landreth Manor folks continue to hold on to their grudge over the trees we cut down. As much as I've tried, I can't change their opinions. The years have taught me that any time you put together a major project like this, someone is bound to get pissed off.

I was in my fifties by the time Forrest Gump's "Life is like a box of chocolates" quote became an oft-repeated phrase in pop culture. I gotta admit though, it certainly seemed like an apt commentary on a number of moments in my life. I joined the Marines to get away from my grandfather and his farm but wound up in the middle of the Cuban Missile Crisis. I left the Marines to keep wife number one happy, yet here I am currently working on making wife number three happy. And when we took on the A. B. Murray project in 1995, our goal was to fulfill the township's request to help get truck traffic out of the nearby neighborhoods. Instead, I found a new home for the RDA. "You never know what you're gonna get," Forrest would have concluded.

CORELL STEEL

START AND COMPLETION DATES:
NOVEMBER 1996 TO NOVEMBER 2003.

LOCATION: The Corell Steel complex was located at the end of Coates Avenue in Bristol Township behind the Coates Avenue School building. It is sandwiched between baseball fields, residential housing, train tracks, and the Pennsylvania Turnpike Bridge. The official address is 805 North Wilson Avenue.

HISTORY OF THE SITE: The story of the Corell Steel site is a proverbial tale of two cities. Originally, it was a 37-acre property with a haphazard collection of single-story industrial buildings and warehouses (some with dirt floors) that totaled almost 500,000 square feet. Trucks coming into the facility drove on stone pathways, as there were no paved driveways between the buildings. Corell processed and fabricated steel products for almost three decades until they ran into money problems and $1,000,000 worth of tax delinquency in the late 1980s. A management company bought 30 of the 37 acres at a tax sale, renamed the campus Crownwood Industrial Estates, and portioned out several large interconnected buildings on that acreage for leasing to other steel processing companies and a variety of other businesses looking for warehouse, office, distribution, and manufacturing space.

Because of perceived contamination in Corell's remaining seven acres, Crownwood had limited interest in purchasing the smaller parcel of the property. Corell continued to own the acreage and the three buildings situated there, but little if any activity was going on. In the early 1990s, a fire broke out in the largest of the buildings—a 50,000-square-foot warehouse and manufacturing facility. It quickly spread to a smaller 5,000-square-foot structure used as an office building, forcing residents of the adjacent neighborhood to be evacuated. The third building, a 30,000-square-foot structure, survived without too much damage.

An aerial shot of Corell Steel's sprawling complex of interconnected buildings.

HOW THE RDA GOT INVOLVED: After the fire, the seven-acre parcel remained vacant and tax delinquent until the RDA attempted to purchase it in November 1996. For some reason, it was taken off the market, but it wasn't for naught: We identified it as one of the original eight properties listed to be remediated in the Bucks County EPA Brownfields Program. In May 1998, we got a second shot at it when it was made available at a sheriff's sale. Crownwood had renewed interest in the parcel and bid

$150,000. We partnered up with the school district on a $200,000 bid that Crownwood declined to challenge. The property was ours. (The partnership with the school district was enacted for a legal reason: The township was never going to be able to collect the delinquent $1,000,000 tax bill from Corell. Owning the property enabled them to legally get that debt off their books.)

ENVIRONMENTAL AND/OR BLIGHT ISSUES: Corell Steel's seven acres had minor petroleum oil issues in the soil caused by three deteriorated fuel tanks. One of the buildings had asbestos problems from old nine-by-nine-inch floor tiles, and the other two were blighted from the early '90s fire.

Corell Steel after the fire.

COURSE OF ACTION FOR THE CLEANUP: In 1999, a year after we purchased the seven acres, we secured several grants for Phase 1 and Phase 2 assessments and remediation of the environmental problems on the seven acres. Additional grants in 2000 helped pay for the removal of the fuel tanks and the demolition of the smaller building.

COURSE OF ACTION FOR THE REUSE: After we cleaned out the larger of the two buildings, we sold it to Crownwood in November 2003. In no time, they rehabbed it and repurposed it for leasing. It is now back on the township's tax rolls. As for the post-demolition three acres, the RDA gave them to Bristol Township as open space.

COSTS AND GRANTS:

- A $200,000 bid from a partnership of the RDA and the Bristol Township School District to acquire the seven-acre parcel at a sheriff's sale. Neither of us had to pay any portion of the $200,000 because the gross proceeds from the tax sale would have gone to the township's school district anyway as partial payment for the property's $1,000,000 in tax liens.

- $125,000 grant for a Phase 1 and Phase 2 assessment of the environmental conditions on the site. Seventy-five percent of the funds came from the state DCED and the remaining twenty-five percent came from federal EPA funds.

- $125,000 DCED grant for the demolition of the burned-out 50,000-square-foot warehouse and the smaller 5,000-square-foot office building.

- $29,000 grant for the removal of the fuel tanks. Seventy-five percent of the funds came from the state DCED and the remaining twenty-five percent came from federal EPA funds.

- $275,000 paid by Crownwood Estates in 2003 to purchase Corell Steel's four-acre parcel and the 30,000-square-foot building.

- Once the project wrapped up and all the costs had been recouped, the remaining funds went to the Bristol Township School District.

POLITICAL ISSUES: None.

CHALLENGES AND/OR SETBACKS: Sometimes, in the pursuit of transparency and serving the public, you have to do things that would seem to make no sense. Residents of the surrounding neighborhoods were convinced that large quantities of hazardous materials had been dumped on the Corell Steel site. To answer their concerns, we paid an environmental company to perform the Phase 1 and Phase 2 assessments.

After four months of spending $125,000 digging six-foot deep trenches all around the campus, their final diagnosis called for a mere $29,000 of remedial costs. They even dug down 10 feet to the water table, and there was nothing there either. Still, we took care of getting the fuel tanks and asbestos tiles removed and then actually cleaned all seven acres, even though no blacktopping or shipping in tons of clean fill to block the contaminants' path were necessary. The process was overkill and it slowed down the site's development for reuse, but it's all part of the game. The public has a right to have a level of confidence that they're not living in a toxic waste dump.

STATUS OF THE SITE TODAY: While Corell Steel is just another of the many Bucks County manufacturers whose moment in the sun has come and gone over the years, Crownwood Industrial Estates—its successor—has been thriving ever since. The campus is a hub of activity, providing a home to numerous businesses while generating jobs and community taxes for Bristol Township.

As for the RDA's participation in this transformation, being straight up with the community about their toxicity concerns was as valuable—if not more so—than the project's ultimate result. There's always another developer somewhere down the road willing to take a piece of property off your hands, but a community's trust is a fragile thing. If you lose it, decades can pass before you get it back. I was proud the RDA chose to be a stand-up organization on the Corell Steel project and had every intention of keeping it that way on every project to follow.

LEVITTOWN SHOP-A-RAMA

START AND COMPLETION DATES:
1999 TO 2002.

SITE LOCATION: Across from the Levittown train station at the intersection of Route 13 and Levittown Parkway in Tullytown Borough.

HISTORY OF THE SITE: In 1951, developers William J. Levitt and his brother Alfred came to Bucks County to assess a large tract of land that stretched across parts of Middletown, Bristol, and Falls Townships. For decades, the locals just saw farmland at that location—five farms, to be specific—but the Levitt brothers had a much larger and ambitious vision. A year later, they broke ground for Levittown, Pennsylvania, a sprawling, self-contained community of low-cost houses that would appeal to local steelworkers at the nearby U.S. Steel mill, GIs who had returned from World War II, and a few years later, Korean War veterans.

Using assembly line construction techniques, 17,311 homes were built from 1952 through 1958. With six models to chose from, these homes could be purchased for less than $10,000, and if you were a veteran of the armed services, you had to put up only $100 to get financing.

Historically, Levittown could be considered a social experiment, but in one respect, it was a bad one: The Levitts would not sell to African Americans. In their minds, they weren't looking at it as an issue of racism.

To them, it was a simple matter of marketing: They didn't want to scare off the majority of potential buyers, who were white. In spite of the protests of the NAACP and the ACLU, Levittown remained a "whites only" community until 1957, when William and Daisy Myers, a black couple, opened the door to people of color when they purchased a previously owned Levittown home.

The development's original master plan included schools, parks, athletic fields, pools, and a shopping center dubbed the "Levittown Shop-a-Rama." Located in the neighboring municipality of Tullytown (Levittown was not, and still isn't, a municipality), the Shop-a-Rama was the largest shopping center east of the Mississippi. No longer would Levittown residents and people from other nearby communities have to travel to Bristol or Trenton to shop.

Built on 60 acres, the Shop-a-Rama encompassed more than 50 stores and businesses, including a supermarket, a gym, a theater, and its flagship department store, Pomeroy's. The simple design featured two parallel strips of stores with a courtyard in between. The Shop-a-Rama had its 15 minutes of fame in 1960 when future President John F. Kennedy and his opponent Richard Nixon both campaigned there to raise funds for their presidential runs.

It was a staple of community life for several decades until it began to decline due to the rise of modern shopping malls in the 1970s. The nearby Neshaminy and Oxford Valley Malls focused an unwanted spotlight on the limited amenities and antiquated facilities of the Shop-a-Rama. The new malls had a much larger and varied selection of stores and restaurants, and most important, the stores and walkways were all *inside*. Regardless of cold, hot, or inclement weather outside, shoppers could comfortably travel from store to store on wide indoor walkways in heated and air-conditioned comfort. By the late 1980s and early '90s, the Shop-a-Rama had become a dilapidated ghost town with fewer than a dozen stores still in operation.

A depressing portrait of lost prosperity: two lone shoppers walking through a virtually deserted Shop-a-Rama.

ENVIRONMENTAL AND/OR BLIGHT ISSUES: The Shop-a-Rama had few specific environmental or chemical contaminant issues past some leaky roofs and broken water pipes that ran off into Route 13. It was their underused properties with their boarded up storefronts and cracked, broken glass display windows that qualified it as a blighted site. Tullytown had been fining the site's owner for years, trying to force him to clean up and restore the property to an acceptable level of commercial operation, but it was to no avail; the owner wouldn't lift a finger to undertake any improvements.

COURSE OF ACTION FOR THE CLEANUP: As a longtime resident of Levittown, Bucks County Commissioner Mike Fitzpatrick had witnessed both the Shop-a-Rama's glory days and its long, slow death spiral. In the late 1990s, he approached the RDA in the hope that it was still possible to turn things around for what was once an iconic Bucks County shopping destination. He wanted us to start the process of designating the site as a "redevelopment area," a long and somewhat complicated process. The Shop-a-Rama involved multiple businesses, some of which were abandoned and blighted and some weren't. Either way, the Shop-a-Rama as a whole

139

was considered a single property. State law mandated that the redevelopment area designation could be applied only to an area that included multiple abandoned and blighted properties.

That hurdle was overcome by including the nearby landfill property owned by Saint Michael's Church (sold to them in 1958 by the Levitts) as part of the proposed redevelopment area. The church's school—while not in the greatest of shape—would not have met the qualifications by itself, but EPA reports from the 1980s listed concerns from students and teachers about odd chemical smells coming from the school building, and the lot itself had an abundance of environmental issues.

COURSE OF ACTION FOR THE REUSE: My job came down to coordinating all the involved parties. A large-scale study was undertaken and numerous meetings took place between Tullytown, the RDA, and Bucks County, during which a wealth of grand, creative ideas were put on the table. At one of our public meetings, a Tullytown resident suggested we restore the site and make it look like a cruise ship. There was also talk of opening the canal that ran across the area near Route 13 and then filling it with canoes. Another proposal called for a centralized gazebo with radiating walkways that would connect all the shops. Perhaps the most ambitious concept was building a pedestrian-friendly connective bridge from the Levittown train station across busy Route 13 to the newly restored shopping center.

No matter how far-fetched, all these concepts brought a great deal of energy and positivity to the project. I've always felt that the only crazy ideas are the ones that are never brought into the light. If you can conceive it, then you can achieve it. Everything looked like a big "GO." The three-way cooperative agreement that evolved between the RDA, the county, and Tullytown was a historic development: Bucks County was going to fund 50% of the project—something that had never happened before. The remaining 50% was to come from Tullytown and any third-party developer brought into the deal.

CHALLENGES, SETBACKS, AND POLITICAL ISSUES: Municipalities can assess fines on property owners, but they can't do much past that to force reluctant owners to improve their holdings. However, the RDA has the power of using eminent domain to force the issue. The Shop-a-Rama's ownership changed hands within their family and was now being run by a gentleman named Stephen Isham of DLC Management in New York. Realizing his company could be forced to relinquish its property, he finally reacted. Mr. Isham came to one of our meeting and asked us to stop the process. We politely told him no but said we'd be more than happy to work with him on the project.

At the same time, there were new elections in Tullytown's town council. The previous administration loved the project, but the newly elected members voted five to three against it. During the elections, *not* moving forward with the project became a talking point. As much as possible— even though I get along well with both Democrats and Republicans—I always try to keep politics out of RDA projects. But the new council brought up issues that were difficult for us to navigate.

Tullytown is an old, wealthy borough, and the council wanted to maintain the quaintness of Old Tullytown. They also wanted someone else to pick up the tab for the eyesore in their midst. When DLC offered to foot the bill, the council wanted to give them the chance to put their money where their mouth was. After doing nothing with the center for years, the Shop-a-Rama's ownership was finally ready to move but at a snail's pace. Their financial offer dangled on the table for two to three years, during which there were numerous meetings, presentations, and hurt feelings. By the time DLC stopped dragging their feet and demolished the Shop-a-Rama in 2002, the RDA was already out of the picture. Finding a creative solution for the Shop-A-Rama had been a losing fight for far too long. Small-town politics helped kill the original concept we'd forged together, but in all fairness, shopping centers are always driven by economics.

COSTS AND GRANTS:

- $6,000,000 would have been the approximate cost of acquiring the Shop-a-Rama ($5,500,000 for the purchase and $500,000 for the subsequent demolition) if the RDA had gone through the eminent domain process. However, DLC stopped that by assuming ownership of the site and finally agreeing to pay for its rehabilitation. After an extended period of citations, fines, meetings, and negotiations, Tullytown had the outcome they'd been hoping for: Someone else was picking up the tab to solve the problem.

- The RDA had a cooperation agreement with the county and Tullytown Borough to pick up our administration fees, so all our sweat equity was not lost when DLC took over.

- We had applied for a variety of grants to lessen the costs for Bucks County and Tullytown, but they were not pursued since the developer finally decided to move forward and rebuild the property.

STATUS OF THE SITE TODAY: During my 25-year tenure at the RDA, we were able to shine a bright light on more than 100 blighted or underutilized properties. Sometimes, nothing got done; sometimes, important, large-scale things got done; and then sometimes, a project got completed but we had to settle for much less than what we had hoped for.

The last of the Shop-a-Rama's stores closed in 2000 to make way for the newly proposed, DLC-financed "Levittown Town Center," which would eventually feature a Home Depot, a Walmart Supercenter, and 25 other smaller stores spread out over nearly 500,000 square feet of retail space. After two years of construction, the Town Center officially opened in 2009. As for the features we'd originally envisioned together—the gazebo and walkways, the canal, the pedestrian bridge from the train station, and the office building—none of them materialized as part of the new plans. In their place was a lot of blacktop and no walkable sidewalks to make the center pedestrian friendly.

See that white van in the lane between the Home Depot nursery awnings and the row of garden sheds? That's all that's left of what used to be the largest shopping center east of the Mississippi. The Shop-a-Rama is just a memory now.

I don't want my comments to appear as sour grapes. DLC eventually did a good job cleaning up and rebuilding the site. The community is now able to utilize a well-thought-out, modern shopping center that is living up to its economic potential and contributing to the area's tax rolls. The final outcome was more of a personal defeat for the RDA and me. Putting three years into a project that had so much promise and then having all our ambitious ideas go up in smoke was not an easy pill to swallow. In the end though, the people won and the RDA did its job by highlighting the situation and using one of its most useful tools, eminent domain, to encourage the Shop-a-Rama's owner to finally bring the center into the 21st century.

STAINLESS STEEL INC.

START AND COMPLETION DATES:
1998 TO 2004.

LOCATION: 219 South Ninth Street in downtown Perkasie, Pennsylvania, one block from the town's old municipal building.

HISTORY OF THE SITE: During the early years of the 20th century, the downtown landscape of Perkasie was dotted with numerous independently owned businesses. A lumber mill, a brickyard, and a variety of small factories that manufactured everything from baseballs to cigars to tiles all coexisted for decades. One of these factories was a silk mill that eventually went out of business and was abandoned. If my memory serves me well, the factory stayed vacant until it was occupied sometime in the 1960s. Its new owner was Stainless Steel Inc., a manufacturing company that produced a variety of stainless steel products. The building itself sat on two acres of downtown Perkasie real estate and housed 25,000 square feet of internal workspace.

Yet, when the property came to my attention during a routine drive-by in the late 1990s, it was once again an abandoned building. Its fenced-in, deteriorated condition gave the impression that it was completely devoid of any maintenance by any individual or business entity. Besides being unfit for occupancy and bringing down property values in the surrounding neighborhood, it also posed a significant public nuisance. Kids—as they always do—found a way to break in and were routinely vandalizing the building.

The reason behind all of this was that after a successful run, Stainless Inc. closed down and the building sat vacant for years. Eventually, it was sold to a Pennsylvania-based corporation owned by a gentleman named Brian Brady. When he purchased the property, it was part of a larger acquisition that involved numerous properties. He wasn't interested at all in continuing Stainless Inc.'s Perkasie manufacturing operation; his principal goal was to get the rights to the technology they used in their stainless steel manufacturing process. After the settlement was finalized, Mr. Brady kept the building closed, protected it with a chain-link fence, and ceased all routine maintenance. After the vandalism problem surfaced, he put the building on the market for $325,000.

If you ever wondered what a textbook example of a blighted, underused building would look like, you can stop your search right here. The Stainless Steel Inc. building in Perkasie checked off all the appropriate boxes under the definition of blight.

Downtown Perkasie was no stranger to challenging times and events that needed creative, determined problem-solving. In 1890, a catastrophic fire that began in a livery stable at Seventh and Chestnut Street destroyed

12 buildings. Almost a century later in 1988, another fire devastated 15% of the downtown, including several irreplaceable historic buildings. The RDA couldn't do anything about the structures Perkasie lost in those bygone eras, but we certainly could do something to improve the sorry state of the current one located on Ninth Street.

ENVIRONMENTAL AND/OR BLIGHT ISSUES: When we first got involved in the project, we thought we were just trying to protect some kids and the general populace from a decaying, blighted building. We had no idea there were much deeper and more dangerous problems lurking in the abandoned Stainless site than just the activities of some mischievous kids.

Trichloroethylene (TCE) is an essential element in the process of manufacturing stainless steel. Primarily a metal cleaner, it was used to inhibit rust in stainless steel. Needless to say, after several decades in business, the Stainless factory and its surrounding grounds were loaded with this highly toxic liquid.

Upon inspecting the building's interior, we also found the second floor was unsafe. At some point in time, long support rods had been bolted down into the floor joists on one side and were connected to the roof beams on the other end. We had no idea whether that stopgap measure had been put in place when the Stainless company was still in business or whether the property's current owner had it done to keep the floor from collapsing. All I knew was that floor was bouncy as all get-out when I walked across it, so I immediately stepped off and retreated to an area that had more solid footing.

POLITICAL ISSUES: Most of the small municipalities in Bucks County occupy approximately one square mile. Because of the county's long history, these municipal downtown areas are usually completely built out, with little new construction going on. Older buildings in disrepair generate limited tax revenues because their property values are not worth much. If you improve and rehab them or tear them down and build new, modern structures, the tax revenues go up because they're worth more. But there's a balancing act involved because if the new or improved buildings are too expensive, it's difficult to get them sold.

This was the problem facing Perkasie. Aside from the concern about the hazardous conditions of the property, the borough knew it had a significant tract of downtown real estate generating nothing—no aesthetic value, no public services, and worst of all, very little tax revenues. Something had to be done, but writing citations and fining the building's new owner would have been the borough's only avenue without the help of the RDA. We had the clout and know-how to acquire the building, clean it up, and resell it to another business for reuse.

I approached Perkasie Borough's council and gave them some general information about ACT 385 and what the RDA could do for them, but I specifically avoided talking about the Stainless building. I didn't have to; they already knew they had a problem there. A large part of my job was educating municipalities on how the RDA could help in matters of grants, funding, and forcibly acquiring properties if necessary—things in which municipal governments have limited capabilities.

It didn't take much coaxing; Perkasie was on board. The same thing couldn't be said for the property's current owner. Brian Brady had never seen the building he'd purchased and had no idea he'd bought seven figures worth of environmental problems. The borough asked us to take the property via eminent domain, but they'd unintentionally thrown a monkey wrench into the works. They had a potential buyer who was interested in the property. Expecting a reuse for the building in the near future, the borough's director of economic development had placed new power transformers on the telephone poles near the old Stainless building.

I was blindsided. I had no idea the borough had done that. When I visited the building's owner at one of his other properties and informed him about the RDA's interest in acquiring the property, he thought the whole thing was a scam. Even worse, because of the transformer situation, he smelled a rat. Brian had every right to feel that way. No one installs new power transformers unless they have an intended use for them in the works. It looked like we were trying to arrange a sale for the building behind his back. It took a while to regain Brian's trust, but after an avalanche of phone conversations with him and his lawyer in Washington, DC, we finally began to make some progress.

Their asking price of $325,000 for the property had not yielded a single bid. That was to be expected. Who would want to buy a property that instantly made them liable for $1,000,000 of environmental cleanup costs? He'd been given a faulty estimate that the environmental remediation would only cost him $200,000, so he was overly confident about the building's salability. Learning that it would cost five times or more than that amount opened his eyes.

The RDA wanted to get the building for nothing by eminent domain, preferably by an amicable agreement instead of resorting to going to court in a long, drawn-out hostile seizure. After six months of negotiations, it was a letter of donation and another letter of indemnification that did the trick.

By donating the building, the owner got a sizable tax write-off, so he was getting some financial benefit out of the deal. Indemnifying his company for up to $1,000,000 in cleanup costs pretty much took him and his company off the hook for any future legal damages—a fair and just outcome, since his company hadn't played any role or contributed in any way to the property's adverse environmental conditions. Once he recognized the benefits of the deal we were offering, we quickly came to terms.

Amicable eminent domain is always a welcome outcome, except for one complication that it sometimes creates: Once the RDA assumes ownership of a property, we become the party responsible for paying its taxes. Having no idea how long it would take to remediate the Stainless building's problems and find a buyer, we asked the borough to take it off the tax rolls to make our involvement in the project affordable. They agreed to our request, which was another strong and positive indication of their financial commitment to the project.

CHALLENGES AND/OR SETBACKS: During my time at the RDA, I never hired a real estate agent or any type of middleman to help find buyers for properties we'd acquired. I always did it myself by word of mouth, public postings in local newspapers, or on the internet. This project was no different. The RDA received numerous inquiries about the property from a variety of sources, but nothing of any substance materialized. Then we caught a lucky break when the First Savings Bank of Perkasie stepped forward and agreed to purchase the property. They were looking for a building in which they could house their administrative offices, and the Stainless Inc. building (after the necessary repairs and modifications) seemed to fit the bill.

But the deal brought about another unwelcome complication: While the bank liked the old Stainless building, they were uncomfortable about the property next to it (also located on Ninth Street). It was owned by the Otto family and was known as the Wispese Building. For an unspecified period of time, some type of manufacturing business operated there, but eventually it just became a warehouse. Large commercial trucks were coming and going there throughout the day as they loaded and unloaded their wares. The First Savings Bank of Perkasie didn't want to set up their administrative offices next to that type of bustling activity, so we had to figure a way to get ahold of that property.

The Otto family valued it at $500,000, but the Wispese Building had TCE issues similar to the Stainless property, plus it had asbestos that needed to be removed. The chances of the Ottos finding a buyer who would pay their $500,000 asking price were slim and none. When the RDA offered them $400,000 plus another tax donation letter (this one for $100,000), they agreed to our offer. We then proposed a two-building package deal for $600,000 that the First Savings Bank of Perkasie accepted in March 2004. All that remained was for the RDA and Perkasie Borough to clean up both sites and get them ready for whatever contractor the bank would decide to bring in to rehab the buildings.

COURSE OF ACTION FOR THE CLEANUP: A Phase 1 walk-through assessment and search of the Stainless property's history confirmed a strong presence of TCE. During Phase 2, two dozen test wells were dug to the first and second aquifers to determine the level of pollution, and report and work plans were submitted to the Pennsylvania Department of Environmental Protection (PADEP) that had to be approved.

We condemned the site in February 2000 and got to work shortly afterward. An earth material test found the source of the problem: A terra-cotta sump drain pipe traveled from the interior of the Stainless building toward an outside two-foot-wide and approximately six-inch-deep tributary. That pipe was the source of the pollutant. Apparently, employees at Stainless routinely spilled TCE in the vicinity of the indoor sump drain during the steel cleaning process.

Some contaminants can be stabilized by capping a site with either concrete or two feet of clean topsoil to keep them from reaching the public via runoff into rivers and streams. However, TCE has a tendency to go straight down into the ground, so that was not an option. Instead, we brought in a machine I call a "stripper." It pumps out the groundwater, filters out the TCE, deposits it into barrels, and then returns the purified water back into the ground. The stripper did a decent job of reducing the level of TCE by 50%, but decent was not good enough. We also employed a chemical agent designed to break down and neuter the TCE to deal with the remaining half of the problem. The Wispese Building also had TCE problems that we remediated with similar techniques.

After all our best efforts, the groundwater still had TCE issues, but we determined that runoff from a third, unrelated property in Perkasie was the source. We discovered the problem after digging some test pits on their property line. We couldn't help them though. Our funding and budget could not cover remediating every environmental problem in Perkasie Borough. Fortunately, DEP guidelines absolved the RDA from any responsibility. As long as the resultant amount of contaminant on the Stainless property (after the filtering) equaled or did not exceed the amount coming in from an outside source, we were good to go. As a final cleanup task on the Stainless project, we complied with the DEP's requirement of eight consecutive quarters of water testing to ensure the TCE problem was sufficiently resolved. A lot of paperwork had to be filed to show all the contaminants were disposed of properly.

COURSE OF ACTION FOR THE REUSE: The contractor that the First Savings Bank of Perkasie hired did a top-shelf job of rehabbing the two properties. The bank paid for the demolition of the Wispese Building behind the Stainless factory and then turned it into a parking lot. The Stainless building itself was a total architectural re-creation, accomplished and financed by the bank without tearing anything down. The second floor was reinforced and augmented with a new addition of almost 8,000 square feet of space (the original second floor did not match the footprint of the first floor), and the rest of the building received a complete facelift with a new facade that wrapped around the building's original exterior.

COSTS AND GRANTS:
- $0.00 for the purchase of the Stainless Steel Inc. building, since it was donated by Brian Brady's company. They received a $325,000 tax donation letter.

- $400,000 paid by the RDA for the purchase of the Wispese building, plus a $100,000 tax donation letter. The $400,000 was cash in theory only, because we already had a two-property purchase deal in place for $600,000 with Penn Community Bank. The owner of the Wispese Building was paid off at settlement by the bank.

- $1,400,000 for the combined cost of the Stainless property's assessment and cleanup. As our principal partner in the project, Perkasie Borough paid $50,000 toward the property's assessment, $250,000 for the cleanup, and the RDA's administration fee.

- $1,200,000 in total from two different ISRP grants ($1,000,000 and $200,000) paid to the RDA for the environmental cleanup.

- $300,000 in additional cleanup funding from Perkasie Borough, which left a surplus of $100,000 above the total assessment and cleanup costs of $1,400,000.

- The Penn Community Bank's two-building $600,000 purchase left a $200,000 surplus over the RDA's $400,000 purchase cost of the secondary building.

- $134,395.14 left in the account as a surplus after the RDA's administration fees were deducted from the project. At a grand, celebratory press conference during the dedication of the newly rehabbed Stainless building, we placed an oversized check on an easel and presented it to Perkasie Borough to pay them back for the funds they'd invested.

THE DEVELOPER: The First Bank of Perkasie was the developer. They took care of hiring the architects and contractors.

STATUS OF THE SITE TODAY: Considering we got the building for nothing and also spent nothing other than sweat equity to acquire it, Perkasie didn't have to spend $325,000 to purchase it. They also didn't have to pay for the acquisition of the Wispese Building (it was paid by the bank), so this was obviously a great all-around deal for the borough. The current occupant of the old Stainless building is Penn Community Bank, the new name coming as a result of a 2015 merger between First Savings Bank of Perkasie and Bristol-based First Federal of Bucks County.

For all parties involved, the transformation of that property was an uplifting experience to be part of. The ugly duckling at that location was once a blighted, contaminated building that posed a danger to the community and brought in little revenue. Today, it's an inspiring piece of architecture that employs over 70 people, contributes a significant amount of money to the borough's annual tax base, and preserves a historic piece of downtown Perkasie for future generations.

It's always preferable to preserve some of the original look and history of an old building if possible. Sometimes, you have no choice but to demolish an old structure and build a new one in its place. Thankfully, this wasn't one of those times. The Penn Community Bank building was a stylish and successful merger of the past and present.

HOWELL HARDWARE

START AND COMPLETION DATES:
2003 TO 2005.

LOCATION: Bridge Street in the downtown business center of Morrisville, Pennsylvania.

HISTORY OF THE SITE: All dynasties crumble over time. The British empire collapsed from their centuries-old burden of trying to maintain colonies all over the world; Lehman Brothers folded in the wake of the 2007–2008 financial crisis they helped create; and even the Yankees' traditional domination of the postseason has become a thing of the past. Now, nobody would ever accuse Howell Hardware of being a dynasty, but to longtime residents of Morrisville, it sure seemed that way.

Through three (and maybe four) generations of Howells, their family-owned hardware store with the red brick facade served the needs of Morrisville while scores of other local businesses went belly up. It seemed they always had everything you needed. You'd walk in and ask for some obscure tool or piece of hardware that hadn't been manufactured in years, and one of the Howells would disappear into the store's basement and then return a few minutes later with the dust-covered relic you'd just asked for.

But then the era of the mega-hardware store arrived. Unable to adapt and compete with Lowe's, Hechingers, and Home Depot, the Howells' family business fell on hard times. As their debts mounted, the family reluctantly closed its doors for the last time in the mid-1990s. All that was left of this deep-rooted Morrisville institution was their single-story, 5,000-square-foot store with a full basement, some dilapidated storage sheds out back, and a twin house with four apartments next door that the family owned and rented.

The end of a Morrisville institution: Howell Hardware, empty and boarded up after decades of serving the borough.

The Howells were so upstanding and honorable that they continued paying off their debts for years, even though their business no longer existed.

HOW THE RDA GOT INVOLVED: One of the many hats I wear at the RDA—perhaps my most important one—is that of a salesman. I can't help Bucks County and its residents if I don't have any projects to work on. So I go looking for them, traveling around to the different municipalities, talking to local governments and townsfolk, making them aware of our services, and asking them what they need. Morrisville had been telling me for a while that they'd like to do something about the abandoned hardware store on Bridge Street.

The trigger that got me involved was a phone call from Joe Conti, a Pennsylvania state senator, whose territory included Morrisville. "Bob, I have three hundred thousand dollars in DCED funding that was intended for a different project, but it didn't work out," he told me. "I don't want to have to give that money back to the state. Do you have any good projects in my district that could use it?"

"I got just the thing you're looking for," I told him.

The RDA formed a cooperation agreement with Morrisville and acquired the hardware store and its related buildings by amicable eminent domain in June 2003. It was sad to take a property from a family I'd known for years, but at that point in time, the decayed remains of their longtime legacy weren't doing any good for them or anyone else.

ENVIRONMENTAL AND/OR BLIGHT ISSUES: Even though the hardware store sold and dealt with a lot of insecticides and lead and petroleum-based products over the years, there were no environmental issues on the property. The RDA conducted our usual tests, but they all came back negative. It was just a run-down property overgrown with weeds and strewn with trash. The worst offender was the twin house next door that was condemned for having an unsafe fire escape.

CHALLENGES AND/OR SETBACKS: None.

POLITICAL ISSUES: Politicians aren't too popular nowadays, but the Howell Hardware store project was an example of the good that elected officials can do when a problem in need of a solution presents itself. It would have been no skin off Senator Joe Conti's back to give the $300,000 grant back to the Commonwealth DCED. It probably would have been less paperwork for him, but instead, he searched for a potential home for those dollars before the deadline was up. A lot of good came out of that search.

COURSE OF ACTION FOR THE CLEANUP: Because there were no environmental problems to deal with, it was a simple demolition job that was performed within 30 days of the RDA's acquisition of the property.

That's me without my usual black attire, talking to State Senator Joe Conti (lower right) during the demolition of the Howell Hardware building. Operating the excavator is Bill Pezza, assistant to State Representative Thomas Corrigan. In the background is the four-apartment twin home the Howells used to rent out, which was razed a few hours later.

THE DEVELOPER: Ed and Chris Cacace were local Morrisville boys who were involved with numerous building projects around town. Since job creation is one of the RDA's primary missions, we always like to do business with local developers and contractors whenever possible. Similarly, we tried to use local demolition companies. It has always been the RDA's position to get a minimum of three bids on every job, but we were lucky to find two Bucks County companies that usually came in with the lowest numbers on the majority of our projects, including this one.

COURSE OF ACTION FOR THE REUSE: The lot that the store, its backyard sheds, and the adjoining twin house had previously occupied sat vacant for two years before the RDA sold it for $135,000 to Cacace Builders. The sale was finalized in March 2005, and within a year, Ed and Chris had built a two-story office building on the site.

COSTS AND GRANTS:

- $135,000 for the cost of acquiring the property (paid as just compensation).
- $25,000 for the Phase 1 and Phase 2 assessment.
- $25,000 in demolition costs.
- $135,000 for the costs of preparing the site for a buyer (grading, seeding, and fill brought in to top off the hole from the basement).
- The $300,000 DCED grant Joe Conti directed our way paid for all the associated costs of assessment, demolition, and site preparation.

STATUS OF THE SITE TODAY: Intended or not, the red brick of the new office building is a subtle nod to the storefront of the site's previous longtime tenant. The current structure is certainly more attractive and significantly larger. Its 25,000 square feet are capped by a stylish, off-white cornice that stretches horizontally across the top of the second floor. I'm sure all that is of little solace to the nostalgic memories of thousands of customers who had frequented the Howell family's hardware store throughout their lives.

The two-story office building built by the Cacace brothers currently occupies the grounds where Howell's Hardware once stood. The new structure may have a similar red brick facade to its predecessor, but it will take decades—if ever—for it to generate the same community endearment.

Along with other businesses to whom they rent office space, the Cacace brothers' headquarters occupy the second floor. The first floor is currently leased to a variety of retail stores and an eatery. The RDA always tries to preserve as much of Bucks County's history, lifestyle, and feel as possible, but the Howell Hardware building just couldn't be saved.

If there's a lesson to be learned from this project, it involves the role of luck. No doubt, it usually plays a significant role in most successful ventures, but you can't depend on that alone. You have to *be prepared to accept the luck* when it comes around. I was very fortunate to get that phone call from Senator Conti, but if I didn't have numerous projects in the pipeline ready to go at a moment's notice, that money would have gone back to the Commonwealth of Pennsylvania or to someone else.

LONGHORN STEAKHOUSE

START AND COMPLETION DATES: 2000 TO
2006, WITH THE MAJORITY OF ACTIVITY
OCCURRING DURING THE LAST TWO YEARS.

LOCATION: The corner of Route 13 and Beaver Dam Road in Bristol, Pennsylvania.

HISTORY OF THE SITE: The site on which the Longhorn Steakhouse was built had a historical record of being a location for ice cream parlors and other food emporiums. The most celebrated of these was O'Boyles Restaurant, which, after a lengthy run into the early 1980s, was succeeded by several other food establishments. Eventually, after some rehabbing and modifications, the Longhorn Steakhouse (no relation to the current chain) opened on the site. It was moderately successful for a few years until it was sold in the late '80s to a new owner, who ultimately ran it into the ground. Mired in debt within a few years, he went out of business and abandoned the building in the mid-1990s.

HOW THE RDA GOT INVOLVED: When the RDA compiled our master brownfield properties list in the mid-1990s, the Longhorn Steakhouse was on it. Its name was later eliminated from the list when we cut it down to just eight larger, more pressing projects, but we revisited the problem a few years later.

Longhorn's owner was delinquent on his mortgage and tax payments to the tune of $2,500,000. That made the property virtually unsellable because of the liens on it. The title couldn't be cleared until some-one paid off those bills. Initially, the RDA's Vacant Property Review Committee received numerous offers for the site, but all the potential buyers were scared off after learning about the associated legal and financial problems.

ENVIRONMENTAL AND/OR BLIGHT ISSUES: The insulation on the Longhorn's heating pipes was loaded with asbestos, but the majority of the blight issues at the site were of the human behavior/societal variety. The building had been abandoned for six years and was a dilapidated eyesore. In its ramshackle state, it also could have posed a potential danger to any adventurous kids who might consider breaking in to explore its interior.

The dilapidated entrance to the Longhorn Steakhouse about to be demolished.

The larger problem, however, was the goings-on behind the building. It had become a haven of illegal activity, particularly drug dealing and prostitution by street hookers who were plying their trade in vans and cars parked out back. Squatters had been using the front of the building as a toilet, and after erecting a lean-to out back, they had become permanent residents on the property. The police were constantly called to the site to clean things up, but as soon as they left, the problems always resurfaced. The situation had become intolerable due to the neighborhood outrage, the misuse of a highly visible community site that was generating no municipal taxes, and the numerous legal and liability issues in play.

CHALLENGES AND/OR SETBACKS: The issue of the liens remained, however. Before we were able to move forward on selling and cleaning up the Longhorn site, we had to convince the Internal Revenue Service (IRS) to transfer the liens from the property itself to the Longhorn's owner so the title could clear. He wasn't taking any of this lying down.

Over the years, he'd received numerous fines and citations from Bristol Township for failing to clean up the site. All of them were ignored. As a blighted site, the RDA was allowed to step in and seize the property via eminent domain for the good of the community. As far as the mortgage company was concerned, this was an amicable eminent domain situation; the owner didn't see it that way. He filed for bankruptcy to hold off the eminent domain process. He was also demanding $1,000,000 to walk away from his bankruptcy and claim of ownership.

The owner's ploy of bankruptcy and the threat of taking us to court worked for three months until we eventually met with a federal bankruptcy judge who ruled against him. The IRS also stepped up and agreed to transfer the liens from the Longhorn property to its owner. From their standpoint, they weren't receiving any taxes from the abandoned building or the owner. They correctly concluded that if the RDA could entice a new business to open on the site, it would be back on the tax register. Due to the positive developments of the federal bankruptcy judge's and the IRS's decisions, we were in business. Our system of justice often moves slowly, but when they finally get moving, things can happen at a rapid pace. After a three-month delay, everything was settled in a single day. The project was moving forward.

POLITICAL ISSUES: Two days after meeting with the federal judge, we held an on-site press conference to announce the commencement of the project. We placed Mayor Sam Fenton on top of an excavator and let him take the first swipe at knocking down the Longhorn sign on the front of the building. He hadn't played a role in bringing the project to fruition, but he was a good man who achieved a lot for the township during his tenure. I was more than happy to throw some goodwill and PR his way. He'd certainly helped me over the years.

COURSE OF ACTION FOR THE CLEANUP: The mortgage company that owned the note on the property was desperate to get rid of it because they were on the hook for any accidents, fires, or other detrimental occurrences that might happen there. The site had been appraised at $311,000, so we offered them two options: The RDA would take the property by eminent domain and pay them $340,000 if they took care of the demolition and cleanup, or we'd pay the appraised $311,000 as just compensation and the demolition and cleanup would be the RDA's responsibility.

The mortgage company accepted the latter option, and best of all, were willing to wait until we found a buyer and closed the deal before paying them. No one passes up an opportunity to work using other people's money (known on the street as OPM), so we closed the deal as quickly as possible. In 2005, the asbestos was removed and the building was demolished and hauled away within five days. One week later, all that remained was a bare lot with topsoil and grass seed.

COURSE OF ACTION FOR THE REUSE: Before the demolition of the Longhorn building had commenced, a neighboring property had offered the RDA $300,000 for the site, which, of course, we turned down since we'd spent more than that on just the purchase price. With no other credible offers on the horizon, I approached the attorney who represented the Dunkin' Donuts Corporation to let him know the property was available and would be a good location for one of their franchises. When Dunkin' Donuts expressed interest in acquiring the property, we asked for $500,000 and said we would clean up the site at our expense. They agreed to the deal, and within a short period of time after we sold off the property, a brand new Dunkin' Donuts franchise stood ready to continue the corner's long tradition of food service.

COSTS AND GRANTS:
- $311,000 paid by the RDA to purchase the property.
- $29,000 in costs for the site's demolition and cleanup.
- $50,000 for the project's legal fees and our administration costs.
- $500,000 paid by Dunkin' Donuts to purchase the site, which covered all costs and allowed for a $110,000 profit that was to be held in escrow in the Bristol Township's project development fund for use on future township projects.
- No grants were needed for this project.

THE DEVELOPER: By the time a developer was needed, the RDA had already sold the property to Dunkin' Donuts, who handled everything from that point on.

STATUS OF THE SITE TODAY: The modern Dunkin' Donuts built on the site may not be a culturally aesthetic marvel, but the clean, well-designed building was certainly preferable to the site's previous situation. Fifteen years after its demolition, the former Longhorn Steakhouse property now serves the community in a positive way, and its current owner and the 30 employees who work there all contribute to Bristol Township through real estate and wage taxes.

From ice cream, to steaks, to prostitution and drug dealing, to coffee and donuts—the corner of Route 13 and Beaver Dam Road has seen it all.

THE A. E. STALEY SITE

START AND COMPLETION DATES:
2005 TO 2008.

LOCATION: Along the Delaware River in Morrisville Borough, Pennsylvania. It's bordered on its landlocked side by East Post Road and Riverview Avenue.

HISTORY OF THE SITE: A. E. Staley is a manufacturer and distributor of starch products for the food industry, particularly high-fructose corn syrup, which they sell to companies like Coca-Cola and Pepsi. Originally founded in 1906 and located in Decatur, Illinois, the company eventually opened an additional 50-acre facility in Bucks County that employed several hundred workers. In 1988, Tate & Lyle PLC, a British liquid warehousing and distribution company, purchased the entire operation for $1,420,000,000.

HOW THE RDA GOT INVOLVED: In 1985, prior to Tate & Lyle's acquisition of the company, changing markets and economic conditions necessitated the downsizing of Staley's Bucks County facility. The site came to the attention of the RDA because half the buildings on their campus had become underused, abandoned, or blighted. These buildings were more of an eyesore than an environmental hazard. However, there were two more immediate problems that concerned the RDA:

- Staley received its raw materials via trains whose tracks ran through Morrisville and then directly onto their site. Local traffic disruption due to these train deliveries had become problematic.

- Thirty-five of the Staley's fifty acres were located in the one-hundred-year floodplain. The company's move to Bucks County decades earlier had preceded the environmental and insurance restrictions that eventually governed building in floodplains. Although essentially grandfathered in, those 35 acres were now out of compliance with current standards.

An aerial shot of the A. E. Staley campus illustrates the flood risk posed by the proximity of the Delaware River.

ENVIRONMENTAL AND/OR BLIGHT ISSUES: Other than the blighted buildings, there were no specific threats from any contaminants, and the few that arose were mitigated by Staley's management.

COURSE OF ACTION AND PLANS FOR THE SITE: Our intent was to move Staley's campus to another location, clean up any of the limited environmental hazards that might have been left behind, and then tear down and remove all their old buildings. During the period when we were in negotiations with Staley's representatives, a flood from the river covered much of their campus, reaching almost halfway up their train cars. If they had any reservations about moving their facilities, this fortuitous flooding was working in our favor. Plans for developing the vacated Staley site included building new condominiums, additional residential housing, a 30-acre recreational park on the river, and a boating marina.

One of the blighted buildings on the A. E. Staley campus.

POLITICAL ISSUES, GOVERNMENT, AND COMMUNITY INVOLVEMENT:
Morrisville Borough was extremely supportive, as was the local populace, who found the possibility of a recreational park and a riverfront marina being built in their town to be very appealing concepts. I was also fortunate to have an "in." I always tried—if possible—to find a way to put a personal touch on every project. In this case, it was Staley's plant

manager: I knew his uncle. It wasn't the strongest connection, but at least the project's tracks now had some grease on them.

COSTS AND GRANTS:

- The only financial investment in the project was the sweat equity spent during meetings and the searches for potential sites.

- A $2,000,000 RACP grant for economic development. The RDA felt that this grant would cover the purchase price of land for Staley's site and any associated cleanup costs.

CHALLENGES AND/OR SETBACKS: The Staley company was amenable to moving their operation to another Bucks County location, the RDA had secured a substantial amount of financing, and the local communities and governments involved were all in. It looked like a done deal. But the Staley organization had four problematic requirements:

- They stored thousands of gallons of corn syrup in on-site railroad tank cars that were opened and inspected every day. Because they were dealing with a food source, local air quality was a critical factor. U.S. Steel had an unused property we felt would be suitable for a new Staley's site, but it was near a landfill. That was problematic because of the potential for harmful airborne particulates from the landfill to get into the railroad tank cars and contaminate the stored contents.

- A second location was selected at the Middletown Industrial Park. The Staley company liked this site, but they needed a massive, readily available stainless steel storage tank to be built before they could move there. It was a big-ticket item that would cost upward of $1,000,000.

- The Staley company wanted a steep price of $3,000,000 for their old site.

- Large railroad freight yards don't deliver. They offload their goods to short lines that handle the task. In Staley's situation, goods were brought in by short lines that ran through Morrisville and then entered the Staley facility, where storage tanker cars sat on the company's dead-end tracks. That infrastructure and procedure was already in existence at their Morrisville campus, but on Staley's newly proposed campus, some of that rail infrastructure would have to be built. We never even spec'd out the exact cost because we knew it would be prohibitive.

Some of the many on-site railroad cars used by A. E. Staley (Tate & Lyle) for corn syrup storage.

DEVELOPER: None, since prohibitive costs kept the project from moving forward.

STATUS OF THE SITE TODAY: After four years of planning, negotiations, and the best of intentions from all the involved parties, we finally threw in the towel on the project at a final 2008 meeting at the Sheraton Hotel next to the Oxford Valley Mall. We'd bitten off more than we could chew. The optimism that came with the $2,000,000 RACP grant dissipated in the wake of Staley's $3,000,000 asking price for the old property and their request for the $1,000,000 stainless steel storage tank. Those pricey up-front costs made it next to impossible to bring in a developer and convince them that they could turn a profit on this project. The loss-leader "X" factor that I needed to bring into the deal was just too big. The RACP grant wasn't large enough to bridge that gap. We had to return it to the state.

Staleys is still in operation as of 2020, but it's just a warehousing operation now. They no longer manufacture any of their products on-site. They just ship them in and out via the small workforce that remains from the hundreds of employees who originally worked there. At this point, moving them to another location wouldn't create any new jobs, since their operation has become nothing more than a large, liquid warehouse. As much as Morrisville would have loved a new park and marina, the lack of job creation didn't justify such a large expenditure of public funds.

For someone who has always felt there's a solution and a way to raise money, the Staley project's final outcome was a tough pill for me to swallow. But you also have to be smart enough to know when to walk away. Just throwing massive amounts of money at a project is not always the best path.

RIVERFRONT NORTH

START AND COMPLETION DATES:
ACTIVE RDA INVOLVEMENT BEGAN IN AUGUST
1994, BUT RIVERFRONT NORTH HAD BEEN
ON OUR SLATE SINCE THE LATE 1980S. THE
PROJECT IS STILL ONGOING.

LOCATION: The Bristol Borough waterfront between Radcliffe Street and the Delaware River and bordered on its north and south sides by Green Lane and Fillmore Street.

HISTORY OF THE SITE: In the ramp-up to World War I, the federal government set up several shipbuilding ports on the East Coast. The idea was to produce more ships than the Germans could blow out of the water. The Merchant Shipbuilding Company, run by railroad heir W. Averell Harriman, anticipated America's entry into WWI, so they opened a shipbuilding facility in Chester, Pennsylvania. In order to fulfill all the wartime contracts for merchant and troop ships, they purchased 260 acres in Bristol Township in 1917 and opened another shipyard along Radcliffe Street on the Delaware River. The shipyard occupied 80 acres of the total property and included a dozen dry docks. The remaining acreage of their 1917 purchase consisted of storage

173

facilities and housing infrastructure for the yard's 3,000 workers and their families. The workforce was primarily made up of women, since many of the area's men were overseas fighting the war.

A dry dock at the WWI-era Harriman Shipyard along Bristol's waterfront.

The $12,000,000 Harriman spent setting up this new shipbuilding facility was not enough to guarantee instantaneous success. The yard's construction was delayed by dredging problems and seven different worker strikes over wages. When the first ship finally rolled off the slipways, the war was already over. By 1922, the shipbuilding industry ground to a halt. The Chester shipyard closed in 1923, and shortly thereafter, the Bristol shipyard began selling off its property to a variety of new manufacturers and industries. By 1926, it was completely shut down after launching only 39 ships. Harriman Township, the name given to the yard's employee housing district, was eventually annexed into Bristol Borough.

The shipyard's misfortune ushered in an extended period of prosperity for the Bristol waterfront, during which it became the economic engine for the county and one of the up-and-coming manufacturing hubs on the East Coast. The most prominent of the new Bristol waterfront companies started out producing airplanes in New York under the name Huff-Daland Airplanes. Several years after relocating to Bristol in 1925, they changed their name to Keystone Aircraft Corporation and switched over to making amphibious, pontoon-style airplanes and airplane parts for the US Navy. After filling in the old Harriman dry docks, they moved into the vacated Harriman Yard buildings and operated along Radcliffe Street until the mid-1930s when the plant closed. Fleetwings Aircraft (and then Kaiser-Fleetwing) continued in the same location until they ceased operations in 1962, ending four decades of aviation manufacturing on Bristol's waterfront.

That industry's demise left an identity vacuum along Radcliffe Street. The door had opened for two vastly different manufactured products to seize the site's spotlight: soap and zinc. While they didn't have the allure and charisma of shipbuilding and aviation, they provided a helluva lot of jobs—as many as 5,000 at Bristol's industrial apex. Over the years, the waterfront had evolved into 52 acres that were subdivided among its most prominent new tenants: the Dial Soap Company (11.3 acres), Purex (33 acres), and the Superior Zinc Corporation (7 acres). An additional half acre just south of the Dial property was occupied by Bristol Steel, a small family-owned business.

Dial's principal products were antibacterial bars of soap and laundry detergent, Purex produced bleach and laundry detergent, and Superior Zinc manufactured zinc powder that was used on inner tubes to keep them from sticking to the insides of rubber tires. All of them were useful, everyday products, but the processes used to manufacture them took a steep toll. By the late-1980s, the waterfront had become blighted and loaded with contaminants. Superior Zinc ceased operations in 1986, and Purex went out of business the following year. The Dial facility was the lone survivor of the big three Bristol-based manufacturers along the Delaware River.

An aerial shot of Riverfront North's "big three" manufacturers in the 1980s. Sandwiched in between Radcliffe Street on the left and the Delaware River on the right are Dial Soap (the large warehouse slightly to the left of the center of the photo and its soap tower close to the river); Superior Zinc (the series of rusted buildings positioned just above the Dial warehouse and stretching to the river); and Purex (the three parallel, white-roofed buildings running north along Radcliffe Street and stretching out of the picture).

HOW THE RDA GOT INVOLVED: When I was hired by the RDA in 1993, a prominent four-by-eight-foot sign on the waterfront property read "RIVERFRONT NORTH PROJECT," but nothing had happened there for years, and there were no plans for the site's immediate future. The RDA's strategy at that point in time was built on waiting for someone to come knocking on their door with an idea.

To be fair, there had been some activity a few years before. The site had been designated as a Certified Redevelopment Area in 1987. Bristol Borough purchased the Purex property in 1988, put it in the name of the RDA, and then asked the RDA to use eminent domain to take the Superior Zinc site in 1990. The catalyst for taking them was the appearance of trash transfer stations on their vacated grounds. The borough was trying to clean up the waterfront. Turning it into a dump would have been a move in the opposite direction. There was also a temporary flirtation by the Borough with riverfront gambling, but that fizzled out after a few years.

It was the biggest project on the RDA's slate when I got there. I asked the board of directors on three different occasions about their long-term plans for the waterfront but came away each time without a definitive answer. I didn't push too hard at first, because I was the new kid in town—their *housing rehabilitation specialist*. But I was emboldened the following year when the board promoted me to the executive director position. I recognized how vast a resource the waterfront could be for the borough and the county, and I was prepared to do everything I could to help it reach its potential.

In my opinion, the sign was a big part of the problem. Labeling the riverfront a "PROJECT" drove away potential developers and public funds. The word implies activity is currently taking place, so they probably figured some other company was already developing the property. Coming from the opposite direction, if it's not really an ongoing project that is moving forward, you can't get grants and public funds.

In late 1994, I added a diagonal strip of wood to the Riverfront North sign with the painted word "AVAILABLE" on it and then sent out requests for proposals (RFPs) to find interested developers. The effect was immediate and potent; people starting coming out of the woodwork inquiring about the site. While all this was going on, we began negotiating with the Dial Corporation to acquire their property so Bristol Borough and the RDA would have complete ownership and control of the entire 52-acre waterfront site.

Every year from 1995 to 2001, I went to Dial to see if they would sell, but they still wanted to remain in business in Bristol. They'd been treading water and buying time since the closures of Purex and Superior Zinc in the late '80s. They were also well aware of the borough's long-term goal of getting rid of manufacturing on the waterfront. Fearful of losing their property to eminent domain, Dial rehabbed some of their more run-down buildings in 1990 and also floated the idea of moving their national corporate headquarters to Bristol if the borough cleaned up the Purex grounds. (Purex was

Dial's subsidiary.) The borough's council changed several times during that period, but nothing happened.

Dial continued to postpone the inevitable for more than a decade, but with a workforce that had dwindled down to 160 employees and their growing fear of being held responsible for any potential environmental problems on their grounds, they finally sold the property to the RDA in 2001.

ENVIRONMENTAL AND/OR BLIGHT ISSUES: Each of the three properties on Riverfront North had different circumstances and varying degrees of environmental issues.

The 33-acre Purex parcel occupied the northernmost section of the site. Three massive buildings longer than a football field stood side by side and ran parallel to Radcliffe Street. Between those buildings and the river was a large, open-space parking area that—after the RDA took over the property—was leased to a local trucking firm to park their trailers on the site. By the time I became actively involved in the project, there were hundreds of them parked there.

The Harriman shipyard had left Purex a reminder from the waterfront's past: Crude oil oozed from the ground close to their border with Superior Zinc's property line. The remaining acreage on Purex's grounds had lead content, some TCE, dozens of buried metal barrels containing petroleum products and other discarded liquid materials, and a lot of cafeteria waste from the company's lunchroom.

Other than an abundance of soap on the grounds, the Dial property posed the least environmental problems of the riverfront's three largest tenants. The centerpiece of the 11.3-acre site was the 183,000-square-foot cold storage warehouse that ran along Radcliffe Street. A parking lot, occupied at most times by a dozen or more trailers, fanned out from the east and southern sides of the building. Close to the river, a 120-foot-high tower surrounded by several attached buildings loomed above the site. The tower was a dryer for the soapmaking process that blew soap mist into the air that floated to the ground as flakes and granules. It was then scooped up and loaded onto carts that ran via tracks into the warehouse where everything was boxed and prepared for sale. The warehouse itself was the site's best asset. It was run-down but structurally sound, and its reuse potential was unlimited. However, we considered it to be underutilized due to its limited function in the '90s as a storage facility with few employees.

Superior Zinc's seven-acre campus was sandwiched in between the Purex and Dial parcels. Three tall chimneys soared over half a dozen mismatched buildings of different shapes that stretched in an unbroken line from Radcliffe Street to the river. By the time their operation ceased in 1986, the buildings were a complete shambles and tons of zinc powder was all over the grounds. When aerial photographs were taken of the waterfront, the white powder made the site look like Alaska in the dead of winter.

Overall, the 52 acres were extremely contaminated. Without the help of the RDA and some public funds, you couldn't give the land away.

COURSE OF ACTION FOR THE CLEANUP:

Purex—With funding from a variety of grants and government programs, the RDA began cleaning up the environmental problems on the Purex site in 2003, but before we could move forward, I needed to get rid of all the trailers that were parked there. It was much more of a cordial undertaking than I might be making it sound. The owner of the truck leasing company and the RDA mutually agreed to end the leasing agreement.

After all the existing buildings were demolished, there was an extensive Phase 1 and Phase 2 assessment performed on the grounds. Numerous meetings with the DEP followed, during which we mapped out our remediation strategy. Removing 33 acres of contaminated soil to an approved landfill hundreds of miles away would have required an army of dump trucks and far more public funding that we could ever raise.

It all came down to determining whether the Purex site—or parts of it—would be intended for commercial or residential use. We knew that some of the contaminants had been dumped on the grounds after 1980. ACT 2 required that we completely remove all of that material to an acceptable off-site landfill. Residential use also required the lead content in the soil to be under 500 parts per million. Much of the Purex ground's soil was nearly double that. So the final decision was based on both safe environmental practices and budgetary considerations. Thirteen acres would be cleaned to pristine residential specs, and the remaining twenty acres would be remediated to the degree necessary for safe, commercial use.

Once we started digging on the 13-acre parcel, we kept finding more and more discarded food cans, plastic barrels, and other assorted trash and waste. By the time we were finished, we were left with a 5-acre hole that was as deep as 15 feet at its worst spots. The hole was filled in with a mixture of clean fill, crushed stone, and crushed concrete from the site's demolished foundations and pads. The earthen materials that contained more than 500 parts per million of lead were moved to the other 20 Purex acres, where it was properly disposed of in a 12-foot-high berm that ran along Radcliffe Street. It was then covered with two feet of clean fill, newly planted trees, and other landscaping material to block any contaminants from reaching the public.

The remaining 20-acre parcel of the Purex property required the removal of several hot spots, including tracing and removing the crude oil we found near the border of the Zinc property. We suspected the oil was coming from a steel pipeline from the river's edge that went to a huge tank near Radcliffe Street for off-loading ships from the Delaware River. It had gone unnoticed for years. The idea was to remove problems like this one and any other contaminants so we could ensure the first two feet of soil on the site was clean and safe enough for commercial use. If the 20 acres were to be used at a later date for residential purposes (which actually happened), a further, more demanding remediation of the grounds would need to be carried out.

Dial—Everything on the Dial site was demolished in 2001–2002 before the RDA had found a developer for the property. Only the three-story warehouse—which was the centerpiece of any future reuse plans for the property—was spared the blows of the wrecking ball. As for the site's other buildings, it was quite a spectacle to see the 120-foot drying tower come tumbling down in an avalanche of disintegrating concrete, mangled girders, and residual soap flakes. Before the warehouse's interior demolition began, Bristol residents were invited to enter the warehouse with large trash bags and take away as much soap as they wanted.

A close-up of the Dial complex after the Superior Zinc site had been demolished and removed. The soap drying tower was still standing, and the warehouse still had the historically "incorrect" windows that resulted from an earlier rehab.

The demolition and collapse of the Dial soap drying tower.

Superior Zinc—After the remains of Superior Zinc's demolished buildings were hauled away, we still had to deal with seven acres of zinc powder. The borough worked with the RDA to remove it, but rather than clean the grounds to pristine levels like the Purex residential housing acreage, we resolved it enough to get the property sold to a developer. It would eventually be blacktopped for parking, which sealed in the remaining zinc and met the applicable PADEP regulations.

THE DEVELOPERS: I always liked to find local developers whenever possible. Of the two we eventually selected, one was in our backyard and the other was located only 30 miles away in Montgomery County.

On the 13 acres of Purex that were intended for 55-plus residential housing, we accepted bids from four different developers. McGrath Homes

Inc. won out with the highest bid. They'd set up an LLC called Riverbirch with plans to build four different 55-plus residential communities in Bucks County called "The Villas." The Langhorne site was the first one on their schedule, followed by additional developments in Bristol, Warminster, and Newtown.

The RDA has flexibility when judging offers that come in from builders and developers. We're not always locked in on accepting the highest bid. Often, we make our selection based on the quality of a builder and their reuse plans, even if other companies offered more money. That was the case with Michael O'Neill's Conshohocken, Pennsylvania–based Preferred Properties LLC. Their proposal for the Dial property, the Zinc site, and 20 of the Purex site's 33 acres was impressive and right in line with the RDA's and the borough's long-term vision for the property. Michael turned out to be a real find. Preferred Properties' development strategy was built around a concept called "Island View One" (converting the Dial warehouse and the Zinc property into a stylish, Class-A, multipurpose office complex) and "Island View Two" (three more Class-A office buildings totaling another 183,000 square feet, to be built on the remaining 20 acres of the Purex site).

COURSE OF ACTION FOR THE REUSE:

Purex—After purchasing the 13-acre parcel on the Purex site, McGrath builders wasted no time. Beginning in 2001, they built 56 luxury townhouses in less than a year and named the new community "The Villas at Riverview."

Dial—The RDA began rehabbing the Dial warehouse shortly after we acquired it in 2001. It was a 36-month-long process that received a major boost when Preferred Properties purchased the property from us in June 2003. It was the start of a very creative and prosperous collaboration.

The luxury townhouses of the Villas at Riverview that McGrath Builders constructed.

One of the largest undertakings during this period involved performing a historic rehabilitation of the warehouse's facade. To do that, we had to remove and replace all the building's windows—no small task in a three-story, 183,000-square-foot structure. Like most large factories and warehouses built in the early 1900s, there were lots of windows. It was an economical way of keeping electrical costs down by using natural light. But when Dial rehabbed the warehouse in 1990, they removed all the original floor-to-ceiling windows and replaced them with much smaller versions. Since the building was a historic structure that would qualify for a significant amount of government funding, the RDA and Preferred Properties quickly agreed that restoring the original early 1900s exterior look of the warehouse was the way to go.

While the windows were being replaced, the warehouse's interior was being converted to a Class-A office facility, which, of course, necessitated the addition of heating and a new electrical grid. Island View One was on its way.

The resurrected Dial warehouse with the historically correct, century-old floor-to-ceiling windows. The parking lot in front is situated on the grounds of the old Superior Zinc site.

Superior Zinc—There was no reuse in the plans for the Zinc site other than the aforementioned blacktopped parking lot that Preferred Properties paid for. Those seven acres now serve the utilitarian purpose of providing parking for the reborn Dial building/Island View One facility.

COSTS AND GRANTS: With the enactment of the 1996 ACT 2 bill, a lot of grants and funding opportunities became available and were used on Riverfront North. The project never could have happened—at least on the same level—prior to 1996.

Property Costs

- $1,500,000 paid by Bristol Borough in 1988 to purchase the Purex property.

- $895,000 paid by McGrath Homes Inc. in 2001 for the 13 acres of the Purex site intended for residential housing.

- $2,100,000 paid by the RDA in 2001 to purchase the Dial property. They wanted $3,100,000 and I countered with an offer of $1,800,000 with no contingencies. The $2,100,000 was the middle ground we settled for. The money came from a $1,500,000 Section 108 loan from the Bucks County CDBG Fund and an additional $600,000 in loans from a private bank. The Section 108 loan was interest-free and had to be paid back within 36 months. We paid it back in the 36th month to the astonishment of many in the county who thought we'd never make the deadline.

- $2,100,000 paid by Preferred Properties (with the help of a HUD loan) to purchase the Dial property from the RDA.

- $900,000 paid by Preferred Properties for the nonresidential 20 acres that remained on the Purex site and the seven-acre Zinc property. As part of the deal, Preferred was required to complete the land development on the additional property. Eventually, they sold some of the acreage to a home builder.

- Approx. $100,000 paid by the RDA as compensation when they took the Superior Zinc site by eminent domain.

Demolition Costs

- A $200,000 DCED grant to get rid of the concrete floors, pads, and foundations to two feet below existing grade on the Purex and Zinc sites.

- A $720,000 revitalization grant obtained by the RDA to demolish the drying tower and all buildings on the Dial site. The lone exception was the large cold storage warehouse, where only the building's interior was demolished.

- The actual demolition costs and associated costs of dismantling all the Zinc site's buildings took place shortly after it was taken by eminent domain in 1990, which was three years before I was involved with the RDA.

Environmental Remediation Costs

- $200,000 DCED grant in 1998 to assess the site conditions, with a 25% match through an EPA brownfields pilot grant. Bristol Borough also contributed funds to the assessment costs.

- An $862,567 DCED grant in 1996–1997 to clean the 13 acres on the Purex site intended for residential housing.

- A $1,000,000 ISRP grant to clean the balance of the Purex site (the other 20 acres) and the Zinc site.

- A $2,500,000 Section 108 Loan to Preferred Properties to rehabilitate the Dial warehouse.

Additional Grants

- $2,000,000 in tax credit funding was obtained by the RDA for Preferred Properties to renovate the Dial warehouse as a historic structure. This required getting the building placed on the National Register of Historic Places.

- $600,000 in opportunity grants, $250,000 in job training funds, $495,000 in job creation tax credits, and $250,000 worth of Neighborhood Assistance Program Enterprise Zone Tax Credits were presented in 2006 to Lenox China as a Governor's Action Team incentive package to persuade them to move into the Dial building. (More on this in the "Status of the Site Today" section to follow.)

- A $2,300,000 EDA grant was obtained by Bristol Borough and administered by the RDA to the developers for paving and land development on Island View One and Island View Two.

POLITICAL ISSUES: None.

CHALLENGES AND SETBACKS: Anyone who has ever worked on a project the size and scope of Riverfront North would tell you challenges and setbacks are daily occurrences. One of the more entertaining tales involved a PECO electric bill.

After we purchased the Dial warehouse in 2001, we assumed responsibility for all the building's utility bills. Being an unheated cold storage facility, I figured the tab on our first monthly statement would be quite modest. *Ten thousand dollars* was not my idea of modest. Apparently, the building's electrical feed came from a PECO substation that ran to a huge transformer outside the warehouse. Whether or not it sat unused in the property's transformer before being utilized in the building was of no consequence. Once PECO sent the power from their substation, it was considered a sale.

With the building being unused for a significant period of time, we had no idea that the electric bill had continued to accumulate. PECO was very understanding and supportive of what Bristol Borough was trying to accomplish on the riverfront, so they let us off the hook. We turned off the transformer and set up a simple, temporary electrical service to power the string of lights that ran through each floor of the building. The following month's PECO bill was a little easier on the blood pressure.

STATUS OF THE SITE TODAY: When I first assumed the job as executive director of the RDA, there were only two projects on the slate: One was Morrisville Rubber, which became my first completed project; the other was Riverfront North, which, when it's fully realized, would be my last.

The Villas at Riverview was an instant success. With a variety of upscale townhouse models ranging from 1,800 to 2,300 square feet that included picturesque views of the river, walking trails, and a beautiful gazebo, McGrath Builders/Riverbirch LLC had no trouble selling every unit within the first 12 months. Those homes are currently valued at twice the original purchase price. Well over 100 more townhouses and condos are planned for the site. Before redevelopment, the 13-acre parcel upon which The Villas was built generated no real estate taxes. Today, each of the new housing units provides approximately $6,000 in annual property taxes to the borough, school district, and county for a total exceeding $300,000.

The Island View One and Island View Two concept died when the bottom fell out of the market during the Great Recession of 2007–2009. But all was not lost: A dazzling, reborn Dial warehouse made its debut in 2004 as Island View Crossing, the name chosen because of the direct sight lines to Burlington Island in the middle of the Delaware River. With the help of a package of over $1,000,000 worth of state-sponsored incentives, Michael O'Neill was able to lure Lenox China into relocating their national headquarters and 450 new jobs to Island View Crossing. They moved in during May 2006 and occupied 126,000 square feet of the building. The remaining footage was leased as office space to a variety of other businesses. More than 500 people come to work at Island View Crossing on a daily basis.

When Riverfront North is completely finished, it will pay over $1,000,000 a year in taxes. It was originally paying $100,000. Thinking over a 10-year period, we spent $1,000,000 (after all the pluses and minuses were settled) to generate $10,000,000. Not a bad return on our investment.

Aside from the RDA and Bristol Borough, numerous other deserving people and organizations have been able to claim a share of the site's success. During her stint as director of the EPA, Christine Todd Whitman came to Riverfront North for a ribbon-cutting PR event in 2002. We really did it up for her, arranging for a tugboat to shoot streams of water several hundred feet into the air while the ceremony took place. It was a fitting celebration of what had already been accomplished and what is yet to come on Bristol's waterfront.

Joel Bolstein and me with EPA administrator (and former governor of New Jersey) Christine Todd Whitman, as she presented a check to Bucks County at the site of the Villas at Riverview.

Hamming it up for the cameras at the Dial warehouse presentation.

The water plume from a fireboat on the Delaware River at the Riverfront North ribbon-cutting ceremony.

BRISTOL STEEL

START AND COMPLETION DATES:
THE MID-1990S THROUGH 2006.

LOCATION: On South Pine Grove Street off Radcliffe Street in Bristol Borough. It was bordered on three sides by the Delaware River, the Anchor Yacht Club, and the former Dial Soap building.

HISTORY OF THE SITE: Many large and small manufacturers came and went during Bristol Borough's industrial boom years. One of them was a small factory that fabricated and treated steel products for the building industry. Known as Bristol Steel, it operated for several decades out of a 40-foot wide, single-story, rectangular building that housed approximately 6,000 square feet of workspace. The long, thin plot of land on which it stood was at most three-quarters of an acre. Sounds like a fairly unremarkable structure, doesn't it? Except for one highly unusual feature: An old, beat-up, 40-foot mobile home had been lifted up via a crane and placed on top of the workshop's roof. It was possibly used as the company's office. I used to jokingly refer to it as a multipurpose property because someone could have lived upstairs in the mobile home and then walked downstairs to work in the shop.

Hands down, the most unique-looking manufacturing site in the history of Bucks County had to be Bristol Steel's piggyback trailer and shop complex. At some point, they must have hired a crane to lift that bulky structure onto the shop's roof.

By the late 1990s, activity at Bristol Steel began to slow down. A skeleton crew working on outdated equipment kept things going until sometime in 2000, when the company went out of business. The building became vacant and no one was taking care of it, so it was condemned as a blighted property.

HOW THE RDA GOT INVOLVED: In the mid '90s, just as the RDA and Bristol Borough were going into high gear with their signature Riverfront North project, Bristol Steel's vacated building came to my attention. How could it not? Here we were, trying to revitalize Bristol's riverfront by doing things like transforming the historic Dial building into a beautiful Class-A office complex and building an elegant new residential housing community, but sitting smack dab in the middle of all this ambitious activity and grandiose planning was a three-quarter-acre junkyard. It stuck out like a sore thumb—like someone walking on stage to accept an Academy Award wearing a stylish Armani tuxedo with a football-sized spaghetti sauce stain on their white shirt. Something had to be done. In 2001, Bristol Borough asked the RDA to try to purchase the property from its owners. An appraisal was done on the site that came in on the low side at $116,700 and on the high side at $291,750. The RDA took it by eminent domain in March 2005.

ENVIRONMENTAL AND/OR BLIGHT ISSUES: Like most manufacturers dealing with metal products, Bristol Steel's property had some TCE issues, but they were minimal. We tested the river nearby to see whether there was any runoff there, but the tests came back non-detect. However, there were some petroleum products in the ground, asbestos issues in the building, and several old rusted tanks that needed to be removed.

These were all run-of-the-mill environmental situations we faced on many of the other blighted properties we dealt with. But the property's taxes were current, and if left alone, the Bristol Steel property wasn't posing much of a threat to the public. The real pressing problem that set the RDA's wheels in motion was the optics—the eyesore problem that needed to be eliminated.

COURSE OF ACTION FOR THE CLEANUP: The borough hired its own contractor to handle the demolition, which took two weeks to complete. Following a Phase 1 and Phase 2 assessment, an ACT 2 environmental remediation began with the removal of the tanks and then the contaminated soil. Clean fill was brought in to replace it and was then graded and seeded. Within two months, there was no sign Bristol Steel had ever occupied the site.

We decided to use the voluntary ACT 2 program to protect all the owners (first the original owner, then the RDA, and finally Bristol Borough) from any future responsibility for any post-remediation contaminants. Environmental testing was conducted over the next eight consecutive quarters to satisfy the Pennsylvania DEP requirements for the remediation.

COSTS AND GRANTS:

- $174,000 for the acquisition of the property, paid as just compensation. It was funded through a loan awarded to the RDA from the Bucks County Department of Community and Economic Development (DCED). In the end, the loan was forgiven, and we eventually sold the property to the borough for $1.00.

- $110,000 in demolition costs funded by Bristol Borough.

- $100,000 for the environmental cleanup funded by a $75,000 DCED grant and an additional $25,000 from an EPA grant fund administered by the RDA.

POLITICAL AND GOVERNMENTAL ISSUES: None.

DEVELOPER AND COURSE OF ACTION FOR THE REUSE: None. Since the project involved only property acquisition, remediation, and environmental cleanup, there was nothing to develop and no reuse of the property.

CHALLENGES AND/OR SETBACKS: Acquiring the Bristol Steel property was not an easy process. We first approached its owner—a gentleman in his midsixties—on a fact-finding mission. He showed no hostility to our plans to acquire the property by amicable eminent domain, pay him just compensation, and help him move. After answering a few questions about what we thought the property was worth, we left and waited to see how things would play out. It didn't go well.

Knowing they owned the last vacant parcel of land on Bristol's waterfront, the owner and his family felt the property was worth far more than what we were offering. Our explanations that the property was probably just going to end up as open space were to no avail. The owner was convinced that some wealthy buyer was going to build a multimillion-dollar waterfront mansion on the site. Complicating matters was his deteriorating health. As time went on, he became more and more uncommunicative and finally stopped returning phone calls. I believe he passed away around this time.

His wife and family inherited the property and claimed they were going to reopen the business. In my opinion, that tactic was a stall to try to drive up the compensation price. By 2004, the site had significantly deteriorated. We condemned it as a blighted property, had it reevaluated by a qualified real estate appraising company (the new figure was $174,000), and then served the family notice that we were taking the property by eminent domain and would be paying them just compensation. They had 30 days to appeal the blight designation and a year to challenge the value of the compensation.

At a 2006 hearing with the County Board of View, they challenged the compensation amount, insisting the property was worth a lot more than what we were offering. The board sided with our valuation. We never set out to create hard feelings, but often, those are the results of the eminent domain process. They had numerous options to hold onto their property. We possibly could have helped them get a state grant or a low-interest loan to clean up the blight and get their company back in business, but that wasn't the family's intention. They just wanted more money.

I didn't take the executive director job at the RDA so I could hurt people. I truly feel we gave the owner's family a good deal. They were paying taxes on a property that was bringing in no revenues and was relatively unsellable and worthless. Taking the property by eminent domain released them from that financial burden, as well as the obligation of cleaning up six figures worth of environmental problems for which they were responsible.

STATUS OF THE SITE TODAY: All that remains of Bristol Steel is a pristine, open space of green stretching from Pine Grove Street straight down to the river. The acquisition and demolition of the property was the final step in the cleanup phase of the Riverfront North project. Bristol Steel was the last of the industrial and manufacturing sites that once populated the waterfront at the northern end of Radcliffe Street.

Although conversations have taken place to build something on the site, nothing substantial has materialized to date. For the time being, it's just a pleasant piece of open green space that has been added to Bristol's waterfront and the adjacent Spurline Park.

All that remains of Bristol Steel's former operation is a grassy plot of land that borders the Anchor Yacht Club.

THE U.S. STEEL FAIRLESS WORKS AND THE PORT OF BUCKS

START AND COMPLETION DATES: 1994 TO 2010.

LOCATION: U.S. Steel's Fairless Works operation was built in the southeastern section of Falls Township in Bucks County. Their port was situated at a point on the Delaware River where it begins to make a sharp 90-degree turn toward Trenton, New Jersey. The borough of Fieldsboro, New Jersey, is on the opposite side of the river.

HISTORY OF THE SITE: Throughout much of the first half of the 20th century, the future location for the U.S. Steel Fairless Works was mostly open space lowlands and farmland, including the extremely successful King Farms. As the Cold War ramped up following World War II, America's steel industry was being encouraged to increase steel production as a bulwark to fend off the communist threat posed by Russia and China. In an effort to comply with the post-war patriotism and nationalistic fervor of the times, U.S. Steel's chief executive officer, Benjamin Fairless, began looking for a location to set up an expansive, full-service steel mill.

He'd had his eyes on land in southeastern Falls Township for some time. It seemed like an ideal location because of the proximity of major highways, rail lines, and the tanker-accessible Delaware River, which—via

197

the Delaware Bay—connects to the domestic and international ship-ping lanes of the Atlantic Ocean. In the late 1940s, U.S. Steel purchased approximately 4,000 acres, broke ground in 1951, and opened a sprawling 1,600-acre facility in December 1952 that immediately began producing steel for worldwide export. A lot of thought and planning had to go into building the site, particularly since a lot of the land had to be filled in to provide solid footing for the enormous buildings that were erected there.

The new campus continued to grow over the years, adding to what started out as a wide assortment of very large and smaller buildings that contained over 1,000,000 square feet of workspace. Eventually, U.S. Steel built two blast furnaces, nine open-hearth furnaces, two coke batteries, an 80-inch hot strip mill, a sheet metal and tin department, and a pipe mill. They even had their own power plant on the premises, and an eight-berth deep-water port was constructed on an inlet off the Delaware River.

By 1954, it began to receive river barges and other ships carrying raw iron ore for offloading into an ore pit right at the dock. A 12-foot elevated rail system was erected to load the ore directly from the pit to a blast furnace 1,000 feet away. That was the shortest run of tracks on the premises. Another 70 miles of internal rail lines wove their way through the maze of buildings and open acreage with the ability to connect to Class I railroad systems like CSX and Norfolk Southern, and a 550-train-car loading area was located right by the port.

U.S. Steel's deepwater port in the early 1970s. After being offloaded from the supply ships, ore was transferred via the elevated rail system directly to the nearby blast furnace.

The entire operation was known as the U.S. Steel Fairless Works, a name that would seem to have been derived from the nearby town of Fairless Hills. However, that wasn't the case; the actual campus is located in Falls Township and was named after Ben Fairless. At its apex in 1974, the Fairless Works expanded to 2,500 acres with a landscape defined by the six enormous smokestacks above the blast furnaces and a tapestry of steam pipes that crisscrossed for miles throughout the complex. Almost 7,000 steel workers were employed there, and another 3,000 people worked on the site as subcontracted truckers and maintenance staff. Many of them lived in nearby Levittown or in local U.S. Steel–subsidized housing.

Much of the company's income came from government contracts. It was an extremely lucrative period for them until a flood of cheap foreign steel imports brought about the decline of the plant in the late '80s. Numerous U.S. Steel workers saw the writing on the wall and started retiring as the Fairless Works began to downsize. (I should know—I provided the flowers for a lot of their retirement parties since I still owned my flower shop at the time.)

In 1986, U.S. Steel was renamed the USX Corporation, but the name change didn't bring about an improvement in the company's fortunes. The downward spiral continued. By 1991, it became too costly to operate the Fairless Works complex. A phased shutdown began, which included closing up their port. The hot side of the plant was the first of the once essential operations to go, and some years later, the pipe mill met a similar fate. In 2001, after changing the company name back to U.S. Steel, all the plant's other activities (including the cold rolling and tin mill operations) fell silent. The lone exception was their finishing plant, which continued to operate with a reduced workforce of 900 employees. Over the next decade, that number fell to 100.

HOW THE RDA GOT INVOLVED: USX brought in a consulting company called Direction Associates to help them repurpose, reorganize, and lease or sell off 1,700 acres of their property to outside companies. At the time,

Denny McCartney was the top dog at what remained of the U.S. Steel Fairless Works. He and Direction Associates' Bob Dusek approached the RDA in 1994 to discuss those same topics, but their principal focus at the meeting was the Fairless Works' closed-up deepwater port. After providing me with details on its history and operation, they wanted feedback on what federal, state, and municipal grants and incentives might be available. They had a basic idea of what reopening the port would cost, but they need our clout, our political and governmental connections, and most of all, our ability to get grants.

In short, they needed me to put together a loss leader package that would convince potential port management companies that getting involved with the Port of Bucks would be a profitable venture for them. Well, they'd come to the right place, because acquiring public funds to create private jobs and business opportunities is what the RDA does best. But on a project of this size and complexity, our skills, know-how, and stamina would really be tested. A huge amount of sweat equity and research would be needed to draft and read through dozens of proposals, to coordinate the project's land development, and to pull in all the necessary big guns—the county commissioners, state and federal legislators, the Pennsylvania DCED, and all the local municipal leaders and community residents.

ENVIRONMENTAL AND/OR BLIGHT ISSUES: For once, the RDA was not involved in the assessment and cleanup of adverse environmental conditions on a site. If there was ever a good time for us to sit on the sidelines of an environmental remediation, this was the one. The Fairless Works site had a formidable array of toxic environmental problems, and U.S. Steel—which had single-handedly created those problems—was legally and financially responsible for all of it. During the construction of their Falls Township facility, numerous borrow pits were excavated (areas where soil, gravel, sand, or other materials were dug up for use at other locations). This fill material was used to raise the Fairless site above the elevation of the 100-year floodplain. Over the ensuing years, large amounts of slag (a by-product of the smelting process), toxins, and various other hazardous materials produced by the mill's steelmaking processes were deposited in those pits.

The history of the Fairless Works' environmental problems went back as far as the mid-1950s. King Farms had an uninterrupted record of prosperity from its debut in 1929, but in 1954, its annual crop yield began to dramatically drop off. In 1958, it was determined that the smokestacks of the Fairless Works were the source of the problem. They were spewing prodigious amounts of toxic chemicals on all the nearby fields. King Farms sued U.S. Steel and received a $1,540,000 settlement.

Three and a half decades later, in 1993, the EPA and USX entered into a consent order for cleaning up the Fairless Works site. The order incorporated the entire 2,500-acre facility. There were 68 areas identified for further investigation, including former production and disposal areas. In addition to the visible, above-the-ground slag problem, arsenic, lead, and various other heavy metals, naphthalene, PAHs, and TCE were in the groundwater.

In 1998, USX expressed interest in obtaining a release from liability for the Fairless Works under the Pennsylvania Act 2 Land Recycling Program. They would have to pay for the cleanup, but releasing them from future liability would aid them and give them an incentive to clean up and redevelop their property. The State of Pennsylvania was eager to grant the request because repurposing the Fairless Works site would help revitalize the residents and economy of Levittown and the surrounding area. Due to USX's downsizing in the 1980s and '90s, 5,000 local jobs had been lost.

COURSE OF ACTION FOR THE CLEANUP: In order to expedite the cleanup and redevelopment of the site, the EPA, the Pennsylvania DEP, and U.S. Steel formed a team to proceed with the necessary environmental investigations. The team focused its first efforts on 450 acres of uncontaminated land that was part of USX's original 4,000-acre purchase from the late 1940s. Since this land had always stood apart from the steel mills and had no significant environmental conditions, it was easily designated for lease or sale under standard real estate transaction procedures.

However, repurposing the land that provided the footprint for the Fairless Works' steelmaking areas required satisfying all the environmental requirements of the EPA and the PADEP. A contractor was hired to begin tearing down the massive buildings that housed the blast furnaces and the rest of the heart-and-soul assembly lines of USX's steelmaking processes.

The demolition of the Fairless Works site began sometime in 1993 or '94 and went on for over a decade and a half. It overlapped the RDA's work efforts at reestablishing the site's port. When I first drove through the site in 1994, they were imploding the six smokestacks from the smelting facilities. The still-functioning parts of the facility coexisted with wrecking crews that were leveling colossal structures only a few hundreds yards away. Hulking slabs of broken concrete and gnarled metal covered the landscape as far as the eye could see. If I didn't know better, I'd have thought I was driving through Dresden, Germany after it was carpet-bombed in World War II.

Hundreds of boxcars, hoppers, and gondola cars filled with junk metal from the demolition stood in silence on Fairless Works' once busy railroad tracks. The fate of their contents—rusted old beams, girders, and steel and copper pipes—would have to wait until their market value rose to a sufficient level to warrant being sold off. Driving through the complex one day in the late '90s, I noticed they were all gone; so was the 12-foot-high elevated rail system that stretched from the port's ore pit to the blast furnace. The wrecking crews' work continued on and off for almost another decade. In 2008, in one of the site's final demolition projects, the Fairless Works' pipe mill came tumbling down.

Concurrent with all the demolition—and in some cases, preceding it—the EPA administered the remediation of the environmental issues both inside and outside the buildings. Toxic items were either removed from the site or blocked from causing harm by encapsulating them under two feet of clean fill. None of what was going on was any of the RDA's business. USX, the EPA, and the PADEP were calling all the shots and spending all the money. The only part of the cleanup procedures that had anything to do with our eventual involvement was the remediation's treatment of the site's groundwater.

One of the demolition company's first moves was to seal up all the port's catch basins (the underground drainage system) with concrete. It was a cautionary measure to prevent environmental contaminants from emptying into the Delaware River. Until the environmental conditions were cleared, the water that flowed through the site had to be treated or contained until it was safe to be released into the river.

I wasn't privy to the cost of USX's cleanup and demolition, but I wouldn't be surprised if it exceeded $10,000,000. In the four and a half decades since the Fairless Works made its debut in 1952, its 1,000,000 square feet of buildings had mushroomed to 5,000,000 square feet. The demolition crew was essentially tearing down a small city. Again, I had no firsthand knowledge, but there's a good chance USX didn't have to lay out a single dime. The resale value of the tons of junk metal in those train cars most likely exceeded the total cost of the demolition.

COURSE OF ACTION FOR THE REUSE, PART I (LEASING THE LAND): The engine that drove the transformation of USX's Fairless Works site was the leasing and selling off of its Falls Township acreage. The land sell-off didn't begin until after the RDA was no longer involved in the project, but the leasing campaign began in 1994. It had two separate large-scale goals: enticing outside companies and industries to set up shop on their former steelmaking campus, and reopening their old deepwater port.

There was no specific theme to the diverse types of businesses that moved to the site during the early leasing campaign: Morton Salt, Toll Brothers Builders, American Water, and two dozen other predominantly domestic businesses moved in during the first wave, bringing in 1,800 new jobs. As the years progressed though, USX's criteria for the type of tenants they were looking for began to evolve. They started avoiding warehousing operations—which bring in few new jobs—and prioritized leasing to heavy industry companies, particularly those with international profiles and ties to wind, solar, biofuel, and other renewable energy products. Gamesa Wind US (a Spanish wind turbine manufacturer), AE Polysilicon (a Taiwanese polysilicon manufacturer), Exelon, and Dominion Fairless Energy are amongst the 50 or so industries that now thrive on the site.

Describing all this activity in two short paragraphs makes it sound as if this transition process was a breeze, but it always takes a lot of incentives to make these types of multifaceted projects work. The new businesses needed assurances they would be able to reuse the property without being responsible for any leftover environmental contamination issues. Big-time grants, low-income financing, and tax abatement programs were also part of the lure the RDA helped put together in order to attract these preferred types of tenants.

COURSE OF ACTION FOR THE REUSE, PART II (LEASING THE PORT): In 1995, the decision was made to find and lease the land around the old port to a port operator. The company Direction Associates found was Atlantic Marine Terminal (AMT). Initially, they leased 20 acres from USX at $5,000 per acre per month. They intended to use the port to ship in steel to sell, which they would then truck out or send via trains to their customers. With the help of a $750,000 DCED state grant, the RDA paved 15 acres around the dock and opened up the catch basins. AMT brought in cranes and heavy equipment to do their offloading, but they had no place to store their steel.

So in their second year as the port's operator, the RDA built AMT a 40,000-square-foot warehouse that we called the "Blue Building." It was funded by a state "Grant to Loan" program. We borrowed $400,000 from the DCED and then loaned it to AMT. The intention was for them to pay it back to the RDA and then we'd use those funds to establish a revolving loan fund for future projects. It seemed like a good, straight-ahead business plan, except AMT defaulted on the very first payment and every payment thereafter. After a little less than three years, they went bankrupt in 1997.

The Blue Building—not the most creative name or design, but it was built to store steel, not works of art.

For the time being, the RDA was on the hook for that $400,000. Fortunately, the state didn't call in the loan; I was able to talk them into letting us use it for the previously mentioned revolving loan. The Blue Building had an ongoing mortgage, but Denny McCartney and USX had a large stake in seeing the port succeed. He allowed us to use the land until we could find a new port operator.

The folks at AMT were good people with the best of intentions, but they were in over their heads. They lacked experience at managing a port, so in no time, they were overextended financially. The next port operator fared much better. A large Ukranian shipping company called Novalog Bucks County Inc. bought out AMT's bankruptcy in 1997 and assumed the $5,000 monthly rental of the Blue Building.

Like their predecessor, Novalog manufactured nothing. They just imported steel and shipped it out. But David Reid, one of their principal owners, had a real feel and vision for what the port could be if properly managed. He was directly responsible for turning it into a world-class success. After creating 199 new jobs at the port in 1999, he won a state award as Pennsylvania's biggest new employer. He was also one helluva salesman. In a short time, after setting up the port's logistical structure, Novalog had four 70-car trains loaded with rolls of steel going out to a manufacturer in Mercer, Pennsylvania—every week! The rolls were mostly used in producing the outer skins of cars, refrigerators, and other appliances.

An aerial shot of the inverted "Y" shape of the Port of Bucks. It can handle anywhere from four to eight ships at a time, depending on their size.

Novolog's successful run ended in 2008, at which point they sold their interests to a bulk shipping company by the name of Kinder Morgan. But before David Reid and Novalog moved on, he set the wheels in motion for what I consider to be the centerpiece of his rich legacy in Bucks County.

From 1996 to 2010, the Army Corps of Engineers (USACE) conducted five significant dredgings of the Delaware River's channel and the port itself. Each dredging lasted a week to 10 days and always took place in the early fall—the time of year determined to pose the smallest threat to the endangered Atlantic sturgeons that inhabit the river. The first of these channel dredgings was to prepare for the reopening of the port. That dredging and all subsequent channel maintenance were the sole responsibility of the USACE. Since the funding came from their annual, federally allocated budget, the RDA had no involvement.

Pennsylvania Congressman Jim Greenwood looks on as I sign the dredging contracts with the Philadelphia Commander of the Army Corps of Engineers. We're in the pilothouse of a tugboat for the ceremony.

Additional dredging of the channel and the port itself was another matter. This was the combined responsibility of the port owner (USX), the port operator (AMT, and eventually Novalog, and then Kinder Morgan), and Waste Management, which owned the GROWS landfill on the opposite side of the port and maintained some berths there. They also helped keep the port's dredging budgets down by accepting the excavated silt for a minimal fee.

What may seem like a workable, amicable arrangement was actually quite the opposite. Nobody wanted to pay for anything; they all looked to the RDA to find funding. By getting everyone together in the same room during once-a-month meetings, I was able to get all the disparate parties on the same page and work things out, but those meetings were where the RDA really earned its money.

The common ground where the USACE and the port's three partners shared costs was whenever the channel needed to be dredged to a new, deeper water depth. Each time, we worked an 80/20 deal. The USACE contributed 80% of the costs, and matching fees of the remaining 20% was a three-way split between USX, the port's operator, and Waste Management. On each of these deals, the RDA was required to act as a nonfederal sponsor by signing a letter of credit to the USACE until the matching 20% of the costs were paid up. As the administrator, the RDA's fees were worked into each dredging's budgeted costs.

On the first run, the original channel was dredged to a depth of 35 feet. Then on subsequent dredgings, it was deepened to 37, and finally 40 feet. But one critical component was still missing: The port needed a turning basin. Novalog's David Reid had been traveling to Washington, DC lobbying for this for some time. When U.S. Steel first opened the port in the 1950s, the barges and freighters coming up the river were much smaller than the 800 to 900-foot behemoths that came into the newly reopened Port of Bucks in the late '90s. The basin was simply too shallow and not large enough to safely handle deep-draft, oceangoing ships. Getting out of the port and turning around was a dangerous maneuver, particularly if there were strong currents. Shipping business was being lost to deeper ports.

David Reid's vision was finally realized in 2001 when the USACE dug a 1,000-foot-wide, 38-foot-deep turning basin. In short time, it became obsolete; larger ships and heavier loads necessitated deepening the channel to 40 feet. The USACE had the project on their radar as early as 2007. Four years later, in 2010, 40 feet became the turning basin's new standard. The reason it took four years to come together was because the administrative and political climate had changed. The people we'd been dealing with at USX, Waste Management, and Kinder Morgan had moved on, and the new administrations didn't like paying RDA fees.

The political climate was also different. Some of my close friends and allies weren't around any more. Mike Fitzpatrick was in Washington, DC where he'd become a member of the House of Representatives, and Harry Fawkes had retired. Things got strange. We were able to get the deal done, but I wasn't happy with the final outcome or the process that brought it about. When a later campaign emerged to further deepen the channel to 45 feet, it was dead before it even started. The can-do atmosphere of the project's earlier years was gone. It was time for the RDA to move on to some of its other projects.

COSTS AND GRANTS:
The AMT Era

- A $750,000 DCED grant to cover the cost of the port's environmental cleanup, reopening the catch basins and stormwater piping, and the paving of 15 acres of the port with 8 inches of asphalt.

- A $400,000 "Grant to Loan" (at 2%) from the DCED to build the 40,000-square-foot Blue Building warehouse.

The Novalog Era

- A $200,000 DCED grant to pave around the dock and office areas.

- A $1,000,000 Pennsylvania Department of Transportation (PennDOT) grant to make improvements to the existing rail systems, which were in bad shape after the years of Fairless Works demolition.

The Kinder Morgan Era

- A $700,000 DCED grant for lighting improvements at the port.

- 2005 Keystone Opportunity Zone (KOZ) designation: In order to make the site more appealing to potential investors, a sizeable portion of the site was given this designation. The KOZ provided state and local tax relief to companies that moved onto the Fairless Works site. It became effective in 2005 and lasted until 2018.

Dredgings

Millions of dollars were spent on the five dredgings under the same 80/20 matching fees deal. The largest individual budget and funding package was for the 2010 dredging of the turning basin to 40 feet.

- $1,580,000 in total budgeted dredging costs. Eighty percent of it was paid by the USACE and 20 percent was divided up and paid by the port, Waste Management, Kinder Morgan, the Bucks County Commissioners, and Falls Township.

CONTRACTORS/BUILDERS CHOSEN: The USACE bid out the job for the port's dredging. An outfit named Norfolk Dredging Co. won the contract.

POLITICAL ISSUES: Even though it was located in Falls Township, USX's Fairless Works was essentially a city unto itself. There was very little political interference of any kind, and they seemed to do whatever they wanted to do.

GOVERNMENT INVOLVEMENT: I purposely left the main event until the end. Of all the massive amounts of government participation involved in every phase of the project, everyone's finest hour came in 1997 when the State of Pennsylvania established a 16-square-mile enterprise zone. Its purpose was to address deteriorated, blighted, and underused industrial and manufacturing areas in six different Lower Bucks municipalities:

Bristol Township, Falls Township, and the boroughs of Bristol, Morrisville, Bensalem, and Tullytown. The zone was in effect for 10 years and then was extended in 2008 when the RDA was successful in convincing the state to give us another eight years. (Penndel Borough was added to the mix at this time.)

The RDA administered the zone in conjunction with an advisory committee made up of representatives from each of the participating municipalities. The intent of the zone was to attract new business while also helping existing businesses within the zone by giving them priority consideration on grants and financial assistance, tax credits, and any other technical and financial resources available from the state.

A high-profile press conference announcing the commencement of the enterprise zone was held at the port. All the political movers and shakers involved showed up: Governor Tom Ridge and Lieutenant Governor Mark Schweiker, State Senator Tommy Tomlinson and State Representative Thomas Corrigan, and all the commissioners of Bucks County, including their chairman, Mike Fitzpatrick, the lead voice in bringing the enterprise zone to fruition. This was no run-of-the-mill photo op; it was a generational event whose significance was not lost on the politicians in attendance. They deserved every bit of recognition the day could offer. They'd all worked their butts off in bringing about Bucks County's single biggest economic development project since U.S. Steel opened the Fairless Works in 1952. (The enterprise zone's extension ran out in 2016. Efforts to reestablish it are ongoing.)

STATUS OF THE SITE TODAY: Currently known as the Keystone Industrial Port Complex (KIPC), the port currently takes up 100 acres and continues to be operated by Kinder Morgan. Oceangoing vessels routinely travel up the Delaware River to KIPC, bringing in 4,000,000 tons of steel, salt, vermiculite, concrete, and a variety of other raw materials. The 130-plus vessels that repeatedly use the port every year represent 5% of all traffic on the Delaware River in the tristate area. KIPC is currently the largest steel distribution center on the East Coast. Its annual figures include revenues in excess of $1,000,000,000 and $26,000,000 in tax revenues while creating more than 4,000 direct and indirect jobs.

Offloading a ship at the Keystone Industrial Port Complex. The large hill on the opposite side of the port is Waste Management's landfill.

As for U.S. Steel, they still own some of the acreage from their former steel mill campus, although only a small finishing facility remains from Fairless Work's boom years. While the RDA is no longer active in the port's current activities, there is no doubt about it: This was the biggest and most impactful project we ever administered.

ROHM & HAAS / MAPLE BEACH

START AND COMPLETION DATES:
1996 TO 2010, WITH 2003–2010
BEING THE MOST ACTIVE PERIOD.

LOCATION: In between State Road and the Delaware River in Bristol Township. The total acreage was bisected by Route 413. The Maple Beach parcel was a quasi-triangular tract of land bordered by Route 413, the Delaware River, and Lake Idaline, which ran diagonally along the site's third side.

HISTORY OF THE SITE: Driving over the Burlington-Bristol Bridge from the 1940s through the 1970s was not a pleasant experience. If you didn't hold your nose, you'd be treated to a noxious dose of a foul-smelling stench that emanated from the land on the Pennsylvania side and floated over the Delaware River. You were entering the 884-acre industrial complex of Rohm & Haas (R&H).

The company had been producing specialty chemicals on the site since 1917—everything from sprays that ripened produce to bases for paints, sunscreens, and various liquid products used in pesticides. Of the 884 acres, only slightly more than 200 were used for manufacturing facilities, which were located a mile or so inland from the river. Much of the other 600-plus acreage was wasteland, although some portions served in previous decades as dump sites for river dredging. A separate 100-acre plot of land called Maple Beach was originally the site of a residential housing community for R&H's employees, but after some years, the company began to repurchase and demolish the houses as they came up for sale. It was a smart legal and business move; R&H reluctantly came to the realization that living downwind from a chemical facility was not a healthy living environment for their labor force. Only four houses from that period currently remain, all of which are still occupied.

Maple Beach viewed from the Pennsylvania shoreline. Spanning the Delaware River on the left is the Burlington-Bristol Bridge.

By 1999, R&H had grown to become the world's largest specialty chemical company, employing over 3,000 workers in the Bucks County and Philadelphia area.

ENVIRONMENTAL AND/OR BLIGHT ISSUES: Less than a third of R&H's property contained the buildings used in their manufacturing process. Since almost all of those buildings were occupied and in use, blight was not really an issue anywhere on their land. However, the same could not be said about their property's environmental condition. The assortment of toxins and other contaminants on the site was substantial, but to get an accurate picture of the environmental conditions, several questions needed to be answered: Which toxins, where did they come from, in what amounts, and what was their current state?

VOCs, SVOCs, PCBs, TCE, acetone, some heavy metals, and ammonia sulfate were found at different locations on the property, particularly around several man-made lagoons formed from the byproducts of R&H's wastewater treatment plant and from the river dredging deposits, which were as high as 10 feet in spots. Some of the lagoons dried up over the years and were covered by dense vegetation. These former wetlands were also environmentally burdened by Buck's County's mosquito control programs of the 1970s, which doused the grounds with pesticides.

As bad as all this sounds, extensive testing and soil screenings were performed at different times from the mid-1980s on by the EPA, the PADEP, and the RDA. There was no doubt about the presence of the aforementioned contaminants, but the overall conclusion was that the levels of their concentration across sizable portions of the 400 acres was low enough to be within acceptable PADEP levels and specs for industrial use. Approximately 240 of those acres could be reused with little or no remediation at all.

The most serious contaminant on R&H's property was an ammonium sulfate plume that was generated over decades from the company's wastewater treatment plant. This is the substance that caused the acrid smell in the vicinity of the facility as previously described. The smell dissipated after discharge of this toxin was discontinued in 1972.

Additional studies were conducted by R&H between 1986 and 2001 on both sides of Route 413, stretching as far as Lake Idaline. While the plume was no longer growing, it still existed approximately 60 feet underground, extending 2,000 feet along the bedrock surface. However, studies found it was immobile, with no immediate or viable pathway for the contaminant to reach the public. While no urgent remediation was found to be necessary, it was decided that the EPA should continue monitoring the site for an unspecified period of time.

HOW THE RDA GOT INVOLVED: The Army Corps of Engineers began dredging the Delaware River in 1996 when the RDA began working on the reopening of the Port of Bucks. Finding somewhere to deposit the dredged river sediment had become a big problem. For technical reasons, the final destination of the dredged materials has to be within a five-mile radius of the pumping system. None of the towns that lined the New Jersey side of the Delaware within that radius wanted the material, and there was also resistance to dumping it on Burlington Island. But just a few miles down the river was the raw, unused riverfront property of R&H.

It wasn't an easy sell. I needed to convince not only R&H's executives on the idea but also Bristol Township. The idea was temporarily put on the back burner, but I made use of the time. From 1996 to 2003, I kept bringing up the topic, picking people's minds, and working on developing a strong relationship with R&H. During those seven years, the Maple Beach concept grew to be much more than just a location for dredged sediment.

COURSE OF ACTION FOR THE CLEANUP: The site was originally below the 100-year flood plain in an area where the nearby Delaware River rises and falls seven to eight feet every day. Decades ago, R&H addressed this precarious situation by building six-foot levees along their waterfront. A Triad study of the river was carried out by the Army Corps of Engineers in the late 1990s that concluded the sediment in the river was clean. If we could use those clean dredging materials to build up Maple Beach and the surrounding acreage to four to five feet above the flood plain, that would prevent any future Katrina-like disasters while also providing two to three feet above the standard two-foot environmental cap of clean fill. That would open the site up to all kinds of interesting reuse possibilities.

COURSE OF ACTION FOR THE REUSE: My primary motivation during every project at the RDA has always been to improve the lives of the residents of Bucks County, but if I said I didn't also have personal goals, I'd be lyin'.

Ego is often the spark plug that turns good intentions into realities; it's what makes us push ourselves past our limits and enables us to find out what we're really capable of doing. For all the communal good I believed a fully developed Maple Beach could create, I also recognized that the signature project of my career was standing right in front of me, daring me to hit its best pitch. I decided to swing for the fences.

A lot of people needed to be convinced of Maple Beach's potential. In my best efforts as the spokesperson and salesman for the project, I couldn't do as good a job as a well-drawn picture, so I hired a design artist. I needed someone who could combine my ideas with all the concepts I'd incorporated from the best minds in the county. The artist's renderings took my breath away.

The artist's rendering that so beautifully captured all the hopes and dreams we had for Maple Beach.

Maple Beach was recast as a self-sustaining community for the 21st century and beyond, incorporating the latest advances in green buildings and solar and wind energy technologies. The acreage on the side of Route 413 that faced Bristol Borough included a wide-ranging development of two and three-story buildings that brought together 2,000,000 square feet of R&D office space and light manufacturing with 700 residential condos. Two bookend, high-rise buildings framed this complex, combining 75,000 square feet of commercial and retail space with an additional 250 condos. A public beach lined the waterfront, and extensive parks and generous amounts of open green spaces breathed life throughout the grounds. As a final touch, Lake Idaline was to be transformed from an unused, neglected body of water into a first-class marina with drawbridge access to the Delaware River.

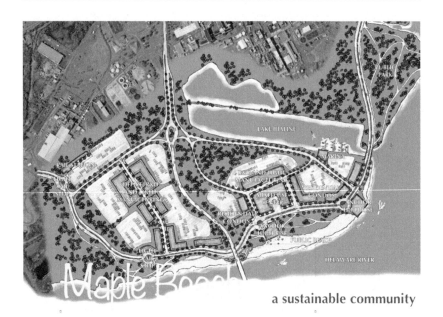

A computer-generated aerial layout of the proposed Maple Beach community that shows its spatial relationship to Rohm & Haas's campus.

The south side of Route 413 included a light industrial manufacturing center, commercial space, and a light railroad station with regional connections to SEPTA and Amtrak. Extensive roadway systems connected both the north and south campuses, and tram service and tram stops were distributed throughout the entire development. Even Bucks County's long-standing goal of having uninterrupted, Bensalem-to-Morrisville riverfront access for its residents was addressed by the walking and bike trails included in Maple Beach's conceptual design.

The price tag for all of this wouldn't be cheap, but a project this ambitious and expansive would be eligible for a multitude of state and federal grant and incentive programs. As the only remaining big open-space area in Bucks County's lower end, R&H's property was a last-chance, can't-miss opportunity for Bristol Township to develop a sizable, stable tax base that could help them for decades. The completed project would allow its residents to live in an adaptive, futuristic community. As conceived, Maple Beach's population could become independent of their cars within the community by walking, riding bicycles, or using the tram service to go to work or visit the site's service and retail areas. There was no doubt in my mind that Maple Beach would serve as a national model for green development and sustainability.

Now all I had to do was convince R&H to sell us 400 acres of their unused property and get the backing of Bucks County and Bristol Township . . . no sweat!

CHALLENGES AND/OR SETBACKS: Right from the beginning, Rohm & Haas didn't really want the project to happen. They were concerned about their liability for any potential chemical spills or any problems caused by contaminants found on their grounds. And they weren't the only ones concerned about the site's toxicity. There were also a lot of naysayers among the governmental decision makers in Bristol Township and Bucks County. It seemed like everyone wanted to believe the environmental issues on the site were worse than they actually were and there was no way it could be cleaned up.

A decade of work and planning came to a head in 2006 during a presentation I put together for all the concerned parties. The EPA provided a conference room at Wanamakers department store in Philadelphia that was attended by more than three dozen representatives from Bucks County, Bristol Township, the Army Corps of Engineers, the EPA, the PADEP, and R&H. I may sound like the village braggart by saying this, but I was really on top of my game that day, and I came armed to the teeth with ammunition.

The Army Corps of Engineers was a strong ally on this project and continued to stress the fact that the dredging materials from the river were tested and certified to be clean; a study from Langan Engineering stated that Maple Beach's 100 acres posed no environmental threat to anyone and required no remediation at all; and the artist's drawings of the proposed site delivered the knockout punch I'd hoped for.

I could feel the tide was beginning to shift in our direction, but the focal point of the presentation was to convince R&H's representatives that there were legitimate ways of absolving the company from any environmental liability. That problem already existed and was not going to go away by just doing nothing. Burlington, New Jersey was a stone's throw away and continued to be at risk from any type of disastrous liquid spill or gaseous leak on R&H's manufacturing site. R&H had been paying hefty insurance premiums for years, and they also were responsible for maintaining the levees and roadways that protected the four remaining houses on Maple Beach.

Because R&H was the original owner that had caused whatever environmental conditions existed on the property, PA ACT 2 wasn't applicable to absolve them from responsibility. I came up with another solution: If the RDA took the property by amicable eminent domain and brought in the PADEP to help us clean up any outstanding problems and certify that the site had been remediated under PA ACT 2 guidelines, R&H could finally free itself from decades of environmental responsibility and the financial obligations that came with it. They would also be unloading 400 acres of unused land while finally giving something back to the community in which they had operated for a century.

A lot of compliments were handed out about the degree of planning and thought the RDA had brought to the table. The room was knee-deep in good vibes and good faith. The meeting finally ended with both sides agreeing to conduct appraisals of the R&H's waterfront property. In 2007, the RDA's appraisal came in at $15,000,000; R&H's figure was more than twice that at $37,000,000. The project died right there.

COSTS AND GRANTS:
- $200,000 from an ISRP grant to pay for the RDA's Phase 1 and Phase 2 inspection of Maple Beach. Matching 25% funds were paid by the EPA.

- $2,400 for the artist's Maple Beach drawings.

- $3,500 for the cost of our appraisal of R&H's property.

POLITICAL ISSUES: There was a lot of political infighting involved in the collapse of this project. I couldn't get the politicians to understand that ACT 2 absolved the township and the RDA from being responsible for the cleanup. We also needed the commissioners from the County of Bucks to issue a bond, but I knew our chances were slim and none. They weren't going to sign off on a $37,000,000 price tag. They never actually said no. In fact, it didn't even come up for a vote. They just didn't want to fight for it.

DEVELOPERS CHOSEN AND WHY: The RDA was temporarily the de facto developer during the planning stage of the Maple Beach project, but since it never progressed past the planning stages, no outside developers were recruited.

STATUS OF THE SITE TODAY: I spent two or three years after the appraisals came in trying in vain to resuscitate the Maple Beach project, but I knew the moment had passed. You usually get only one shot on a deal of this size and scope. Fears of perceived toxicity had crept back into people's minds, and the $37,000,000 price tag for unused, undeveloped land with no water, sewage, or electrical service was a nonstarter.

Sometime in 2009, R&H's Bristol Township operation was acquired by the Dow Chemical Company. They were extremely difficult to work with. I'd exhausted every trick in the book to try to change their minds, including offering to build only the industrial and commercial portions of our plan in exchange for their changing the wording of their property deed that prohibited residential use of any kind on the site. We wanted them to include a sunset date that would permit residential use of the site if and when Dow ever moved their operation out of the area. We even offered to provide no opening doors or windows on the side of the Maple Beach development that faced the chemical plant. But Dow wasn't really interested in hearing any counteroffers or rebuttals. They let me know in short time that they had no interest in proceeding any further with the Maple Beach negotiations. That was the final stake in the project's heart.

Little has changed in the sale's aftermath. Plastics, chemicals, and agricultural products are still produced at Dow's Bristol Township facility, although with a significantly reduced workforce. The same decades-old environmental conditions still exist on the grounds, particularly the ammonia sulfate plume that the EPA and the PADEP periodically monitor. Dow's liability problems continue to exist, yet while ownership of the 80-acre Croydon Woods on the western border of the site was transferred in 2016 to the Heritage Conservancy for preservation purposes, Maple Beach's 100 acres still face an unfulfilled and uncertain future.

This project really wore me out. It was the only challenge I ever took on in which I had to completely give up. But . . . not really. We hit a brick wall when that $37,000,000 R&H appraisal came down the pike, but within a few months, Maple Beach started gnawing at me again. Every so often, I find myself trying to figure out a way to get it going and rewrite history—like a fisherman returning to a mountain lake every season, casting for that monster catfish that got away from him years before when his line snapped during a titanic struggle.

Vince Lombardi once said, "We didn't lose the game; we just ran out of time." He was preaching to the choir. I have just started my eighth decade, so I realize I'm in the fourth quarter. Still, it's tough to let go of a generational project that could have had so great an impact on the county and its residents. You can call the Maple Beach Project Bob White's great white whale if you want, but I won't believe that until the clock reads 00:00.

THE GRUNDY POWERHOUSE

START AND COMPLETION DATES:
IDENTIFIED AS A PROBLEM IN 1999;
COMPLETED IN 2016.

LOCATION: Canal Street near Jefferson Avenue in Bristol Borough, one block from the SEPTA train station.

HISTORY OF THE SITE: For more than a century, the 186-foot-high clock tower on Canal Street has stood watch over Bristol's rise and fall as one of the East Coast's most important manufacturing centers. Through it all, the tower evolved into one of Bucks County's most iconic symbols. It was never a stand-alone structure. It was added on to the Grundy textile mill, a 300,000-square-foot complex of interconnected buildings, the tallest of which is seven stories high. Built by the Grundy family, construction began in 1880 and continued over the next three decades. After the death of company founder William H. Grundy in 1893, his son Joseph—who eventually became a US senator—took the helm of the family business for the next half century and was responsible for building the clock tower in 1911.

He also built a secondary building a few hundred feet away that supplied the heat and energy for the mill. The signature feature of this 28,000-square-foot, three-story powerhouse was an imposing, 180-foot-high chimney with the Grundy name prominently displayed in vertical block letters on its sandstone colored bricks.

During the 1930s—the Grundy Mill's most prosperous period—more than 850 workers were employed there. The mill and powerhouse stayed in the family and continued to operate until 1946, when they were sold. The main complex continued to be used for various industrial purposes until 1981, when a businessman named Fred Baumgarten purchased it as a distribution center for his own textile company. After a few years, he stopped producing textiles and turned the property into a state-of-the-art, multifaceted business complex whose new tenants included a whiskey distillery, a boxing gym, a dance studio, and a manufacturer of robotic systems.

The powerhouse's ultimate fate was not as impressive. By the early 1990s, it had ceased to be used as a heat and power supply for the compound next door. An elderly couple had purchased the property and was renting it out to an overhead door company who used it as a warehouse. In 2000, they moved out and the building was abandoned. The structure and the half-acre site on which it rested continued to deteriorate for another decade and a half.

The Grundy Powerhouse after it had fallen on hard times.

HOW THE RDA GOT INVOLVED: Alarmed by its decayed state, Bristol Borough brought the property to our attention in the late 1990s and asked us whether we could clean it up and repurpose it. When the RDA tried to purchase the building, its owners asked for $400,000. Due to the poor condition of the property and some internal environmental issues, it wasn't worth anywhere near that amount. The owners protested that we were overstating the property's problems. On appeal, the Bucks County Board of View sided with us. We acquired the property in 1999 by eminent domain and, after getting the final just compensation figure, we paid the former owners $110,000.

In 2001, the RDA listed the Grundy Powerhouse on its "big eight" DEP list of brownfield properties to be worked on.

ENVIRONMENTAL AND/OR BLIGHT ISSUES: The powerhouse had been decaying for decades. There were asbestos problems in the basement, and the main floor was in bad shape. It was part wood and part concrete—a bad mix that almost always results in rot at the point where the wood and concrete meet. There were also tons of discarded and outdated parts, fixtures, guide tracks, and fasteners left behind by the overhead door company when they moved out. All of them would have to be moved out and trucked to a dump.

COURSE OF ACTION FOR THE DEMOLITION AND CLEANUP: There was a six-year lag period before we began any environmental remediation or cleanup activities. During that time, we were waiting on the final verdict from the Board of View, and we were also looking for a developer to take on the project. A 2005 grant enabled us to clean up the asbestos in the basement, and EPA and DEP funding paid for cleaning out and securing the remainder of the building over the next few years. The RDA was flush with funds in the early 2000s due to having so many simultaneous projects going on. We could move money around from one project to the next without having to slow down the conveyor belt of progress.

The powerhouse's rotted wooden floor was left for the time being, awaiting a final design for the building's reuse. It made no sense to repair a floor without knowing how it would be used and what might be built on top of it.

COURSE OF ACTION FOR THE REUSE, PART 1: Tom Corrigan was a Bristol Borough councilman who went on to become a state representative in Harrisburg. He was a history buff with a big dream: He wanted the powerhouse to become a museum—an adjunct extension of the Mercer Museum, which was located in Doylestown. Since they owned a lot of Bucks County historical artifacts, the Mercer Museum was thrilled with the idea. Tom also wanted to reopen the Delaware Canal, which ran past the Grundy Commons and ended directly in front of the powerhouse. It had been a pet project of his for years, but he felt tying it in with the proposed museum would be great for tourism.

In 2003, a review team was set up to do a feasibility study, but Tom wasn't sitting on his hands. He used the down time to get an approval for a $5,000,000 grant. This was big! We had the right property; a brilliant, creative concept; and best of all, *the money*. There was no stopping us, or so we thought; then everything began to fall apart. The Mercer Museum couldn't get funding for the operating costs. A $5,000,000 museum with no one to run and staff it was not going to work.

DEVELOPER: We were down but not defeated. Moving on to plan B, we showed the building to a lot of people in hopes of finding a developer to take on the project. There were a lot of tire kickers interested in converting the property to a wide array of commercial uses. This went on for quite a few years and ended up with no serious takers. Then we caught the break we'd been looking for: We were approached by Keystone Heritage Group LLC, a developer that had scored a recent success in Bristol by converting the old Mill Street Theater to condos. They had instant credibility with us, and we had our second wind. We sold the property to Keystone in

2006 for $200,000 with the understanding that they had to give us a plan and a timeline.

COURSE OF ACTION FOR THE REUSE, PART 2: Keystone came up with an ambitious reuse proposal that involved 36 condos, restaurants, shopping, and a novel idea to convert the powerhouse's chimney into an observation deck for the condo tenants. Unfortunately, their proposal met the same fate as Tom Corrigan's museum concept. The recession killed the housing market, and Keystone was unable to land enough condo pre-sales to get a bank loan. They kept trying for another four or five years but, in the end, couldn't deliver the goods. In 2013, the property reverted back to the RDA and we had to return their $200,000.

Powerhouse
Luxury Residential Condominiums on the Canal's Edge

Keystone Heritage Group's vision of what the powerhouse condo complex would look like.

Finally out of options, and at the request of the Bristol Borough Council, the RDA gifted the powerhouse to Fred Baumgarten for $1.00 with the understanding that he had six months to tear down the building and another six to improve the property by developing the land and building a parking lot. Fred delivered on both ends in 2016, spending $300,000 to demolish the powerhouse and its chimney and then another $400,000 on building a 50-space parking lot where it once stood.

After more than a century, all that remained of the powerhouse was a pile of twisted girders and concrete rubble.

COSTS AND GRANTS:

- $110,000 paid by the RDA as just compensation for the acquisition of the powerhouse.

- $200,000 paid by Keystone for the conditional purchase of the property.

- $200,000 paid back to Keystone to reacquire the property after they failed to deliver on the specified purchase conditions.

- $200,000 of DEP and EPA funding granted to the RDA for the purpose of securing the building and remediating its interior problems, including the removal of the asbestos and the disposal of its interior contents.

- $1.00 paid by Fred Baumgarten in the gifting of the property by the RDA.

- $300,000 paid by Fred Baumgarten to demolish the powerhouse.

- $400,000 paid by Fred Baumgarten to develop the post-demolition powerhouse land and build the parking lot.

POLITICAL ISSUES: None.

CHALLENGES AND/OR SETBACKS: There were no battles on this one. There were good relations all around with a lot of good people. We just couldn't get it done. In the end, prohibitive costs and the financial climate that followed the Great Recession left our dreams unanswered.

STATUS OF THE SITE TODAY: Tom Corrigan's vision would have been a spectacular addition to Bristol Borough, but it was not to be. We all had to settle for much less. After the investment of more than 1,000 manpower hours, you can imagine the disappointment Tom, the borough, and everyone associated with the RDA and Keystone Heritage Group LLC felt at the final result. We didn't get what we wanted, yet I can't say the project was a complete loser. We got rid of a blighted, decaying building, and the parking lot was sorely needed by Grundy Commons. For far too long, their tenants had been forced to park significant distances away from where they worked.

Both Keystone and Fred Baumgarten were invoiced for the RDA's administration costs, but that provided little satisfaction. In show biz, romance, and even the construction business, timing is everything. The Grundy Powerhouse had passed its moment of resurrection. It just wasn't in the cards for it to come back.

Grundy Commons as it looks today. The Commons is a successful hub of economic activity, the parking lot is a useful addition, and the undeveloped canal is still a picturesque site, but it's hard not to lament the demise of Tom Corrigan's dream. If it had come to fruition, the entire Grundy complex would have been transformed into a major destination for the county.

THE U.S. MAGNET FACTORY

START AND COMPLETION DATES:
THE RDA'S INVOLVEMENT BEGAN IN THE
LATE 1990S. ACTIVITY STEPPED UP AFTER
2005, WHEN A DEVELOPMENT DEAL WAS
REACHED BETWEEN YARDLEY BOROUGH,
THE DEVELOPER, AND THE RDA. A LENGTHY
PERIOD OF ENVIRONMENTAL REMEDIATION
AND LAND DEVELOPMENT FOLLOWED THAT
WAS COMPLETED BY 2013.

LOCATION: Off of North Main Street in Yardley Borough.

HISTORY OF THE SITE: As its name would suggest, the U.S. Magnet Corporation was a company that manufactured magnets, but it also produced batteries for cars and trucks. Its factory was situated on a 23-acre plot of land in Yardley Borough with a few extra acres stretching into Lower Makefield Township. Magnet wasn't the first occupant at that location. Cold Spring Bleachery, a company that bleached cloth for industrial use, had a successful run at the same spot that lasted from the early 1900s into the first few years of the 1970s. When I was 25 years old in 1965, I actually used to plow snow from the site with a backhoe. The bleachery had a snow removal contract with my dad's construction company.

233

Magnet purchased the site from Cold Spring in the mid-1970s and began manufacturing their products in the same old building its predecessor used. After a decade in business, competition from Chinese and other overseas manufacturers who produced similar products ended U.S. Magnet's run. Done in by the lower-priced goods that flooded world markets (as well as the cheap labor forces that produced them), Magnet quit paying their mortgage and abandoned the property sometime in the mid-1980s. It stayed vacant and in disrepair for almost a decade and a half. The lone exception (and only safe part of the building) was where Magnet's administrative offices used to be located. A beer distributor had set up business there shortly after the company left and was apparently paying rent to the bank that held the mortgage. By the time the RDA began to focus its attention on the property, the remainder of the building had been abandoned for over a decade.

A late-1990s aerial photo of the U.S. Magnet site. By that time, it had become a ghost town in the middle of Yardley Borough.

HOW THE RDA GOT INVOLVED: The property first came to the attention of the RDA in late 1997, when it was identified as one of the original eight properties listed on the brownfield sites list we compiled. Our active participation began in the late 1990s, when we were approached by a developer who was interested in the property.

ENVIRONMENTAL AND/OR BLIGHT ISSUES: The U.S. Magnet building itself was a haphazard collection of old, single-level structures that were all connected together. It was in very poor shape when the RDA became involved. The roof was rusted and leaking, and overall, the entire structure was unsecured and in danger of collapsing.

Contained within the building's 200,000 square feet of surface area were numerous jugs and bottles of chemicals, as well as almost 50 barrels that contained unknown substances. The manufacturing process of the company's production of car and truck batteries left a great deal of waste on the property, including acid, plastics, lead, and other metals. After occupying the site and being in business for almost half a century prior to U.S. Magnet, I'm sure Cold Spring Bleachery also contributed to the property's collection of contaminants.

People were parking boats, RVs, and tractor trailers on the grounds, and—as if there weren't enough waste on the property—individuals would sneak in and illegally dump their own materials on the premises. With the building and its surrounding property being unsecured, the Magnet site was also the subject of random acts of vandalism. For far too long, it was an eyesore and a ticking time bomb that was getting worse year by year.

THE DEVELOPER: A company called Cold Springs Investment Group LLC (CSIG) became interested in purchasing the property for development in the late 1990s. Most likely, they heard about the opportunity when the beer distributor's original owner passed away and another distributor took over. After an initial inspection of the site, during which they became aware of the degree of environmental challenges on the grounds, CSIG came to the RDA for advice and assistance. There was no way they could turn a profit without the help of the state grants we specialized in obtaining.

This was a large-scale project that we could really sink our teeth into. A mutual cooperation agreement was struck with CSIG, in which they bought the title from the mortgage company and temporarily transferred it to the RDA in a voluntary eminent domain deal. Since no one wanted to own the property, it had never been fully foreclosed. The bank was happy to unload the site.

As bad as the site looked in the previous aerial photo, this close-up of one of the abandoned U.S. Magnet buildings accurately portrays the degree of deterioration and decay throughout the complex.

The RDA agreed to obtain state grants for the project and work at getting the local community and government officials on board. The developer agreed to pay all costs of the cleanup, land development, and the RDA's administrative costs. The overall financial setup was our typical 75/25 deal: We supplied 75% of the total budget in state grants, and the developer paid the remaining 25%—all of which was targeted to pay for the environmental cleanup portion of the budget.

POLITICAL AND COMMUNITY ISSUES: I was always of the opinion that "no" was not an answer, but if any project could make me revise that optimistic outlook, it was this one. In spite of whatever power of positive thinking I brought to the table, I have to confess that, at times, I thought it might never happen.

The U.S. Magnet site was the last piece of open land in Yardley Borough, so everyone wanted to make the right decision. Numerous promising ideas for the property were brought up, ranging from industrial usage to residential housing to creating a municipal park. Despite each concept's relative merits, the local community and its politicians contested every proposal. One roadblock after another impeded our path forward. The borough was concerned about significant increases in local truck traffic that could arise due to an industrial reuse of the site; many people felt the property's environmental problems could never be resolved enough to be safe for residential usage; and while many residents liked the concept of transforming the Magnet site into a beautiful recreational park, others in the borough didn't like the thought of spending a lot of money to create something that would generate no tax revenues.

It became obvious that education and community relations would need to play a significant role to get this project off the ground. It's very common for the principal deciders on a project to come in with an arsenal of negative ideas and wrong information. To counter this, the RDA put together two large-scale promotional presentations to explain our plans to the community. One of them was a public meeting at Yardley Borough Hall, where the PADEP and our environmental engineers addressed everyone's concerns about any existing toxicity on the site. Regardless of the professionalism and logic of their detailed and convincing arguments for the eventual safety of the site, the community was still not satisfied; they battled us on everything.

I began pounding the pavement in Yardley to create some enthusiasm and give the townsfolk the comfort level they needed to feel their concerns about the site's future use were being taken seriously. The borough's council members, in particular, needed to be convinced that if they approved the development of the Magnet site—which in their minds was a risky project—they wouldn't be putting their reelection chances in jeopardy. Another essential part of my public relations blitz was befriending the chief of police and asking him to assist the RDA in providing security for the site. Recognizing that the proposed project would be a major asset for Yardley Borough, the chief and the police department eagerly complied with our request.

Putting on our thinking caps, we also pursued a strategy of trying to convince the community they would have to give up something to get something back. The RDA brought two peripheral projects into the mix. One had to do with a deteriorating local dam. The Quakers have had a longstanding presence in Yardley that goes as far back as the late 1600s. Their meetinghouse was next to Lake Afton, where they liked to meditate to the sound of the water running over the dam. CSIG agreed to repair it to the tune of $250,000, and they also agreed to build a footbridge over a creek on the Magnet site to connect the property to North Main Street.

It's difficult to determine whether sweetening the deal with these two off-site improvements turned the tide or it was just our years of tenacity and patience, but after more than a decade of effort on everyone's part, we finally reached an irrevocable development plan with Yardley Borough in 2005.

COURSE OF ACTION FOR THE CLEANUP: The RDA and CSIG took on the site's environmental issues with the utmost seriousness and were prepared to use whatever means necessary to ensure the future safety of the site. In particular, to take on the environmental issues within the footprint of the building, a cleanup crew wearing hazmat suits was recruited to rid the building of the barrels, jars, and various other containers of known and unknown chemicals within.

Finally, after years of negotiations, investigation, testing, planning, and remediation, the U.S. Magnet grounds and building had been cleaned to PADEP standards. Residential housing was now a realistic possibility. Demolition of the building began in 2005 and was completed by early 2006.

CHALLENGES AND/OR SETBACKS: While the lengthy cleanup phase was progressing, Cold Springs LLC wasn't sitting on their hands. They were looking ahead, working with their engineers and consulting team to come up with a land development plan the borough would feel good about approving. Many submissions and eventual modifications and revisions were presented in hopes of offsetting the community's negativity surrounding the project.

From the start, the RDA and CSIG expected and made plans for dealing with this particular challenge. What we didn't expect was the necessity of acquiring and adding a small additional piece of land to the project to meet PennDOT (Pennsylvania Department of Transportation) requirements for roadway access to the property. Some homeowners near the site were fearful of being forced to move. Others feared a drop in the value of their real estate. During the year it took to resolve the situation, the future of the Magnet site project was in constant jeopardy.

Because of this hurdle and numerous others, the security of the site during this long, drawn-out process became a major issue. From the very beginning, the RDA was quick to recognize the dangerous conditions the site presented. The last thing we needed was any lawsuits that might arise due to someone getting injured on the property—regardless of whether they were on the premises legally or not. The official posting of the property along with all the "*NO TRESPASSING!*" signs displayed around the site weren't proving to be enough of a deterrent to any kids or curiosity seekers who might want to explore the abandoned building. We finally brought in security guards to ensure everyone's safety.

At the end of the cleanup phase, the final approval for residential housing on the site was obtained from the PADEP. That satisfied everyone's concerns about what the site's end use would be, particularly in regard to its suitability and safety for a future housing community.

COSTS AND GRANTS: The timing couldn't have been better when CSIG approached the RDA. The State of Pennsylvania had recently started their Industrial Sites Reuse Program (ISRP).

- $250,000 for the property's environmental assessment. Seventy-five percent of this was paid by an ISRP grant we obtained. The remaining twenty-five percent was paid by CSIG.

- The cleanup and demolition were well over $1,000,000. Through another ISRP grant the RDA obtained, we covered the first $1,000,000. The remaining cost, which approached $600,000, was paid by CSIG. Approximately $400,000 of that $600,000 contribution was used to pay for the demolition.

- $250,000 paid by CSIG to repair the dam at Lake Afton.

STATUS OF THE SITE TODAY: After almost 15 years of development, CSIG and the RDA sold the former U.S. Magnet site to Orleans home-builders in 2013. Ground was broken in 2014, and after three years of construction, Yardley Walk—a residential enclave of 63 luxury homes in the $700,000 to $800,000 range—made its debut in 2017. As a sign of how proud one of CSIG's general partners was regarding what his company had accomplished and the quality level that was delivered, he purchased and currently lives in one of Yardley Walk's houses.

The quadrangle at the center of Yardley Walk.

The windfall of tax revenues these new homes continue to generate for Yardley Borough has been a major boon to the local economy, the school district, and the variety of services the borough is able to offer to its citizenry.

The time spent on this project and the immense satisfaction of all who participated in its completion cannot be overstated. It seemed at times like the project would never get finished, but we all kept the faith and persevered. Not all of the RDA's successes happen in days, months, or even years. Some projects took a decade or more, requiring important contributions from committed communities, government officials, and several different developers, all bringing their ideas and dreams to the process. This was a great, long-term success for the RDA and all involved.

When you look at the luxury condos and elegantly manicured grounds of Yardley Walk, it's difficult to fathom that a site like the U.S. Magnet factory ever existed within the same space.

THE PENN SALT
MANUFACTURING COMPANY

START AND COMPLETION DATES:
1996 TO 2017.

LOCATION: Between State Road and the Delaware River in Bensalem, Pennsylvania.

HISTORY OF THE SITE: The World War II mini spy drama narrated in this book's preface depicted Penn Salt during its most significant period of operation. After the war, the company gradually moved away from aluminum refining and cryolite production but still remained in the chemical business. Its new products included refrigerants, hydrochloric acid, and cleaning and lubricating agents for the laundry and metalworking industries. Sometime during this period, Penn Salt changed its name to the Pennwalt Corporation and then merged in 1989 with a French chemical company called Elf Atochem. Production continued until 1997, when all manufacturing operations at the facility ceased, equipment was removed, and the buildings were vacated.

HOW THE RDA GOT INVOLVED: Penn Salt was one of the eight original properties identified on the RDA's 1996 brownfield sites list, but we really didn't get involved until 2000 when Bensalem Township and Atochem brought us into the mix. They were looking for help in remediating the site's environmental problems. In spite of the RDA assuring Atochem that ACT 2 got them off the financial hook, they feared what could be found on their grounds and its resultant economic consequences.

They were working with an environmental engineering company that planned to accept ownership of the property from them in exchange for cleaning the environmental contamination on the property. The environmental company began assessing the property in 2003 and was preparing a cleanup plan, but as time dragged on, a new developer stepped to the forefront. Mignatti Companies wanted to purchase the property and was willing to accept the obligation of remediating it to the satisfaction of all concerned.

Mignatti knew early on they were looking at a $6,000,000-plus cleanup bill, and they needed help on the financing end. In 2006, a cooperation agreement was worked out with them in which the RDA was asked to accept the title to the property (after Mignatti's purchase) in order to assist them in obtaining public funding and carrying out the remediation. We eventually took the property off the tax rolls, which also helped lessen their financial burden while the project moved forward.

ENVIRONMENTAL AND/OR BLIGHT ISSUES: In all my years at the RDA, this was the most contaminated property we ever faced. More than six decades of chemical production had deposited tons of toxic cryolite on the site, along with TCE, PCE, PAHs, PCBs, pesticides, and arsenic. The environmental problems weren't limited just to land: A canal coming off the Delaware River that fed into the property also exhibited some of the same problems.

All of this had taken a heavy toll on the Penn Salt compound. During World War II, grass, weeds, and all other vegetation were completely absent from the grounds surrounding the site's buildings. As the years passed, Mother Nature made a modest comeback. By the 1990s, a hint of life had emerged once more on the property, but it was a stretch to describe the existing scrub brush as "life."

Atochem had done a preliminary study of the soil and groundwater at the site in 1996. Numerous other tests were conducted and supervised by the RDA, the EPA, and the Pennsylvania DEP. Due to the extent of the environmental problems, the testing went on for almost a decade. The unanimous conclusions indicated that the concentration of contaminants far exceeded acceptable Pennsylvania DEP ACT 2 cleanup levels.

Penn Salt was still a busy, thriving business when this picture was taken. Because of the proximity of the Delaware River and the canal that ran into the river (situated along the far left of the photo), it's easy to see why Bensalem and Atochem had environmental concerns that extended past the Penn Salt property.

The distinctive sawtooth roofs of Penn Salt's buildings had a structural basis and also provided natural lighting during the daytime.

COURSE OF ACTION FOR THE CLEANUP: At the same time the environmental assessments were going on, Bucks County and the RDA were conducting a riverfront study that included all the municipalities that bordered the Delaware River from the Philadelphia line all the way north to the 330-foot "Trenton Makes The World Takes" sign on the bridge connecting Morrisville to Trenton. I rented a boat to take pictures from the river looking toward the land to help in our determination.

The signature "Trenton Makes The World Takes" bridge across the Delaware River that was the northern boundary of the Bucks County and RDA riverfront study.

The study included possible reuses for the Penn Salt property. The overwhelming verdict was that industrial usage had dominated the waterfront for far too many years; it was time to turn Bensalem's valuable riverfront property into a residential housing community.

That goal made it absolutely necessary to go all-in on cleaning the property. The specs required for safe, human habitation would be far more stringent than those used for industrial reuse. We were taking no chances on this project. Two different environmental companies were working on the site and were employing double testing. One company performed the remediation while the other verified the first company's results.

The site's cleanup began in 2006 and continued for several years. Penn Salt's campus consisted of two long, single-story buildings with high ceilings and sawtooth roofs that ran parallel to the river. They were surrounded by several other smaller buildings with similar profiles. All of them were razed, and their concrete was crushed and used as a portion of the fill material needed to replace the 43,700 tons of contaminated ground soil that was removed and sent to an EPA-approved landfill.

Numerous smaller details also had to be dealt with, like the removal of underground fuel oil storage tanks that were discovered near one of the smaller buildings. After all the heavy lifting was done on the site, several years of monitoring the groundwater and soil gas followed.

DEVELOPER CHOSEN AND WHY: The RDA didn't choose Mignatti as their developer; *Mignatti Companies chose the RDA.* They needed our assistance in what they knew would be a massive, complex undertaking. The project caught a lucky break when they stepped forward, because their presence got Atochem off the hook. Mignatti was a well-respected, qualified home building company that had been in business since the early 1900s. They also had a history of building several other town house communities in Bucks County and nearby Montgomery County.

COURSE OF ACTION FOR THE REUSE: Mignatti's master plan didn't involve just the Penn Salt Property. The overall project covered three parcels in Bensalem that totaled 45 acres. Penn Salt was the largest of the three. With the township's approval, Mignatti presented an ambitious plan to build 700 luxury townhouses (250 on the former Penn Salt site and 450 on the other two parcels) along with 40,000 square feet of commercial, retail, and office space. A marina was also proposed, and an abundance of green space was conceptualized to make the residents feel like they were living in Bucks County.

The cleanup phase was well underway, and it looked like Bensalem would have a terrific new upscale riverfront community in record time . . . but then the Great Recession hit in 2007 and 2008.

Although land development continued on the site, construction was held off for six years, during which time Mignatti partnered up with a Los Angeles real estate investment and management company named Resmark Land and Housing. Construction finally began in 2014, and Mignatti built more than 100 new homes over the next three years but eventually sold off everything to Lennar Homes in 2017.

The expanding Mignatti/Lennar townhouse development is getting close to reaching the open space in the photo's forefront where the main Penn Salt buildings were situated. The new community is called Waterside.

COSTS AND GRANTS: The former Penn Salt property was located in an area designated as a state enterprise zone, which enabled the RDA to obtain priority consideration in getting grants.

- A $200,000 ISRP grant from the DEP to the RDA to clean up the canal coming off the Delaware.
- A $250,000 EPA Brownfields Grant in 2005 for cleaning up the site.

- A $975,000 EPA loan awarded to Mignatti through the RDA Environmental Revolving Loan Fund at 2% interest. It may seem like a sweetheart deal for Mignatti, but remember, they wound up having to carry the financial burden of the site for years, and even though our fund did not require payments of principal during this timeline, it did require Mignatti to pay the interest each year.

- The RDA also helped Mignatti get a Commonwealth of Pennsylvania PENNVEST loan of more than $5,000,000 for the cleanup. It began as a low-interest loan with payments of interest only (no principle) for the first 10 years. After that, PENNVEST required the developer to begin paying principal payments along with an increased interest rate.

- Financing for the construction of the townhouses came from a private source after the RDA was no longer involved.

CHALLENGES AND/OR SETBACKS: *Time* itself was the biggest challenge on this project. The RDA certainly wasn't planning on owning the Penn Salt site for 14 years, but that's how it worked out. Atochem spent six or seven years determining whether it wanted to take on the responsibility and cost of cleaning the environmental problems. Another three years passed before the cleanup began in 2006, and then the recession paralyzed Mignatti and everyone else, placing a seven-year delay on any construction. The only thing that wasn't subject to the delays that the passage of time imposed on everyone was the monthly payments and interest on all the loans—specifically the PENNVEST loan. Because of the financial hardship imposed on the developer by the Recession, we tried to get PENNVEST to lower its interest rate, but they declined to do so (probably because that same recession was hard on them too).

STATUS OF THE SITE TODAY: A spectacular town house community has been constructed on two of the three parcels. Lennar continues to build on the property and plans are still in place for the marina and the mixed-use office, retail, and commercial structures, but as of 2020, they have yet to be built. After more than half a century of stifling toxicity, the Penn Salt parcel is finally clean as a whistle, and—miracle of miracles—beautiful green grass has finally returned to its former grounds. Chalk one up for Mother Nature.

Between its waterfront location and the variety of well-thought-out town house designs, Waterside feels more like a resort than a suburb of Philadelphia.

That's me speaking at the press conference for the Waterside community, during which I presented a check to Mignatti Companies to help fund the cleanup of the Penn Salt site. As usual, we always tried to make press events out of these types of ceremonies to publicize the new project and bring attention to the services the RDA was able to provide to Bucks County. This particular ceremony was covered by Channel 6 ABC News.

ACTION MANUFACTURING

START AND COMPLETION DATES:
JULY 2011 TO JANUARY 2012.

LOCATION: The original location for Action Manufacturing was an aging building next to St. Christopher's Hospital in the Erie Avenue section of North Philadelphia. Its new home is in the Keystone Industrial Park in Bristol, Pennsylvania.

HISTORY OF THE SITE: Maybe it was the Marine in me that was the reason this project captured my imagination and drew me in. Action Manufacturing is a company that designs and produces military ordnance, specifically firing caps (known as fuzes). In other words, they manufacture the triggers that make artillery and rockets go *boom*. Action had been in business since 1946. Its owners and front office had a great deal of pride in their history—and with good reason: They were survivors. After navigating the rough waters and up and down budgets of the Department of Defense for six and a half decades, it was still a solvent, productive company. Some of its income also came from state department–approved, "friendly" foreign customers like Canada and other US allies.

In 2011, Action decided it was time to move from its longtime North Philadelphia facility to a new location. North Carolina was considered as a potential destination, and Governor Bev Purdue tried her best to lure Action and its 350 military industrial jobs to the Tar Heel State. One of the primary reasons they were considering a 450-mile move to the South was they were getting no traction from local commonwealth government agencies like the Industrial Development Authority (IDA) and the Economic Development Corporation (EDC).

Action had been shopping for someone or some agency that could help them make a smooth transition, find the right property, and aid them in maneuvering through the gauntlet of planning commissions, engineering requirements, zoning restrictions, and above all, ease community apprehension about having a weapons manufacturer in its midst. The initial "someone" they were looking for was State Representative Tina Davis of Bristol Township.

ENVIRONMENTAL AND/OR BLIGHT ISSUES: There were no environmental or blight issues involved. Action just wanted to move from an old, out-of-date building in a dicey neighborhood to a modern facility that fit its current needs and enabled its workers to work night shifts without fear of getting mugged.

HOW THE RDA GOT INVOLVED (COURSE OF ACTION, PART 1): Within two days of when Tina Davis and I spoke about the project, I set up a meeting that included Action's front office people, the governor's action team, State Senator Robert Tomlinson's office, Tina Davis's office, Bristol Township's manager William McCauley, its zoning officer Tom Scott, the EDC, and the staff of the RDA. Action's executives got the chance to ease everyone's fears about the safety issues and security of the military products they manufactured, and then, on behalf of the RDA, I gave my patented pitch about the services we could offer. In a meeting that lasted several hours, the legislator's offices and Bristol Township's staff offered their assistance while the economic agencies offered little more than their usual, "Fill out the forms and we'll get back to you in a few days."

Tina was very concerned, and we agreed in private that we had to do something quickly or Bucks County was going to lose Action Manufacturing and its 350 jobs to North Carolina. While flirting with the move down south, Action had also been simultaneously shopping for sites in Bucks County. They had found a promising location in Bristol Township's Keystone Industrial Park, but could we get the county to move fast enough to convince Action to pull the trigger and select it as its new home?

CHALLENGES AND/OR SETBACKS: At first, the primary challenge for me was to bring all the economic development and planning agencies to the table to see what incentives were available to assist Action in making its move to Bucks County. Each of the agencies had different programs to offer, but the paperwork to get them was far too involved and cumbersome to help expedite the impending move Action was contemplating.

A personal matter further muddled the waters. The RDA offered Action a 2% loan to help with the costs of moving all their equipment from Philadelphia to Bucks County. The company executive who would be responsible for filling out the mountainous pile of the loan's application forms had a close relative who was dying. Under his current circumstances, there was no way he had the time or energy to spend days filling out the technical and financial data requested on the forms. Besides, Action wasn't looking for funding or financial incentives anyway. They had all the money they needed courtesy of their affiliate AMC Investments. What they were short on was time and guidance.

COURSE OF ACTION, PART 2: Realizing going through the normal channels and procedures wouldn't get the job done, the RDA bypassed them and fast tracked Action through all the bureaucracy of land development and local governmental agencies' procedures and requirements.

Instead of waiting for Action to obtain its own private inspector to see what it needed, I suggested they ask the township to provide that service.

In no time, Bristol Township and its zoning officer Tom Scott were all over it. This alone was a major leap forward because it enabled Action to determine what needed to be done to obtain its required certificate of occupancy. (A business can't move into a property without a township issuing that document.) Sometimes all you need to do is offer some TLC, a helping hand, and the convenience of one-stop shopping. Simplifying things helped Action Manufacturing decide Bucks County would be its new home.

COSTS AND GRANTS: No public money was spent on this project, there were no grants involved, and no money was earned by the RDA. There was nothing to invoice. You don't always need to throw around money or other incentives as an enticement to make a deal happen. The entire process consisted of just sweat equity over a short period of time—all of which benefitted Bristol Township and Bucks County in the end.

DEVELOPER: No developer was involved.

GOVERNMENT AND POLITICAL INVOLVEMENT: I'm a lifelong Republican, and throughout much of my career, I've relied on Republican power brokers like Harry Fawkes and Mike Fitzpatrick. Senator Tomlinson is also a Republican, but Tina Davis is a Democrat. So are Bristol Township's William McCauley and Tom Scott, and historically, Bristol Township has generally been a Democratic stronghold. Yet we were all able to work together for a beneficial common cause. I've always taken great pride in my ability to get along and work with everybody, regardless of their political affiliation.

Bristol Township has always been extremely business friendly and very supportive of the projects the RDA has brought them over the years. This one was no exception, but the excessive paperwork situation disturbed me. As diplomatically as possible, I brought up the issue with the county's various economic agencies and planning commissions. I knew it would go nowhere, but I'm always looking for ways to be more efficient and make things happen. That's difficult to do sometimes when procedures and regulations hold things up.

The engineering firms that review projects for municipalities are often the primary culprits for bogging down projects, but I don't want to be too harsh in that assessment. There's a fine line between being taking sufficient time to be thorough and padding billable hours by stretching things out. Sometimes they cross that line; sometimes they don't. Either way, I have no doubt those are problems every municipality in the country deals with on a daily basis.

Action Manufacturing's headquarters in Bristol's Keystone Industrial Park.

STATUS OF THE SITE TODAY: After only a few months, Bucks County welcomed Action Manufacturing and its 350 jobs with open arms. With no interruption to its business activities, it began the relocation process in January 2012, and by October, the move was complete. The gratifying feelings of accomplishment and teamwork that resulted from the overall experience were well worth the price of admission.

MILLER TRAILER PARK

START AND COMPLETION DATES:
2015 TO 2017.

LOCATION: Near the Croyden train station at the intersection of Cedar and Main Avenues in Croyden, Bristol Township, Pennsylvania.

HISTORY OF THE SITE: For almost half a century, 50 trailers occupied a three-acre site in Croydon that had formerly been the home of the Quaker Rubber Company. Most, if not all, were inhabited on a rental basis. Over the years, the trailers' conditions had deteriorated, making this mobile home community a local eyesore. The property was owned by a Bucks County commissioner who sold it in the mid-2000s to a development company.

The intent was to clear the land and build a community of new town houses. By 2007, the trailer park was shuttered and the developer began the work of demolishing and removing the old trailers. That's when their problems began.

ENVIRONMENTAL AND/OR BLIGHT ISSUES: Before demolition started, neighbors began complaining of scrap metal being strewn around the site from people stripping the vacated mobile homes. Once demolition commenced, scraps of rubber waste product were also discovered on the property that had been dumped there during its Quaker Rubber period.

257

Miller Trailer Park during its last year of occupancy.

HOW THE RDA GOT INVOLVED: The developer wasn't prepared to handle blight and environmental conditions, so they came to us to help clean up the site. In 2015, we formed a cooperation agreement and got to work. In order for us to get involved in the cleanup, the RDA had to own the property. We accepted the book value of the mortgage but didn't pay anything. The developer continued to be responsible for making the mortgage payments, there was no closing, and no money was exchanged in the transaction since the RDA acquired the property by amicable eminent domain.

COURSE OF ACTION FOR THE CLEANUP: Cleanup began in summer of 2015. Phase 1 and Phase 2 investigations confirmed the rubber and metal waste, but no toxic environmental conditions were detected. Upon completion, the cleaned site was left as an open, grassy space.

CHALLENGES AND/OR SETBACKS: The developer had approached Bristol Township and presented a proposal to build 30 townhouses where the trailers had once stood. Since the mid-2000s, the township had wanted to see the trailers removed, and now it had finally happened. The engineers and planning commission had only heard or seen sketch plans on the proposed development. Now, they had a full set of plans submitted for their approval. But they approved only 26 of the requested 30 new townhouses. That killed the developer's profit margin, and with it the proposed housing development.

The community really didn't want more housing, but they were willing to compromise. The 26 homes figure was their concession position. The developer had been too quick on the draw in demolishing the site. Once the trailers had been removed, they lost their principal bargaining chip. The township dug in its heels and waited. But time was a luxury the developer did not have. They had to continue making the mortgage payments on the site while negotiations plodded on. They had already invested a sizable amount of capital on the demolition and couldn't afford to play the waiting game. Their bank account was hemorrhaging money.

Following the hauling away of the trailers and the cleaning of the site, the removal of the trees in the center of the grounds was the last task that needed to be completed before the development phase of the park project began.

COURSE OF ACTION FOR THE REUSE: As time passed with no progress being made, the empty lot became overgrown with weeds and brush. It was benefitting no one. After more than eight years, the point had arrived where the developer just wanted out. With the townhouse concept dead in the water, the developer was hoping the RDA could get them out of the deal and find a reuse for the property.

Discussions with the township indicated it wanted to build a recreational park on the site. I became the middleman facilitating the sale to the township of what, at the time, was the RDA's cleared and cleaned property. The $663,000 sale price went to the developer. In 2018, the township secured partial financing for the construction of the park through a DCED grant. By the end of the summer, Croydon had a beautiful new recreational facility.

COSTS AND GRANTS:

- The RDA acquired the property in March 2015 via amicable eminent domain for the remaining amount of the mortgage, which was $663,000. This was by no means an easy task. We had to negotiate with the mortgage company and the developer so everybody would be in agreement. The money came from open space funding from Bucks County and Bristol Township.

- $100,000 to clean up the rubber and metal waste on the site. Seventy-five percent of that figure came from an ISRP grant to the RDA. The developer paid the remaining twenty-five percent.

- $240,000 DCED grant to Bristol Township to redevelop the former Miller Trailer Park into a recreational park. The remainder of the $700,000 cost of creating the park was paid by the township.

POLITICAL ISSUES/AND OR GOVERNMENT INVOLVEMENT: State Rep. Tina Davis and Senator Tommy Tomlinson helped the township land the grant for developing the park.

STATUS OF THE SITE TODAY: Cedar Avenue Park was dedicated in 2018. Three acres of blighted mobile homes had been replaced by professionally landscaped grounds with shady trees, conveniently placed benches, and a well-lit, paved path for jogging or leisurely walks. Nearby street parking was improved, and a classy-looking black metal fence fanned out from a stone entry wall and surrounded the entire park. This is a really exceptional facility. The township did itself proud.

The developer didn't fare quite as well. They had invested a significant amount of money and time on the project and come away with nothing. The RDA did a good deed helping them out of their financial predicament before the losses got any worse. I wish we could have done more for them, but on the positive side of things, I was very happy we had played a role in significantly improving the quality of life for Croydon's residents.

After years of tolerating the run-down trailer park, the surrounding neighborhood welcomed the newly constructed Cedar Avenue Park with open arms.

ALL IN A DAY'S WORK

Author's note: By no means was this book intended to be a complete history of every RDA project that took place during the years I worked there. For that, I'd need to add several more volumes. The work of cleaning up a county's past and repurposing it for the future evolves just as much from the sum of lots of small and medium-sized projects as it does from the multimillion-dollar, headline-grabbing affairs you read about in the previous files. The following assortment of redevelopment projects reflects typical, year-to-year RDA activity over a two-decade time span. Some are mundane, and some are historic and transformational. A few of the projects involve quick fixes, while others show important thought and foresight, but all were united by the dedication and commonality of purpose of the county's politicians, municipalities, and of course, the staff of our redevelopment authority.

LOCKHEED MARTIN (1996) – A potentially invaluable opportunity presented itself to Bucks County: Aerospace and advanced technologies giant Lockheed Martin was interested in building a large facility in Newtown Township that would employ 1,200 local workers. It would take a substantial incentive package to make it happen. The primary obstacle holding up the move was a lack of infrastructure on the property they were looking at. The RDA was asked to apply for a DCED grant in the amount of $2,000,000 to bring water and sewer service to the site. The state agreed on the condition that Lockheed Martin had to provide us with annual financial reports to verify the job creation statistics. The company operated out of this 57-acre facility for almost two decades until cutbacks in US government contracts caused them to downsize and close up some of their operations.

BATH STREET APARTMENTS (1996) – The RDA assisted the Borough of Bristol in a program that required the purchase of several properties that had been converted into apartments. The principal objective of the program was to improve the quality and appearance of these buildings by converting them from apartments to privately owned homes. The reasoning was simple: Homeowners take care of their properties; landlords don't. Landlords will usually do the absolute minimal number of repairs they can get away with to maximize their property's earning potential.

Our first project was a four-apartment brick twin on Bath Street. The RDA borrowed $160,000 from the First National Bank in Newtown and used $80,000 for the building's purchase and the remaining $80,000 for the property's rehabilitation back to a twin home. It was sold to two new homeowners at $80,000 each. The deals contained five-year soft mortgages of $5,000, and the new owners had to agree not to lease their homes during that period of time. (Soft mortgages are secondary mortgages at below market interest rates that help homeowners make down payments and pay for closing costs.)

EPA, DCED, AND ISRP GRANTS (1997) – Chinese culture has a long tradition of naming years after their zodiac animals. We've all heard slogans like "Year of the Dragon," "Year of the Monkey," and "Year of the Dog." If I had to choose a name for 1997, it would have been "Year of the Grant." All those grants I referred to in connection with many of our large-scale projects—they didn't just materialize out of thin air. A lot of paperwork, manpower hours, and political maneuvering preceded every grant authorization, especially in 1997 when all those efforts went toward obtaining grants to pay for large-scale projects like the renovation of the A. B. Murray building, dredging the turning basin for the Port of Bucks, and the costs of researching and compiling the final EPA brownfields list.

UNION CAMP PAPER CORP. (1998) – New Hope Borough asked the RDA to assist them by designating a certified redevelopment area in the portion of their community that included the former Union Camp property. Two large water towers loomed over the sprawling, run-down facility of interconnected buildings that were situated on a canal right next to New Hope's passenger train station. The company had discontinued its paper products operation several years earlier and had not been successful in selling the property. Once the RDA shined a bright light on the project, several developers became interested. Eventually, a private developer named George Michaels purchased the site and turned this sow's ear into a silk purse. One row of Union Camp buildings was torn down and the other was refurbished. The site is now home to a retail center with half a dozen stores.

THE BRISTOL BOROUGH TRAIN STATION (1999) – A group from the Bristol Cultural & Historical Foundation came to the RDA for assistance in rehabilitating the Bristol Borough passenger train station. It was an important piece of Bucks County's past, but it had become abandoned and blighted. After obtaining some grants, I managed and scheduled the entire renovation of the building. It currently looks just like it did in the days when it was a stop on the Southeastern Pennsylvania Transportation Authority (SEPTA) train system. For several years, the rehabbed building was home to a bagel restaurant and now serves as a day-care center.

THE RED LION INN (2000) – In 1781 on their way to the Battle of Yorktown, George Washington and his troops camped out behind this historic inn. More than two centuries later in 1991, a lot of that history was erased when the Red Lion Inn—a popular restaurant at the time—burned to the ground. The site was left with probable but unknown environmental conditions. Upon inspection, four large fuel tanks filled with cement and other materials were found on the site. They were probably left from an adjacent gas station that had been abandoned long ago. All four were removed and the property was deeded to the Township of Bensalem. Plans are in the works to turn the site into a water pumping station for a utilities company called Aqua.

MORRISVILLE FREIGHT YARD FEASIBILITY STUDY (2000) – The RDA and the Bucks County Planning Commission conducted an exhaustive two-year study to assess the feasibility of building a passenger train station at the Morrisville Freight Yard. The objective was to get New Jersey transit to provide Bucks County commuters with on-site parking and direct rail service to Trenton and their Northeast Corridor trains to New York City. It was determined that the project could be done, but prohibitive costs resulted in no action being taken by the county commissioners. The study remains at the offices of the RDA.

BRISTOL BOROUGH HIGH SCHOOL (2000) – State Representative Thomas Corrigan asked the RDA to administer a $250,000 grant to upgrade and improve the borough's high school track and field facility. The existing track had been outdated for years, and the field itself was in sore need of attention and sodding. The project was a instant success with the community, as was everything Mr. Corrigan got involved with.

THE MILL STREET SHOPPING DISTRICT (2001) – The Borough of Bristol asked the RDA to acquire four blighted, dilapidated buildings in the 400 block of Mill Street. After the acquisitions, all of them were demolished. A Delaware Canal visitor center was planned for the site, but that never materialized. The property was deeded back to Bristol Borough and is now a part of the "Bristol Borough Raising the Bar" campaign to help stimulate business activity by improving the municipality's Mill Street shopping district.

THE CLOVERLEAF RESTAURANT (2001) – Morrisville Borough approached the RDA to acquire the abandoned Cloverleaf Restaurant located at 850 Pennsylvania Avenue. At the time, there were several agencies looking to purchase the property and convert it into low-income housing—an outcome the borough wanted to avoid. The RDA was able to obtain a grant to pay for the amicable purchase from the owner and the subsequent demolition of the building. It was converted it into a grassy field that was added to what is now a 12-acre parcel that is under agreement of sale. That land is the focal point of ongoing discussions for a large-scale project that would transform downtown Morrisville.

DELAWARE RIVER ACCESS FOR MORRISVILLE (2002) – There was a vacant property on Riverview Avenue that was up for sale after the owner died. This parcel of land went straight from Riverview Avenue to the Delaware River's edge. If someone bought and developed it, the borough would never have access to the river at that point. That threatened Morrisville's long-term plans to be part of an uninterrupted recreational pathway that would run through all the lower Bucks County municipalities that bordered the river.

As a preventative measure on the borough's behalf, the RDA purchased the property, demolished the home, and subdivided the lot into five parcels. Four houses now occupy the four parcels running from Riverview Avenue toward the river. The fifth parcel—the one bordering the river—was deeded to Morrisville Borough, ensuring it will always have access to the river along the length of their waterfront.

BRISTOL BOROUGH RECREATIONAL FACILITIES IMPROVEMENT (2002) – This was another one of State Representative Thomas Corrigan's numerous pet projects for Bristol Borough. He asked the RDA to apply for and administer a state grant to upgrade the local community track, storage room, and restroom facility. The RDA obtained the grant, hired the contractors, and managed the project.

THE SPREAD EAGLE INN (2002) – Northampton Township wanted to improve the flow of traffic in the center of Richboro, specifically near the corner of Almshouse Road and Second Street Pike. They wanted to widen the road, but that's where the old Spread Eagle Inn was located. The inn had been vacant for some time, so the township manager asked the RDA to acquire it. Under normal circumstances, we would have just demolished it, but the centuries-old Spread Eagle Inn had historic signif- icance. Because of that, we demolished only the portion of the building that was an add-on structure. For the original part of the building, we obtained a grant to help pay for jacking it up and moving it 50 feet away onto a new foundation. Northampton paid for the property's acquisition and contributed to the costs of moving the building. The original build- ing still exists, but it is no longer an inn. It was sold to a developer for approximately $800,000.

COATES AVENUE SCHOOL PARKING LOT (2003) – Working with the Township of Bristol and its mayor Sam Fenton, the RDA was able to purchase one acre of land from Crownwood Estates for use with the town- ship's parks and recreation. Fenced off and paved, it now serves as a parking lot for the neighborhood and park area at the Coates Avenue School.

LOWER BUCKS HOSPITAL (2003) – State Senator Tomlinson and State Rep. Thomas Corrigan obtained a $5,000,000 RACP grant to construct a new emergency room for the Lower Bucks Hospital. The RDA prepared all the documentation and administered the grant for the project. It was a huge success because it provided the hospital and the community with a state-of-the-art emergency room facility.

318 AND 320 OTTER STREET (2004) – Bristol Borough asked the RDA to acquire and demolish these two run-down Otter Street homes. The land was sold to RPM, a private developer that built a single-family home.

THE NORTHAMPTON SENIOR CENTER (2005) – The RDA applied for and received a $500,000 RACP grant for the Northampton Senior Center. We administered the grant and provided progress inspection while the center was being constructed. The grant was used for the final payments for the center's construction.

PENNRIDGE COMMUNITY SENIOR CENTER (2005) – The RDA applied for and received a $500,000 grant to help build the Pennridge Community Senior Center. However, they could not accept the grant because it called for paying all workers the prevailing wage scale as set by the commonwealth. That requirement, which was in line with prevailing union labor costs, broke the senior center's construction budget. The unfortunate part was they waited until the last minute to decline the grant, so we were unable to repurpose the funds to another project.

DELAWARE RIVER LAND USE STUDY (2005) – The RDA was asked to cohost a study with the Bucks County Planning Commission's executive director, Lynn Bush, and the six county municipalities that border the Delaware River from Bensalem to Morrisville. It was a long and detailed study that required committee meetings be held for the public and each individual municipality so we could be sure everyone had a say on the future land uses examined in the study. We developed six opportunity zones with acceptable land uses, and I am proud to say this is one of those rare studies that did more than just collect dust on a shelf. As of this date, four of the opportunity zones are in process and in line with the study's results.

30 JOLLY LANE, LEVITTOWN, PENNSYLVANIA (2005) – This home burned down and was left vacant and unattended for years. It was also set ablaze several more times after the initial fire. I first read about it in the *Bucks County Courier Times* and then contacted Bristol Township, which asked us to acquire the property, fill in the pool area, demolish the home, and find a new owner to rebuild in the same location. After many inquiries about the site, we finally found a developer willing to take on the challenge. When it was completed, a beautiful new home occupied the property, and as you can imagine, the surrounding community was pleased to be rid of the eyesore. This was one of those situations in which numerous outstanding liens were at play, so no one came forward to accept the just compensation. Instead, it was paid to the county court, which would ultimately decide where and how to distribute those funds.

ROUTE 13 TRAILER PARK (2006) – This project was a job within a job. There was an old abandoned trailer park on Route 13 whose grounds were scattered with deteriorating trailers, assorted debris, and an array of environmental contaminants. Because the park's owner had refused to take care of these problems, Bristol Borough asked us to take the property by eminent domain and remediate the site. The cleanup was progressing nicely until someone dumped 100 gallons of heating oil on the property. After consulting Joel Bolstein and Environmental Consultants Inc., we brought in a pump truck to collect the puddled oil and then dug down three to four feet to remove all of the earthen material that had become contaminated. It was a good thing we found the spill before it sank too deeply into the ground. Once the entire property was remediated, it was regraded, mulched and seeded, and then transferred to the Bucks County Parks and Recreation Department for inclusion in Silver Lake Park.

PARX CASINO (2007) – Gaming came to Bucks County in a big way. PARX Casino was scheduled to open next to the old Keystone Racetrack on Street Road in Bensalem. Scores of meetings were held to discuss how increases in traffic, crime, extra police and security needs, and the necessary road and infrastructure upgrades would impact the surrounding municipalities. How were Bensalem and the surrounding municipalities going to pay for all this? Through smart public relations, good neighborly behavior, and profit sharing, that's how. Due to being the host community,

Bensalem worked out their own deal with PARX. The surrounding municipalities were to receive 1% of the PARX Casino's gaming profits.

It was a great solution that was eventually written into law (PA 71, the Gaming Act.) For the first 10 years, the money went to the County of Bucks, which then transferred the portion for the impacted communities to the RDA. It was our baby from there. I was charged with developing the program from start to finish, and the RDA did pro bono work taking care of its administration. Our payoff came in 2017 when the law was changed; the money would now come directly from the commonwealth to the RDA, and we were allowed to charge up to 5% of the total funds for our annual administrative fees.

CORELL STEEL (2008) – We closed out the last remaining portion of the Corell Steel property by transferring it to Bristol Township. It was to be used as open space within their park system at Coates Avenue.

THE RICHBORO SCHOOL BUILDING (2009) – A local bank wanted to build a new branch on a Northampton Township site that was occupied by an old vacant schoolhouse. The property was located on Second Street Pike and belonged to a developer who hadn't done anything with it for years. The RDA took it by amicable eminent domain and removed it from the tax rolls to help get the building sold, but because the schoolhouse went back to the early 1900s and had historical significance, the township would not allow it to be demolished.

The solution we arrived at was the same one that was applied to another historic Richboro structure: Like the Spread Eagle Inn, the schoolhouse was lifted from its foundation and moved (a little further this time) 200 feet back from the street. The bank built their branch, and the old schoolhouse was renovated and is now occupied by Dumack Engineering Inc. The RDA was the conduit that brought all the different parties together to bring about a good result. One abandoned building was replaced by one new building, a second rehabbed building, and two businesses paying taxes and serving the community.

THE SALE OF ONE NORTH WILSON AVENUE (2010) – After 14 years of RDA ownership, I decided to sell our One North Wilson Avenue office building to our tenants. To make the sale work for them, I negotiated a lower sale price in exchange for six years of free office space for the RDA. It was a big change for us, since we went from collecting $60,000 a year in rental income from our tenants to just paying for our utilities and phone costs. It was better for the RDA to have the money in hand and not have the headache of maintaining the building.

LOWER BUCKS HOSPITAL (2010) – When the Lower Bucks Hospital fell on hard times and was on the verge of closing, the RDA stepped in to save it by establishing a certified redevelopment area, taking ownership of the property, and developing a creative financing plan for a buyer to purchase and renovate the Hospital. This financing plan required the County of Bucks to back a bond issue, and the buyer had to complete 10 million dollars of improvements over the first five years of the deal.

Without these needed funds, the hospital would have been forced to close down, causing local residents to travel to hospitals in Falls Township or Philadelphia for their health care needs. State legislators really got behind this project and saved the hospital. A lot of good people were working together on various charitable projects during this period.

BEAUTIFICATION GRANTS FOR THREE BOROUGHS (2011) – At the request of State Senator Tomlinson, the RDA successfully applied for a $1,500,000 RACP beautification grant for the boroughs of Penndel, Langhorne, and Langhorne Manor. Although it took several years to complete the process, each municipality received $500,000. They all had a variety of different nuts-and-bolts-type projects that needed attention—everything from providing better signal lighting at intersections to working on storm sewers to fixing up old municipal buildings. We had to provide continual, in-depth administration of how the grant money was being used and how the jobs were progressing.

MECHANICSVILLE ROAD PROPERTIES (2012) – The RDA paid off the mortgages on two homes in Bensalem Township that were in foreclosure. After acquiring them, we demolished both homes and graded and seeded the grounds. The township agreed to take care of the maintenance of the properties while we negotiated their sale to a company that would develop and provide homes for military veterans. When the properties were finally sold, the RDA recovered the money it spent on the mortgage payments and demolition.

ELEMENTARY SCHOOL ON BATH STREET (2013) – Bristol Borough School District approached the RDA to see whether we could help them remove a large pile of contaminated earthen material on an elementary school site. The school transferred the property to the RDA, and we took it through PA ACT 2 to remediate it in accordance with DEP regulations. Because children would be playing on or near the site, the contaminated material needed to be spread out and encapsulated. We were able to obtain an ISRP grant for the remediation, but it came with a problematic precondition: The site had to have a history of industrial use at some point.

I thought that would count us out, but after researching the site, I found it had indeed been a location for some past industrial usage. With that knowledge in my back pocket, we began the process. We even added a driveway, a parking area, and a basketball court paved with bituminous material that provided the needed cover to prevent human contact with the contamination. The total cost was $1,250,000. The school district paid $250,000 of that amount.

THE MILL RACE INN (2013) – The inn had suffered back-to-back floods and remained closed for over a decade. The property was deemed to be blighted by Northampton Township, and the RDA acquired it by eminent domain. We received several inquires from developers and eventually reached an agreement with a restaurant company. For three years, they tried but failed to get the project going, so the agreement of sale was canceled. The RDA is still marketing this property along with the township.

AMETEK US GAUGE PROPERTY (2014) – AMETEK is one of the world's leading suppliers of high-quality pressure and temperature gauges. For many years, they operated out of a 250,000-square-foot building that occupied 5 acres of a 45-acre plot they owned in Sellersville. When they eventually decided to close up the operation and relocate, AMETEK demolished the building, leaving a 5-acre concrete floor, a 5-acre parking lot, and a lot of TCE on the property. The Bucks County Industrial Development Authority (the BCIDA) had been eyeing the property with the intention of creating a business campus there.

The BCIDA contacted us to help develop the property, but they were also looking to solve a potentially nasty problem. Three small, privately owned properties were situated within the 45 acres. The owners thought they were holding onto gold mines and were in the driver's seat. The situation could have proved to be an encumbrance to the IDA's plans to install a roadway throughout the campus, so we took the properties by eminent domain after negotiating in good faith and paying out $20,000 in compensation.

With no further impediments, we managed the project for the first year, during which we installed water, electric, and gas service and also built a roadway and a cul-de-sac. After that, our job was done. We transferred the deeds on the three small properties to the BCIDA in 2015 when they took over as the developer. For the foreseeable future, AMETEK is responsible for a pumping station on the property that handles the TCE problem. One 70,000-square-foot building has been built on the campus to date. It houses Solar Manufacturing, a company that designs, manufactures, and maintains vacuum furnaces.

AMPOL WINDOW MFG. CO. (2014) – Hubbell Lighting ran a manufacturing plant on Beaver Street in Bristol Borough, but they also owned 30 acres on Route 13 that they wanted to sell off. They had a buyer in AMPOL, a window manufacturing company that wanted to build a 250,000-square-foot facility on the site that would employ 200 workers. But when AMPOL began digging test pits on the property, they found some environmental problems and a lack of some fundamental infrastructure components. They came to the RDA to help carry out an ACT 2 remediation and to also install water and sewer service for the proposed building's fire suppression system and bathrooms.

We were successful in securing $1,850,000 worth of grant money to pay for all these needs: $1,000,000 of RCAP funds for the water main, a $400,000 PennWorks grant for the sewer pump station and sewer mains (with matching fees from the owner in the amount of $100,000), and a $350,000 ISR grant to clean up the environmental problems.

Sounds like it was a done deal, but as an old Scottish poet once said, "The best laid plans of mice and men often go awry." When we started this project, Route 13 was undergoing reconstruction. That made our work a lot harder since we were not allowed in the roadway and had to bore under the super highway to connect the new sewer pump station to the existing sewer service lines. The RDA had to put our name on the property's deed and take it off the tax rolls to get everything done. The project is still in development and the RDA will continue to own the site until all the work is completed.

6401 MCPHERSON STREET (2015) – The 35,000-square-foot building at this address had been blighted and abandoned for many years. The structure was so run down, you could look right through the roof and see the sky, and the surrounding property was littered with numerous abandoned vehicles and boats. The PADEP had already performed nearly $1,000,000 of environmental cleanup at the site, but with their blessing and the cooperation of Bristol Township, the RDA was able to take the property by eminent domain. Working with our selected developer, the property was completely rehabilitated and renovated in an unusually short period of time. There are currently five condos there occupied by various businesses that employ more than two dozen workers.

HELLBERG'S GREENHOUSE (2016) – This was a thriving greenhouse operation for decades that was located on Route 152 North in Chalfont, Pennsylvania. When it went out of business, the owner had trouble selling it because of arsenic and other contaminants on the site. In cooperation with the owner, a selected developer, and the municipality, the RDA acquired this property to remediate it and turn the site into residential housing. The greenhouses had to be taken down and hauled away, and the environmental cleanup was extensive enough for us to hire Environmental Consultants Inc. to handle the job. The RDA coordinated all the involved parties and negotiations. The proposed housing community is currently in development.

THE BARREL SITE (2017) – Sometime in the 1980s, someone disposed of a lot of barrels containing various toxins on a property in Bensalem Township that did not have a listed owner. The RDA acquired it by eminent domain with the intention of performing the environmental remediation. Once cleaned up, it will become open space parkland for Bensalem Township. Even though the EPA had previously moved some of the barrels, approximately $300,000 worth of work to remove all the contaminants still remains. The site's remediation is not on the fast track, although applications have been filed for state funding from the Industrial Sites Reuse Program. No one wanted to take credit for ownership of the property because of all the contamination, but I'm sure long-lost owners will come out of the woodwork once it's cleaned up.

PART FOUR

CHAPTER 12

FINISHING TOUCHES

My 24-year tenure as executive director of the Bucks County Redevelopment Authority officially ended on July 9, 2018. It was a tough year for me and not just because of the career and lifestyle changes that came with the end of my term of service. My son Randy passed away in February of the same year at the age of 56. He was a great kid, but he was never the same after his move to Connecticut with his mother. Coming from a broken home didn't help him, and neither did my habit of working two or three simultaneous jobs.

I took him in when he was 14, after he got in trouble for throwing some smoke bombs into a building that stated a fire. His hard partying and hell-raising ways followed him back to Pennsylvania. Even though he ultimately moved out, got married, and had a career of his own, Randy's out-of-control lifestyle finally caught up with him when he suffered a life-ending heart attack. We'd been estranged for a number of years, yet I always thought we'd have time to bury the hatchet at some point. That lofty goal was done in by a serious miscalculation on my part: Like every parent who loses a child, I never thought he would die before me. I miss him very much.

My son Randy, doing what he loved best.

My brothers Cooper, Bill, and Jerry all lived into their seventies and then died off one by one. Jerry fought off cancer for seven years but not before selling off Grandad's farm for several million dollars. My younger brother Dick is still alive and well, living in Harvey, North Dakota. My sister Mary Jane is also, thankfully, still with us. We all keep in touch regularly even if we don't see each other that much.

The last gathering of all my siblings in 1996 for my brother Jerry's sixtieth birthday celebration. From left to right: Cooper, Bill, Jerry, me, Dick, and Mary Jane.

When it comes to emotional pain, saying goodbye to family and loved ones will always rank at the top of the list, but when your work is your life, dealing with its demise ranks a close second. I deeply miss not being the head of the agency anymore: the daily action, the friends I made along the way, steering the ship in what I felt was the right direction, and the gratifying feeling that I was performing a valuable service for the community in which I grew up.

My exit was not a sudden one. The writing had been on the wall for a while. In 2015, we'd outgrown our North Wilson Avenue Offices, so we purchased and renovated the old Bristol Jewish Community Center on Pond Street. The RDA's move there reflected the county's changing times, politics, and economics. The support of the county commissioners I'd enjoyed during my first two decades at the RDA was no longer there. It became harder and harder to get things done. When I started out, there were exceptional people like Harry Fawkes and Mike Fitzpatrick in the Bucks County hierarchy who could not only say *yes* or *no* but could actually make things happen. (Harry had retired, and Mike left his position in the county to represent the State of Pennsylvania as a Congressman in the US House of Representatives.) Most of the engineers I'd worked with were also gone. They were "field guys" who were often on-site and could adapt their course of action to a property's less-than-perfect conditions—an essential skill, since engineers' and architects' plans are often drawn up to be correct under "perfect" conditions.

Regrettably, as the years marched on, these people were gradually replaced by committees, lengthy studies, and engineering firms who would rarely show up at work sites to make field decisions. Endless paperwork and reviews rule the day now, routinely disrupting projects and adding significant time delays and costs for the developers.

RDA board member Pat Bachtle used to joke around and say, "Bob White hits a lot of home runs, but he doesn't always touch all the bases." No doubt, my style of doing things made some municipal and county government folks nervous, but I saw the results of the new micromanaging procedures that replaced the way I used to work. It took nearly five years to get the funding and approvals to install extensions to a public water and sewer system for a new manufacturing building—even though it promised to provide up to 250 new jobs! The same thing happened with the rehab and transformation of the old Delaware Valley Hospital into the proposed Angel Star assisted living facility. With 250 to 350 new skilled and unskilled labor jobs waiting in the wings, you'd figure everyone would do their best to keep bureaucratic delays to a minimum. Not so—the project has been going on for five years and it's still not finished.

The RDA's new headquarters in the old Bristol Jewish Community Center on Pond Street.

This wasn't the work environment I was accustomed to. I felt less and less important, and for the first time in my life, I began to experience a feeling of helplessness. It began to affect my health. The thought of stepping down became more real by the day. I discussed my decision with some of the RDA's board members and finally made the tough choice. I turned the helm of the RDA over to my Deputy Director Jeff Darwak and accepted the county's offer of a two-year deal to be an advisor and special consultant.

Pat Bachtle and me at my 2018 retirement party.

I'd be lying if I didn't admit that, in spite of it all, my current life is pretty darn good. On the third try, I finally got the marriage thing right. I met my current wife, Gladys Mendieta, in 1995. A native of Ecuador with two children, she was running the Latino Leadership Alliance of Bucks County when Mike Fitzpatrick introduced us. We were married in 2006 and have never looked back. She's my soul mate and has influenced me and made me a better person in so many ways. Through much of my life, my attendance at church services was governed more by rote than because of any deep spiritual need or commitment. Since Gladys came into my life, I hardly ever miss a Sunday mass, and this time around, it's by choice as opposed to habit.

Like anyone who has lived through almost eight decades, I have a few regrets. I still smart a bit over losing the letter President Lyndon Johnson wrote that thanked me for the work I did on JFK's funeral. In the wake and confusion of two divorces, it was one of the things that just got misplaced. I certainly could have been a better husband and father—I still have no relationship with my daughter—and if I had my druthers, I'd have liked to stay in the Marines for life. But that's about it.

Not too long a list, although some of my regrets had a profound effect on me, mostly in a positive way. I spent the second half of my life trying to make people view me as a "good guy," mainly because I wasn't always a good guy in my younger years. I think I did a decent job of attaining that goal, which is a current source of pride and contentment for me.

As you can imagine, many things have changed quite a bit since the day I left Bucks County to join the Marines in 1959. Some buildings from Grandad's farm still exist, but what used to be his land is now bordered by the recently built Washington Crossing National Cemetery in Upper Makefield Township. At some point in the future—ironically less than 1,000 yards from where I was born and used to milk cows—I'll be buried there, along with other military veterans from the Philadelphia metropolitan area.

Grandad's farm had been downsized to just 10 acres. The Washington Crossing National Cemetery is just a few hundred yards off to the right of the picture.

The lush, natural beauty of Bucks County and many of the important historical buildings I grew up with are alive and well-preserved for future generations. Most of the county's heavy industry from the post–World War II boom is gone now, although Dow, U.S. Steel, and several other companies are still alive in the area, operating on a reduced basis. New innovations and business models have taken their place.

When I was born in 1940, the population of the county consisted of approximately 100,000 people living in an agrarian and manufacturing-based economy. It's now over 600,000, and the economic landscape has changed considerably. A cottage industry of bed-and-breakfast inns has brought about a major surge in tourism, and the retail shops, boutiques, and upscale restaurants of the Oxford Valley and Neshaminy malls, Peddler's Village, Doylestown, and New Hope draw millions of people from neighboring states, as well as Bucks County's own boroughs and townships. Considering its previous economic manufacturing-based roots, it's remarkable that Bucks County is now a major hub for the biotech industry, rivaling established technology centers like San Francisco and Boston.

For more decades than I'd like to count, I've had a front row seat to all this growth and transformation. Although I no longer do official drive-bys looking for potential blighted areas and properties that could be rehabilitated, I still live in Bucks County and travel through many of its boroughs and townships. There are always sites that could be improved, but I'm not at the helm anymore. As a consultant to the RDA, I may make some recommendations, but jumping in with both feet would no longer be appropriate.

Nevertheless, some of the old sites I see still resonate deeply in my soul. On the occasions when I happen to drive past some of the original locations of factories and businesses like Corell Steel, the Grundy Powerhouse, Dial Soap, or U.S. Magnet, it's impossible for me not to be overwhelmed by a deluge of memories: the faces of people who worked with me on those projects; the mental snapshots of how run-down those properties were and how beautiful they became; the challenges and hurdles that had to be overcome; the successes (the Port of Bucks) and, yes, even the dreams and best-laid plans that never materialized (Maple Beach).

My initial goal was to leave Bucks County in better shape than it was when I came in. As of today, all eight properties on my old brownfields list of the mid-1990s have been cleaned up and redeveloped and are continuing to make major contributions to the economy and welfare of Bucks County and its residents. I've tried to keep that in mind when dealing with the emotional aftermath of my departure.

When I retired, the *Bucks County Courier Times* reported, "Bucks County's man in black rides into the sunset after spending the last 25 years building the Redevelopment Authority into a self-sustaining, economic change engine." It took the sting out of my departure for a brief moment, but overall, ego gratification has never had much appeal for me. It's a short-lived need that requires constant feeding and renewal or it disappears into thin air. The Marines taught me that true accomplishment has more staying power:

The only worthwhile accolade is the satisfaction
that comes from doing your job well—without the
expectation of a pat on the back.

Time marches on. I'm not trying to paint myself as a character out of Grant Wood's iconic *American Gothic* painting. Lord knows, my days of holding a pitchfork are long gone. There are many things about our current technology and culture for which, as the saying goes, "I'm all in." My iPad and I are inseparable. I have two different cell phones that ring off the hook, and my SUV probably has more technological advances built into it than the early Apollo space capsules. I'm amazed at the vast array of subjects and educational opportunities colleges offer young folks today, but some lessons can't be learned on a blackboard or in a lecture hall. I miss many aspects of my earlier Bucks County life, particularly the daily reminders and appreciation of the simple value of someone hard at work in a field making things grow.

I don't know where my new consultant status will lead me. Maybe I can make something grow out of it—maybe not. Either way, I'm sure there are some good projects awaiting me somewhere if I work hard and keep my eyes open. Nothing's guaranteed. For all I know, I could have a heart attack helping a neighbor dig a drainage ditch next to his house. At 80, I should be slowing down, but I've always said, "If I'm gonna die, it's gonna happen when I'm doing something I love."

Somewhere in the back of my mind, I think I might have heard that before . . .

APPENDIX

BOB WHITE-ISMS

People tell me all the time I should write a book of my old-school mottos, adages, and business tips. I don't have enough for a book, but I do have a few pages worth, so for better or for worse, here they are:

I like to tell the truth because it's too much effort to try and remember the lies and who you told them to.

If 51% of people like me, I'll be all right.

If things were as easy to do as some people think they are, everyone would be doing it.

Try to avoid forcing a square stick into a round hole.

If you're not going to be the best, then at least try to be different.

You can't win over the past, but you can win today.

Always watch what you say, because you can't put toothpaste back in the tube.

If you wanna learn something, take an old guy out to lunch and listen.

Strangers are friends you haven't met yet.

You can lead a horse to water, but you can't make 'em drink. *(The cliché of clichés, but it was one of my grandad's favorites, so I had to include it.)*

It's OK to not know everything, but it's *not* OK to not know where to find the answer.

The reason we all have two ears but only one mouth is because God wants us to listen twice as much as we talk.

More often than we'd all like, the saying "No good deed goes unpunished" winds up being true, but do the good deeds anyway.

When you meet someone for the first time, you're just meeting that person's representative; the real person may show up sometime later when you least expect it.

Knowing what you don't know is as important as knowing what you do know.

Never be afraid to steal an idea or a quote.

If it's possible, someone is probably already doing it; and if it's impossible, someone will still be trying to do it.

BUSINESS TIPS

Always be the first one on the job and the last one to leave.

Treat every job you have as if the business or project were your own.

Whenever possible, use other people's money (OPM).

Ask lots of questions. If you don't ask, you can't succeed.

A business with no sign is a sign of no business, and a project with no plan is a plan for no projects.

Try to know when things are over before they're over.

Learn to be a good loser. You never know when you may have to deal with the same people on a future project.

Sellers and buyers are usually liars.

Never leave a job without having another job waiting for you.

Money usually follows you if you like what you're doing.

Look at the solution—not the problem. It's never about what you can't do; it's about what you can do.

When trying to pitch an idea, keep asking questions until the guy runs out of reasons why something won't work—or you come to the realization that he's right and it doesn't really work. Whatever conclusion you arrive at, just make sure you do everything in a calm, courteous, and non-overbearing way.

Never turn down a meeting. Good things often occur when you least expect them.

Fake it until you make it. You have to rep your project with confidence.

Deadlines come at you like the morning freight train and they wait for no one. (In other words, don't put off things until the last minute.)

Never participate in negotiations unless you have the authorization to make a change.

Find any problems before a job is done. Finding out afterward is the worst time.

Giving an employee more money will not necessarily make them more productive.

Working unconsciously is when you respond automatically to something you have become conscience of.

I saved my best advice for last. Learning how to communicate with people in an effective and constructive way is the key to almost everything—not just in business but in life in general. Scores of books have been written on the topic, and they're helpful, but age and experience are the best teachers. It's a skill that's best learned through lots of interactions and seeing what works and what doesn't. Here are the two rules of communication I've always lived by:

RULE #1: NEVER START CRITICIZING SOMEONE BEFORE PRAISING THEM FIRST. In my experience, it's never been a constructive method for making corrections and improving performance. I'd prefer to approach someone on a project and say something like, "Steve, you did a great job straightening out the roofing problems on that house, but what happened with the dry wall in the living room?" They'll always appreciate the compliment and will usually be more receptive to the criticism.

RULE #2: VERY OFTEN, THE WAY YOU CHOOSE YOUR WORDS IS THE KEY TO GETTING SOMETHING DONE. There was a highly visible, signature, five-story building in downtown Morrisville that was in disrepair. The owner wouldn't fix it, and the borough's council wasn't doing anything about it either. Neither of them wanted to spend the necessary time and money to make things right. If I ranted and raved about the building looking like crap, I wouldn't have gotten anywhere with them. Instead, I calmly pointed out, "You know, if a piece of plaster falls off an upper story of the building's facade and someone gets hurt, you'll have one helluva lawsuit on your hands." So the borough blocked it off with barricades. And wouldn't ya know it, in no time at all, the building's owner took care of the problem.

TESTIMONIALS AND ACCOLADES

A FEW KIND WORDS FROM
MY COLLEAGUES AND CO-WORKERS

In 1989, Langan came to Bucks County with a tradition of innovative engineering solutions for shuttered, complex, former manufacturing sites. Something we called "Industrial Site Redevelopment." When I arrived during the spring of 1995 to support Langan's growth, I began asking around as to who within the county might have the interest and knowledge in redevelopment. Multiple people told me, you need to get to know Bob White. Boy, were they *right!*

Immediately it was clear that Bob was a man on a mission who was well-versed in the real estate development process within the county. He had a unique blend of hands-on experience, connectivity, and creative approaches to address these underutilized sites. Almost simultaneously, the USEPA birthed its Brownfield Redevelopment Grant program. Before you knew it, a team of public and private sector talent was formed to support Bob's vision. The Bucks County Redevelopment Authority brownfields initiative was underway.

In the ensuing years and through all his accomplishments, Bob has become a kindred spirit to many, with the common desire to see a revitalized Bucks County reach its full economic and quality of life potential. And I am most proud of all to call Bob White my friend.

Ed Geibert

Senior Business Development Consultant, Langan Engineering

In 1995, Pennsylvania put its award-winning brownfield program in place. Back then, I was the deputy secretary who led the team at PADEP that was responsible for putting the program together and rolling it out. We needed allies to get it passed, and we needed economic development leaders with vision to help us implement the program. Right out of the gate, Bob White led the charge to use that new program to reclaim old industrial sites in Bucks County.

Through his efforts, the Redevelopment Authority of Bucks County became a national leader in brownfield redevelopment. It began with his idea of creating an inventory list of all the vacant and underutilized industrial properties in the county. He and his staff prioritized that list, applied for and obtained funding for environmental assessment and remediation grants, and then found private developers to partner with to help bring those properties back to life, creating new jobs and economic opportunities.

The fruits of that work can be found throughout Bucks County, and as someone who lives in Bucks County, my fellow citizens and I will be forever grateful to Bob White for all of his hard work. In my mind, Bob White is larger than life. He enters a room wearing his big cowboy hat, and he is so well respected because of his knowledge, his experience, and his perseverance in always getting the job done. No one has done more to breathe new life into brownfield properties in Bucks County than Bob White. He is a true visionary.

Joel Bolstein

Partner, Fox Rothschild LLP

I met Bob White in the fourth quarter of 1997. He was executive director of the redevelopment authority. At that time, I was working on a project called the U.S. Magnet Site in Yardley, Pennsylvania, the 23-acre site that is described in this book. After the first meeting, I really thought it would be a one-and-done business deal, both with the RDA and with Bob White. I was wrong.

The Magnet site in Yardley from beginning to end took 15 years. Bob was there the entire 15 years, always available, helping and guiding the development from an abandoned industrial site to townhouse development. The site, along with many others we worked on together, would not have been completed without the intimate knowledge Bob brought to the practical and professional problem-solving of brownfield site development, the new Act 2 law, and what was needed to complete an Act 2 site.

I had no idea in 1997 of the tremendous benefit of working personally with Bob and the long-term professional and personal relationship that would develop over the next 25 years.

When you work with Bob on a brownfields project, the meeting usually includes local town officials, engineers, and concerned neighbors. He fills the room with his presence and knowledge. Everyone in the room listens out of respect because they know he knows what the site was, what it is now, and the damage it is doing to the community. They do not doubt his commitment to a solution or what he believes professionally and personally the site can be. As a result, the project gets done.

Bob was the key to the redevelopment of many of the sites we worked on. Having him on the team gave confidence to private and public entities that the site would get developed and benefit the immediate neighbors and community.

After meeting Bob in 1997, my confidence in the redevelopment of brownfields projects grew. With that confidence, we were able to develop millions of square feet of vacant and underutilized brownfield industrial properties in Bucks County.

I know that the success of the Redevelopment Authority of Bucks County during the past 30-plus years could not have been done without his knowledge, support, and enthusiasm.

Tony Cino
Mnop, Inc.
Managing Partner of Cold Springs Investment Group LLC

Dear Bob,

Truly, I cannot begin to express my gratitude for your advocacy on the borough's behalf concerning the $100,000 grant request for our police facility project. During the borough's attempts to develop an economically viable project, you offered me an unbiased and practical perspective. In expressing your belief in the value of the RDA's mission and your palpable commitment to it, you were a friendly and encouraging face.

Thank you for sharing the borough's vision. Thank you for supporting the borough's residents and police department. Thank you for giving me your time and interest. Above all, thank you for being a man of action and integrity. Your advocacy on behalf of the borough for this project was truly exceptional. It speaks volumes about your commitment and honor. Candidly, although I hoped you would advocate for the borough as you did, I had no reasonable basis or expectation that you should do so. Honestly, Bob, you have impressed me in a very special way. On behalf of current and future residents and police officers of Langhorne Manor Borough, I offer my heartfelt appreciation for your interest and attention toward the borough and me, and also your genuine commitment to the RDA's mission.

Kind regards,

Bill McTigue
Council President

Bob White is a superstar in economic development. Many in the field have hit-or-miss skills. Not Bob. He has a unique skill set borne out of a lifetime of experiences that tested him as a man and as a professional. I am not aware of any courses or university programs that teach what Bob has learned to do, so I pleaded with him over the years to share all his experiences and the knowledge he's accumulated. He's too modest to ever say or even think it, but this book is a gift to this and future generations. We all thank Bob for the many jobs he has created over the years, along with the civic, cultural, and historic legacies he has preserved in many of Bucks County's towns. I feel privileged to have been able to watch it all happen.

James P. Gorecki
Senior Vice President, Fidelity Commercial Real Estate Alliance, Inc.

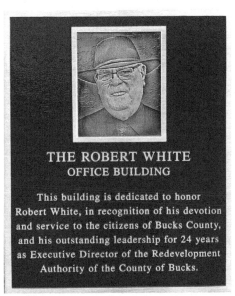

In 2019, the RDA Board of Directors affixed this plaque at the entranceway of the authority's Pond Street headquarters.

What is a doer? A doer is a person who works tirelessly to achieve success in spite of risk, opposition, and criticism. In the field of community redevelopment, a doer is someone who is committed to transforming an abandoned building or factory into a vibrant destination—in spite of the naysayers and the critics. A doer pushes through all obstacles and impediments to achieve progress.

Bob White epitomizes the type of doer a community needs in order to transform a project from a conceptual dream into a finished reality. I am honored to have worked with him over the years and have witnessed and admired the many great accomplishments he's achieved on behalf of the citizens of Bucks County.

Sam Kucia

Environmental Consulting, Inc. (ECI)

In 1992, I was appointed to the Bucks County Redevelopment Board of Directors. At that time, the Authority hired a firm to find projects for us. We had only one environmental cleanup, and our budget was minimal. When Bob White was hired, it wasn't long before the Redevelopment Authority 'blossomed.' It may sound like a strange word to use in the context of the Authority, but it's the only way to describe it.

Bob did not wait for townships and boroughs to contact us. He could look at a rundown factory and visualize innovative new businesses thriving in the same footprint. A neighborhood full of blighted houses? No problem. Bob could instantly conceptualize how they could become a beautiful new development, whether the community's need called for quality low-income housing or upscale townhouses.

These weren't just pipe dreams swirling around in his head. He would contact borough councils and supervisors with realistic, well-thought-out plans that would win over even the staunchest of skeptics. His perseverance enabled him to always find a way to "git 'er done," as he was fond of saying.

You can drive almost anywhere in Bucks County and see the results of his plans and perseverance, from the reborn Dial warehouse in Bristol to an economic powerhouse like the Port of Bucks in Falls Township to a tidy little municipal park that emerged from the rubble of a deteriorated trailer park in Croydon.

It has been an honor and privilege to work with this man. I know whatever endeavors he pursues going forward, he will always git 'er done.

Pat Bachtle
Chairwoman of the Board of Directors, The Redevelopment Authority of the County of Bucks

My association with Bob White began when I was a Bucks County commissioner. Over a period of many years, we developed a warm friendship and working relationship that I value to this day. Bob is a true son of Bucks County, with a connection to both its past and future. His strong personal work ethic and values are, no doubt, rooted in growing up on his family's farm in Bucks County and were further solidified during his honorable service in the United States Marines.

Bob came to the Redevelopment Authority of Bucks County at a time of great need. Overall, the county was looking for a maestro who could successfully orchestrate its three regions: Upper Bucks, Central Bucks, and in particular, Lower Bucks, where the infrastructure and aging abandoned industrial sites had been deteriorating throughout the 1970s and 1980s. With his vision and his desire to work and make change, Bob more than fit the bill. (And he had a heckuva good time while doing it!)

More than 50 major improvement projects were completed during his tenure as the Authority's executive director. He succeeded because of his uncanny ability to enlist the support of local municipalities and the public-private partnerships needed to turn some of these sites and community districts into new businesses and growth opportunities. He had the unique ability and judgment to hire very good people, and his communication skills were unparalleled. Because his county roots and history were so deep, everyone respected him; they knew he understood them and their needs, and if he promised something, it was as good as done.

Notably, politics never played a role in the way Bob did business, as he would often say. And I agree. He was a lifelong Republican, but he consistently made friends "across the aisle" and worked equally well with all our political leaders, in all municipalities, and for the good of Bucks County. Bringing people together may have been his greatest skill.

I'm proud to call him a friend and to, again, acknowledge his ongoing contributions to the county we love.

Mike Fitzpatrick

Former Bucks County Commissioner and United States Congressman

A HEARTFELT THANK-YOU

Throughout my professional career, I've always tried, as much as possible, to maintain an awareness and appreciation of the people around me who played significant roles in everything I ever achieved. Their many contributions have been magnified during the introspective process of writing this biography. I could turn this opportunity to express my gratitude to all these folks into a full-blown chapter all by itself, but I'll keep it brief.

I was blessed over my 24-year tenure as the BCRDA's executive director to work with numerous gifted, talented people in our office staff. Heather St. Germain, my first hire, was an ace of an administrative assistant and the person who helped me bring the RDA into the computer age. Patricia DeLorenzo, my first bookkeeper, who unfortunately became ill and had to resign, and her successor Joe D'Adamo, guided me through all of our bookkeeping concerns and helped ensure there was always enough money to pay our staff. Because of their attention to detail, the RDA passed every one of our annual audits with flying colors. Midge Wagner spent 15 years working at the administration of the agency, and I can't forget about the contributions of Jeffrey Darwak, my deputy director and heir to the executive directorship. All of these good folks own a share of the Authority's success.

I'd like to thank all the legislators and public officials—from both parties—who came together with their respective communities to help make all the projects we worked on come to fruition. In particular, I'd like to cite some of the very special people in this group for their steadfast confidence in my ability to get the job done:

The thought of working for the RDA would never have occurred to me without Pat T. Deon Sr.; Harry Fawkes always stepped up to the plate and made the hard decisions that most people of lesser intestinal fortitude would have avoided; and both Senator Robert Tomlinson and State Representative Thomas Corrigan not only supported our projects but often went above and beyond the call of duty to identify and deliver every possible source of public funding.

Our board of directors, particularly board chairwoman Patricia L. Bachtle, always had my back during my years with the RDA. If not for the always welcomed advice and direction of Joel Bolstein, our special environmental counsel for more that two decades, I doubt I would have been as successful in repurposing all the brownfields sites we turned around. Time after time, Joel helped me get the job done.

A few other very important pieces of the puzzle included environmental consultants Sam Kucia, Nick DeRose, and Ed Geibert, developers Tony Cino and Ed Cacace, and contractor Brian Bzerinski. And most of all, my heartfelt thanks to my good friend, county commissioner, US congressman, and lifelong Bucks County resident Michael G. Fitzpatrick. You are sorely missed by me and the entire county.

Shaking hands with my good friend Mike Fitzpatrick.

To the many other names I wish I could have included but were not mentioned due to time and space limitations, you may not be on these pages, but that doesn't mean you and your contributions are not in my heart and mind. We did a heckuva lot of great things together, didn't we?

—Bob—

ABOUT THE CO-AUTHOR

ALLAN SLUTSKY is a Grammy award–winning musician, author, and film and record producer whose books include *Bobby Rydell: Teen Idol on the Rocks, The Funkmasters: The Great James Brown Rhythm Sections*

1960–1973, and *Standing in the Shadows of Motown: The Life and Music of Legendary Bassist James Jamerson.* In 1989, *Standing in the Shadows of Motown* won the *Rolling Stone*/BMI Ralph J. Gleason Music Book Award and was the basis for a 2002 motion picture of the same title that Allan co-produced. In 2003, it received Best Non-Fiction Film awards from the National Society of Film Critics and the New York Film Critics Circle. Allan has been a member of Stockton University's music faculty since 2012.